FROM THE INTRODUCTION

When Gina was deported to Tijuana, Mexico, in 2011, she was scared. Although she was born in Mexico, her only memory of being there was a fuzzy, dreamlike recollection of falling off a burro—a donkey—when she was three or four years old. Her parents brought her to the United States when she was young; she's not sure how old she was. She knows she was born in Guerrero, one of Mexico's poorest states. After explaining this, she quickly says, "Don't ask me more because I don't know." Her childhood memories revolve around her life in the U.S.—going to school, attending birthday parties at Chuck E. Cheese, and dancing at her high school prom. As an adult, she gave birth to three children in the U.S. and celebrated countless holidays with her parents and siblings, all now U.S. citizens. . . .

Following her deportation, she was alone in Tijuana—separated from her children and all of her earthly possessions. Everything felt foreign and intimidating. She explains, "I got scared when I first got in to TJ [Tijuana]. I was in shock." . . .

Six years after her deportation to Mexico, Gina still misses home. "I miss everything about it," she explains, "my kids, my family, the food, the places, the clothes, the jobs. Everything. This is not what I'm used to."

DEPORTED
AMERICANS

DEPORTED AMERICANS

LIFE AFTER DEPORTATION TO MEXICO   BETH C. CALDWELL

Duke University Press   Durham and London   2019

Printed in the United States of America on acid-free paper ∞
Designed by Courtney Leigh Baker and typeset in Knockout
and Whitman by Westchester Publishing Services

Library of Congress Cataloging-in-Publication Data
Names: Caldwell, Beth C., [date] author.
Title: Deported Americans : life after deportation to Mexico / Beth C. Caldwell.
Description: Durham : Duke University Press, 2019. |
Includes bibliographical references and index.
Identifiers: LCCN 2018037350 (print)
LCCN 2018049803 (ebook)
ISBN 9781478004523 (ebook)
ISBN 9781478003601 (hardcover : alk. paper)
ISBN 9781478003908 (pbk. : alk. paper)
Subjects: LCSH: Immigrant children—Legal status, laws, etc.
—United States. | Children of illegal aliens—Legal status, laws, etc.
—United States. | Illegal alien children—Legal status, laws, etc.
—United States. | Mexicans—Legal status, laws, etc.—United States.
| Emigration and immigration law—United States. | Emigration
and immigration law—Mexico. | Deportees—Family relationships.
| Deported children—Mexico. | Deportation—Social aspects.
Classification: LCC KF4848.M48 (ebook) |
LCC KF4848.M48 C35 2019 (print) | DDC 305.9/0691—dc23
LC record available at https://lccn.loc.gov/2018037350

COVER ART: Families separated by the two countries chat along the U.S.-
Mexico border fence at Border Field State Park, California, U.S., November
19, 2016. REUTERS/Mike Blake.

TO MOM AND DAD,
Thank you for your unconditional love,
support, and generosity

CONTENTS

ACKNOWLEDGMENTS

This book has benefited greatly from the generosity of many people who have shared their time, experiences, and expertise.

The theoretical contributions of the book have been improved by comments and suggestions offered by colleagues in the field of immigration law and deportation studies. Deborah Boehm, Ietza Bojorquez, Jennifer Chacón, César Cuahtémoc García Hernández, Joanna Dreby, Ingrid Eagly, Tanya Golash-Boza, Linda Kerber, Elizabeth Keyes, Jennifer Lee, Hiroshi Motomura, Stephen Lee, and Yolanda Vázquez commented on chapters, talked through ideas, and provided key insights.

In addition, I benefited greatly from the guidance and support of my colleagues at Southwestern Law School, especially Danni Hart, Hila Keren, Gowri Ramachandran, and Rachel VanLandingham. Thank you for so generously sharing your time and suggestions. I appreciate Dean Susan Westerberg Prager's ongoing support of this project and am also indebted to Warren Grimes, Southwestern's associate dean for research, for his support of this project. Margaret Hall and Linda Whisman in Southwestern's library have been a tremendous help with research. And thank you to my LAWS colleagues and the clinical team at Southwestern for your friendship and encouragement.

I am very grateful to the two anonymous reviewers who provided detailed feedback and ideas through the review process. The manuscript improved tremendously from your thoughtful comments.

I conducted the initial interviews for this project with funding from a Fulbright Garcia-Robles grant and continued the research with support from the Open Society Foundations as a Soros Justice Media Fellow. Thank you to Adam Culbreath and Christina Voight of the Open Society Foundations, and to el equipo dorado: Erin Siegal McIntyre and Joel. I also appreciate the tremendous work of everyone at Duke University Press, including Gisela Fosado, Lydia Rose Rappoport-Hankins, and Liz Smith.

Earlier versions of some chapters were published in law review articles, including "Deported by Marriage," which was published by the *Brooklyn Law Review*, "Banished for Life," which was published by the *Cardozo Law Review*, and "Expanding Constitutional Protections to Functional Americans," which was published by the *Whittier Law Review*. Many of the ideas in this manuscript benefited from conversations with colleagues at Thomas Jefferson School of Law, where I initially began writing this book. Special thanks to Meera Deo, Ilene Durst, Luz Herrera, Linda Keller, Brenda Simon, and Kaimi Wenger.

Thank you also to my family for their love, support, and technical assistance with this project. I am grateful to my parents, Dan and Lora, and to my sister Ellen for reading through multiple drafts, offering not only encouragement, but also questions that helped me to think more critically about my work. Thank you also to my brother John for his love and support, and to the Medina family—Maribell, Imelda, Vanessa, Marie, Carlos, John, Jeffrey, Angel, and Steve. And to Carolina—thank you for everything.

Joel, thank you for your tireless research assistance and insights, and for dedicating so much of your time to helping me with the interviews. And to my children, Evie and Emiliano—I hope that this book will contribute to "changing laws that are not fair," as Evie says.

INTRODUCTION

I am an American at heart and in many other aspects. It's the
paperwork stating that I am an American that I regretfully lack.
—deported U.S. veteran

In Mexico, especially along the border, the consequences of deportation are
impossible to ignore. American children who speak limited Spanish inun-
date Mexican schools; camps of homeless people filled with deportees crop
up in border cities; call centers owned by foreign companies set up shop
to capitalize on the influx of native English speakers who, once deported,
will work for under two dollars an hour. Hundreds of thousands of American families have relocated to Mexico, leaving the U.S. to stay together
after a parent or spouse is deported. In border cities like Tijuana, American
spouses of deportees wait in border-crossing lines for hours every morning to get to work in the United States or to take their children to school.
Other families are divided by the border—parents separated from their
children, spouses from one another. Among deportees with strong ties to
the U.S., loneliness, depression, and thoughts of suicide are prevalent.

Although the troubling consequences of the U.S. deportation regime are
visible virtually everywhere on the Mexican side of the border, they remain
largely invisible to most people on the U.S. side. Once deported, people
who were previously integral members of U.S. society fade from the country's collective consciousness. Banished from the boundaries of the nation

they once called home—often permanently—the millions of deported disappear. However, people who have been part of the social fabric of the United States should not be so easily forgotten.

The United States has embarked on a massive deportation effort over the last decade; its scope exponentially exceeds deportation efforts of the past. During President Barack Obama's eight years in office, the United States deported more people than it deported in a 108-year period between 1892 and 2000.[1] President Donald Trump has set out to deport even more. Many who have been deported in recent years belong to American families—a quarter of the people the U.S. has deported in recent years are parents of American-citizen children, and still more are married to U.S. citizens. The majority have been deported to Mexico—over 2.6 million people in the ten years between 2007 and 2016 alone.[2] At least half a million U.S.-citizen children now live in Mexico. Deportees who grew up in the U.S.—and their family members—struggle to adapt to life in Mexico because they feel they have been forced out of their homeland.

WHEN GINA WAS deported to Tijuana, Mexico, in 2011, she was scared. Although she was born in Mexico, her only memory of being there was a fuzzy, dreamlike recollection of falling off a burro—a donkey—when she was three or four years old. Her parents brought her to the United States when she was young; she's not sure how old she was. She knows she was born in Guerrero, one of Mexico's poorest states. After explaining this, she quickly says, "Don't ask me more because I don't know." Her childhood memories revolve around her life in the U.S.—going to school, attending birthday parties at Chuck E. Cheese, and dancing at her high school prom. As an adult, she gave birth to three children in the U.S. and celebrated countless holidays with her parents and siblings, all now U.S. citizens. After she left Mexico as a child, she only returned once, driving down to Rosarito Beach from Los Angeles like thousands of other American tourists for a weekend getaway in Baja California.[3]

Following her deportation, she was alone in Tijuana—separated from her children and all of her earthly possessions. Everything felt foreign and intimidating. She explains, "I got scared when I first got in to TJ [Tijuana]. I was in shock. I'm like, 'Oh my God,' especially seeing the mountains with houses and then all the people outside." The "mountains with houses" are hillsides lined with makeshift shelters, some pieced together from scraps of wood and cardboard, roofs patched with pieces of scrap metal. Even after being in Mexico for months, she still doesn't feel comfortable in Tijuana. "I'm scared too. I don't like going to the *centro* [downtown Tijuana]. I get scared walking over there. I don't like it. I feel like someone is going to rape me or rob me. You walk and all the guys [are] staring at you like if they wanna do something or they're planning to do something to you." The area of town she is referring to is otherwise known as the Zona Norte. It's the part of the city closest to the border—the place where deportees arrive if they keep walking straight from the entry to Mexico where Border Patrol leaves them. It's also a haven for drugs and prostitution.

Gina experienced her so-called return to Mexico as a foreigner. She expressed discomfort, fear, and shock with many things she saw—a lot like other Americans might feel if dropped off in Tijuana with no warning. Gina is not technically American, although she almost was. She had a green card for many years. In legal terms, she was a lawful permanent resident on track to become a citizen. "I passed my citizen test and everything," Gina reports in our first interview. "Congratulations," she remembers hearing, "you passed!" The next step was to attend a swearing-in ceremony, but she was told she would need to appear in immigration court before being sworn in. She never made it to the ceremony. Rather than becoming a citizen, Gina was deported.

Her path to citizenship was derailed because she had been in an abusive relationship with the father of her children. Although his abuse was so severe that she suffered two miscarriages following beatings, Gina was the one who was arrested and convicted of domestic violence. She fled Los Angeles to get away from him, going to Colorado where her parents lived. After the move, she missed a critical immigration court appearance in Los Angeles. In her absence, the judge issued a deportation order due to the criminal conviction. Gina still had her green card, but unbeknownst to her, it was no longer valid. Six years after her deportation to Mexico, Gina still misses home. "I miss everything about it," she explains, "my kids, my family, the food, the places, the clothes, the jobs. Everything. This is not what I'm used to."

THE EXPERIENCES OF Gina and other deportees who grew up in the United States raise complicated questions about what should happen when legal definitions governing citizenship contradict people's identities. How do people develop identities tied to a country that does not recognize them as members? What happens when people are rejected and expelled by the country they consider home? Morally and legally, should the United States deport people whose lives are inextricably tied to it?

This book addresses these issues by focusing on the experiences of deportees and their family members. It highlights how the law has fueled mass deportation in the past decade and examines the consequences of this policy choice. It combines primary research with legal analysis in order to explore the real-world consequences of the law and to identify potential legal challenges to current policies based on people's life experiences.

At its core, this book is about membership, and its opposite—exclusion. The title *Deported Americans* is meant to challenge traditional notions of what it means to be American, and to highlight the contradiction of banishing people who feel like they belong within the territorial boundaries of the United States. By documenting deported people's feelings of identity, their attachments to the United States, and the stigma and rejection they feel in Mexico, I examine inconsistencies between legal definitions of citizenship and people's life experiences. Although the Statue of Liberty articulates an inclusive stance toward immigrants, welcoming the "huddled masses yearning to breathe free," this inclusive rhetoric is a myth because it so clearly conflicts with the nation's history of excluding people of color and other socially marginalized groups.[4] Deportees' life experiences demonstrate that this history of exclusion persists. The concept of deported Americans also captures the experiences of citizens who, although legally included in U.S. society due to their citizenship status, are simultaneously excluded from accessing many of the rights that typically accompany citizenship because of their relationships with noncitizens. The term encompasses both the experiences of deportees who are functionally American but have been deported under the law, and the experiences of their family members—many of whom are Americans under the law but have been functionally deported.

Many people who have been deported grew up in the same households as brothers and sisters who are citizens. Although the childhoods of these sibling groups are parallel, they occupy different citizenship statuses based on their location of birth or their age at the time of a parent's naturalization. The law draws lines between members of the same families whose identities and attachments are virtually identical, labeling some citizens and others aliens. It operates as a powerful tool that extends membership status to some while denying it to others.

DEPORTED AMERICANS

At the Casa del Migrante in Tijuana—a temporary shelter where many deportees find themselves sleeping in the days following their deportation—a glass bowl sits on a shelf, filled with deportees' key chains. It is a visual representation of all that people have left behind. The keys that fill the bowl used to unlock people's homes, offices, cars—the places where they spent the most time, and that filled their lives with meaning. After deportation, key chains that at one time felt indispensable become so meaningless that they no longer serve a purpose. The keys people have left behind represent lost families, homes, jobs, property, and lives. These losses are no less profound because of one's location of birth.

The people I interviewed all migrated to the United States as children and were primarily socialized there. Some came when they were infants, one or two months old. I call them deported Americans because they identify themselves as Americans. People in Mexico perceive them as Americans as well. They are members of the 1.5 generation of immigrants (who arrived between the ages of six and twelve) or the 1.75 generation (who arrived prior to age six). The majority fall into the second category—they came as very young children. Sociologist Rubén Rumbaut has found that the "experience and adaptive outcomes [of 1.75 generation migrants] are closer to that of the U.S.-born second generation" children of immigrants, "pre-school children who retain virtually no memory of their country of birth, were too young to go to school to learn to read or write in the parental language in the home country (and typically learn English without an accent), and are almost entirely socialized here."[5] An estimated 2.1 million members of the 1.5 or 1.75 generation immigrants of Mexican descent reside in the U.S.—almost half are now adults.[6] In his book *Lives in Limbo*, Roberto G. Gonzales explores the life experiences of undocumented members of this population while they are living in the United States, uncovering the complex nature of their membership status in U.S. society. This book looks at the other side of this generation's experiences by examining what happens after people who have been primarily socialized in the United States are deported.

Deported Americans are similar to the people the DREAM (Development, Relief, and Education for Alien Minors) Act set out to protect, and to the young people who have been protected by DACA (Deferred Action for Childhood Arrivals), which has provided temporary relief from deportation for people who migrated to the United States as children.[7] Some deportees in Mexico even call themselves "los otros Dreamers"—the other Dreamers. Yet many have no hope of ever lawfully returning to the United States. When President Obama announced the creation of DACA, he highlighted the strong affiliations with U.S. society that young people develop when they migrate as children. He stated, "These are young people who study in our schools, they play in our neighborhoods, they're friends with our kids, they pledge allegiance to our flag. They are Americans in their heart, in their minds, in every single way but one: on paper."[8]

Many people the United States has deported were also educated in U.S. schools and recall beginning their school days by pledging allegiance to the American flag. Some even served in the U.S. military. According to one deported veteran, "I am an American at heart and in many other aspects. It's the paperwork stating that I am an American that I regretfully lack." Why are so many people permanently barred from returning to the United States despite relatively widespread support for protecting from deportation those who came to the United States as children?

The line that divides most (but not all) of the people I interviewed from their counterparts who have been allowed to stay in the United States is that they have been defined as criminals. People with criminal convictions are disqualified from most protections in immigration law, including DACA.[9] While excluding people with criminal convictions may seem like good public policy on the surface, the criminal alien label has been used to manipulate public support for deportation practices that have consequences so cruel and inhumane that they would likely raise more concerns about the legitimacy of deportation if the population most affected were not so dehumanized.

This book aims to humanize people who have been deported based on perceptions of criminality and dangerousness in an effort to push back against the totalizing narrative that frames the lives of "criminal aliens" as less valuable. Thus, I deliberately place the experiences of people who have been deported due to criminal convictions at the center of my analysis, highlighting their stories in order to demonstrate the human costs of framing an ever-expanding segment of the population as disposable. I focus not only on the experiences of deportees but also on their family members, thus challenging the false dichotomy between felons and families that has been drawn in popular discourse.

Although my research focuses on Mexico, its findings are relevant to understanding the broader phenomenon of people who grew up in the United States but have been deported to countries around the world. Scholars have started to refer to the widespread displacement of deportees who identify as American as a diaspora—"the movement, migration, or scattering of people away from an established or ancestral homeland."[10] Although not typically used to refer to those who have been deported, the term fits for those deportees who identify the United States as their homeland. Daniel Kanstroom, the preeminent legal scholar on deportation, frames the phenomenon of this "forcibly uprooted population of people with deep and cohesive connections to each other and to the nation-state from which they were removed" as a "new American diaspora."[11] Nancy Landa, who grew up in Los Angeles but was deported to Mexico, refers to the phenomenon as "the Dreamer diaspora."[12] Although most of the members of this deported American diaspora now live in Mexico, others have been scattered across the world, with documented concentrations in El Salvador, Guatamala, the Dominican Republic, Jamaica, and Cambodia.

Accounts from deportees who grew up in the United States and have been deported to various countries echo the sense that they are essentially American. In an ethnographic study focused on deportees to El Salvador, Susan Bibler Coutin explains that "King," an immigrant from El Salvador who came to the United States as a young child but was deported as a young adult, "experienced deportation not as a return but as a departure, [in his words], 'leaving, you know, the country you were raised in.'"[13] Similarly, in their book about deportation to the Dominican Republic, David C. Brotherton and Luis Barrios found that for deportees who had "emigrated as children and who were socialized from an early age in the norms, rituals, and ideologies of the United States, . . . it was difficult to see themselves as anything other than 'American.' . . . Their cultural reference points, their most important memories, and the narratives they repeated to themselves were still embedded in New York."[14] One woman who had grown up in the U.S. but was deported to Mexico identified so strongly with the U.S. that she misunderstood the immigration officer's asylum screening question— where they ask if she was in fear of returning to her country of origin. In her words, "They asked me, 'Are you afraid that somebody's going to hurt you in your country or something?" And I told them no, because I consider the [United States] as my country, you know? Not anywhere else. . . . I don't know anybody [in Mexico]."[15]

Legal scholar Cristina Rodríguez argues that "membership can turn on the extent of one's earned connection to U.S. society and may not be merely a function of legal status."[16] She uses the term "functional Americans" to refer to noncitizens with particularly strong ties to the U.S. who are essentially American.[17] Deportation is particularly cruel for functional Americans. It not only undermines family connections, career paths, and other attachments but also strikes at the core of people's identities.[18]

RESEARCH AND METHODOLOGY

I did not set out to write a book documenting the consequences of deportation to Mexico. Rather, my interest in the subject unfolded organically, fueled by both personal and professional experiences. From 2005 to 2009, as deportation numbers were beginning to spike, I worked as a public defender in Los Angeles. Many of my clients were not citizens of the United States. Thus, advising people about the immigration consequences likely to flow from their criminal convictions became a central part of my practice as a criminal defense attorney. For many, the most serious consequences of their criminal cases were not the sentences they faced in criminal court, but the immigration consequences that would follow their convictions.

I represented a nineteen-year-old whose family had moved from El Salvador when he was a toddler. He was lawfully in the U.S. under a humanitarian program that provides temporary relief for people from designated countries experiencing conflict or environmental disasters. He was charged with a relatively minor misdemeanor for engaging in disorderly conduct. He had been binge drinking with friends, like many of his peers on college campuses across the country. However, he was apprehended by police for acting drunk in public. As is typical in criminal court, the city attorney's office had charged him with two separate but related crimes for his conduct that night. He had a choice—he could take his chances at trial or he could plead guilty. If he took the plea bargain, the prosecutor was prepared to drop one of the misdemeanor charges and to offer a sentence of community service rather than jail time.

People convicted of two misdemeanor offenses were ineligible for Temporary Protected Status, so he would risk deportation if he went to trial and lost, because he could have been convicted of two misdemeanors. He decided to plead guilty because the immigration consequences were too serious to risk. I sat with my client and his mother and discussed the potential immigration problems he could face if he were convicted of another crime in the future. I offered potential scenarios that could saddle him with a new offense—things I often saw with other clients his age, like riding in a car with someone who had contraband, or carrying drugs, a pipe, or a pocketknife. I tried to impress upon him the gravity of his position—any second misdemeanor offense would render him ineligible to stay in the country. A couple months later, he was back in court, charged with a second misdemeanor offense. A different attorney was assigned to represent him on this case, and I do not know what the outcome was. But his situation highlights just how tenuous lawful presence can be—and just how quickly someone can go from being a typical American teenager with lawful status in the U.S. to being a potential deportee, facing forcible removal from his home and his family. As a public defender, I witnessed the front end of the deportation process, as people became aware that they could face removal as a result of an arrest or conviction.

I started to see the other side of deportation—what happens after people are deported—when I moved to Mexico in 2009 to research criminal justice reforms with funding from a Fulbright Garcia-Robles grant. I traveled around Mexico quite a bit that year and encountered people all over the country who had grown up in the United States but had been deported—people who spoke English using American slang and colloquial expressions, and who dressed in a uniquely American style. I started to have casual conversations with others about their experiences, which unfolded naturally, driven partly by a tangible excitement to talk about the place we both considered home. I met several deportees from Los Angeles, where I grew up; this gave us common ground. People would tell me about the things they missed the most—foods, people, places. Their memories were intertwined with a sense of despair because they had been physically removed from the people and places that were so important to them. These conversations shaped my understanding of the unique challenges facing deportees who had spent their formative years in the U.S.—I was struck by how American many people who had been permanently banished from the U.S. were.

In the capital city of the southern state of Oaxaca, I met a woman who hadn't seen her nine-year-old son since he was six because he remained in

Los Angeles with his father to continue attending school there. She taught at a prestigious language school in the center of the city and spoke with an American accent. "I'm more comfortable speaking English than Spanish," I recall her telling me. In a small coastal town on Oaxaca's coast, I met a middle-aged former gang member who had grown up on the Eastside of Los Angeles but had settled into a job managing a hotel perched on a cliff overlooking the ocean. "From the streets of L.A., I never thought I'd end up here," she said, while I ate breakfast on a cliff-side patio with a spectacular view of the Pacific Ocean. "The pay isn't great, but I get to live *here*, so it's not bad."

Although these conversations arose naturally, I started to take notes. I knew the stories were important. I was honored by the intimate details people shared and was inspired by their hope that people back home would pay attention to what was happening to them after they were "kicked out." People did not want to be forgotten. Each individual's experience was unique, but at the same time, I started to see common themes running through their stories—themes of family separation, struggles with identity, stigmatization, and loss. I didn't have a prescribed list of questions. Instead, I listened to people as they discussed the aspects of their deportation experience that stood out most to them. I spent several months in the central state of Jalisco in 2010, where I ran into deportees working primarily in the tourism industry. They were particularly visible in Puerto Vallarta—a popular tourist destination for Americans and Canadians—where native English speakers lined the streets offering information about time-shares and tours. I arrived in Tijuana later in 2010 and was struck by the sheer numbers of Americanized deportees. Their numbers were exponentially larger in the border area than in the rest of the country.

In 2011, I began to interview people in the Tijuana region more formally, gathering information from more and more deportees. I found people primarily by word of mouth, with one person referring me to others. Service providers who work with the deported population put me in touch with some people. Others I located rather accidentally. I approached people I encountered in their daily lives—people who seemed American because of their dress or the ease with which they spoke English—with the assistance of my husband and research partner, Joel Medina. With his charm and insight, Joel opened doors to interview people whom I never would have been able to interview alone. I interviewed people in their homes, at their jobs, and in shelters, bars, restaurants, and coffee shops.

Between 2009 and 2016, I interviewed 112 deportees, mostly men but some women.[19] I deliberately limited the population I interviewed to include people who spent their formative years in the United States—those who came to the country when they were children. Most of the interviews took place in person, although a few occurred over the phone or via video-conferencing. The majority took place in the border area of Mexico—particularly Tijuana and Rosarito—but I interviewed people throughout Mexico in Oaxaca, Guanajuato, Sonora, Jalisco, Michoacán, Mérida, and Quintana Roo. I also interviewed fifteen spouses and twelve children of deportees. Some I located online through discussion forums and Facebook groups; others I found through word of mouth. The people I interviewed ranged in age from twenty to sixty-eight years old. Some had been undocumented in the U.S.—without lawful status. The majority had been lawful permanent residents (green card holders) or had some other kind of lawful permission to be in the United States, mostly because they were in the process of acquiring lawful permanent resident status through a parent. Almost all entered the U.S. without inspection, meaning that they entered without a visa and without permission. A few of the people I interviewed were not sure whether they entered with a visa. Most were Mexican nationals, but I also interviewed twelve people who had been born in El Salvador or Nicaragua but settled in Mexico after their deportation.

One of this book's central contributions is the longitudinal nature of my research with a subgroup of deportees. I followed a core group of fifteen deportees over the course of five to seven years, checking in with them over time to see how their lives were unfolding. The book explores the experiences of six of these individuals in depth—Gina, Edgar, Jose, Frank, Mike, and Luis. I interviewed them all on several occasions and spent time with them as a participant observer in their homes, at their jobs, in parks, and in restaurants.[20]

My interest in deportation has been shaped by personal as well as professional experiences. My husband's family is from Mexico. Through our marriage, I became part of a mixed-status family, meaning that our family includes people who are U.S. citizens, lawful permanent residents awaiting citizenship but whose immigration status is not as safe as that of citizens, and people who do not have lawful permission to be in the U.S. Having a personal connection with deportation—or the threat of deportation—is not unusual. A 2008 study by the Pew Hispanic Research Center found that 68 percent of Latinos worried that they themselves, a family member, or a close friend might be deported.[21] Several members of my extended family were deported to Mexico while I was researching and writing this book; experiencing the pain of deportation firsthand has deepened my understanding of the phenomenon.

ORGANIZATION OF THE BOOK

Chapter 1 gives background and context, providing an overview of the laws governing deportation and examining how the evolution of deportation law has been shaped by race. I explore the connections between racist historical immigration restrictions and the current politics of exclusion directed toward people labeled criminal aliens. This exclusionary stance toward immigrants has informed the law. Immigrants in deportation proceedings are systematically denied standard constitutional protections. The chapter highlights the lack of due process protections in deportation proceedings and the dramatic erosion of protections for people with criminal convictions faced with deportation. Using narrative examples, the consequences of being deported without the opportunity to appear in court to contest one's removal are explored, as are the consequences of the extremely limited scope of judicial discretion in the current legal schema. Although the chapter's primary purpose is to provide context and history, it incorporates narrative accounts of deportees' experiences with the legal process of being deported, thus contributing information that will be of interest to specialists. Deportees' perspectives on the legal process highlight the consequences of a legal framework that systematically underprotects immigrants' rights.

Chapter 2 describes several people's experiences with arriving in Mexico and explores four common themes that emerged in their narratives: culture shock, lack of family ties, barriers to social integration, and stigma. Their arrival experiences show the extent to which their lives and identities are deeply tied to the United States and, conversely, disconnected from Mexico. The presence of a signficant group of deportees of Central American origin who have settled in Mexico's border region is also discussed here. The rationales of these Central American deportees for living in Mexico's border region highlight the unique identities of deportees who associate more strongly with U.S. culture than with the cultures in their countries of origin.

Chapters 3, 4, and 5 present the major qualitative findings of my research in Mexico. Chapter 3 focuses on how people's life trajectories continue in the months and years following their deportation, identifying three primary paths: (1) descending into substance abuse and/or depression; (2) rebuilding lives in Mexico by working, starting businesses, or attending school; and (3) returning to the United States despite the risk of death or incarceration if apprehended. This chapter makes important contributions to the existing literature by examining the crimogenic conditions deportation causes from a structural perspective. Through this lens, higher rates of substance abuse among deportees in Mexico's border region are understood as a predictable result of deportation, rather than as a justification for the practice.

In addition, the longitudinal nature of my research allows me to explore how some people have been able to overcome the obstacles deportation creates and have built relatively successful lives in Mexico. For example, a number of deportees have launched small businesses or have embarked upon professional careers in Mexico, a phenomenon that has not been fully explored in other academic research. The success of some deportees demonstrates the shortcomings of deportation policies that do not allow a path to return even when an individual can demonstrate rehabilitation. My research also uncovers that feelings of loss, depression, and anxiety are persistent even among deportees who have been successful at rebuilding their lives in Mexico in the years following their deportation. Consistent with Ines Hasselberg's research on deportation in the U.K., where she describes deportation as a process that unfolds through a series of events over time, the consequences of being banished from the country people consider home extend far beyond the moment of deportation.[22]

Deported Americans' primary motivation to return to the United States—family ties—challenges the legitimacy of incarcerating and deporting people for doing something as natural as returning to one's family. In addition, narratives reveal how, in many cases, prison does not function as a deterrent to reentry because (1) people are often willing to risk anything to reunite with their families, especially if a family member faces some kind of crisis; and (2) many people report they would prefer to be in prison in the United States than deported to Mexico in order to be closer to family.

Chapters 4 and 5 delve into the experiences of deportees' children and spouses, discussing the myriad ways in which their lives are affected by deportation and describing how the law has failed to protect their rights, in part because courts have failed to adequately consider the harm families experience due to deportation. Although they are citizens, they lose many of the privileges of citizenship because of their relationships to deportees. Chapter 4 specifically focuses on the experiences of spouses of deportees and compares the current experiences of women married to deportees to the historical practice of divesting American women of their citizenship if they married a foreigner. This chapter highlights logical inconsistencies in the law, which protects the right to marriage from prohibitions on interracial marriages but does not similarly protect binational marriages in cases involving deportation. Chapter 5 explores how children are affected by deportation by describing the experiences of children who are separated from their parents, those who move to Mexico, and those who go back and forth. This chapter explores several ways in which the law fails to protect children's right to family unity, and their best interest, when a parent faces deportation.

The conclusion considers solutions, recommending both judicial and legislative changes that could minimize some of the harmful consequences of deportation described in the previous chapters. The first part focuses on two areas where legal challenges in court have potential to change deportation policy. In the past, an incomplete understanding of the consequences of deportation shaped legal precedent; research on people's lived experiences now has the potential to change the rules governing deportation. Specifically, the experiences of people who grew up in the United States but have now been deported challenge traditional constructions of American identity and reveal how, in many ways, deporting members of this population is akin to denationalizing citizens. The reality of their lived experiences opens the door to reconsidering case law that draws a bright line between deportation (which is allowed under the Constitution) and denationalization (which is forbidden). In addition, the suffering that families endure when a member is deported demonstrates how previous court decisions (which have downplayed the effects of deportation on family members) are based on a fundamental misunderstanding of the meaning of deportation in people's lives. The experiences of deportees and their family members highlight the critical need for courts to reconsider prior decisions that have concluded that deportation does not compromise the rights to marriage or family unity for the family members of deportees.

In addition to exploring these two potential legal challenges to current deportation law, the conclusion recommends legislative reforms that would reincorporate a balancing test in all deportation cases, so that judges could weigh the harm of deportation against the government's interests in deporting an individual, even in cases involving criminal convictions.

IN A WORLD where increasing numbers of people (and families) live transnational lives, traditional definitions of citizenship warrant reconsideration. As anthropologist Deborah Boehm explores in *Returned*, her book about deportation to Mexico, "As places of departure and destination blur, migrants, deportees, and other transnational subjects describe 'going' and 'coming' in ways that challenge traditionally linear understandings of migration."[23] In the modern world, the physical boundaries of nations may no longer be the best way of capturing membership in a particular country. Scholars increasingly focus on the cultural aspects of citizenship and identity that are not tied to physical territory, and a loosening of international borders, as evidenced in experiments like the European Union. The experiences of deportees who identify as American highlight the need to think about different ways of defining membership, and even citizenship, so that formal definitions correspond to people's lived experiences.

The emergence of a body of scholarship decoupling theoretical understandings of citizenship and belonging from territorial presence butts up against a hardening of borders, perhaps in response to the international move toward transnationalism. This hardening of borders is tied to a desire to exclude immigrants deemed socially undesirable, as evident in the rhetoric surrounding popular support for Great Britain's leaving the European Union and as physically manifested in the U.S. border with Mexico.

Along the U.S.-Mexico border, a series of fences stretches for hundreds of miles, dividing "us" from "them." Over the past twenty years, the U.S. government has greatly expanded the resources it allocates to finding, detaining, and ejecting Mexican immigrants. Border Patrol's funding increased tenfold—from $363 million to $3.5 billion—between 1993 and 2013, and the Department of Homeland Security's budget for interior immigration enforcement increased 73 percent between 2003 and 2013.[24] Border enforcement has become increasingly militarized, to the extent that drones are now used to patrol several regions along the U.S.-Mexico border.[25] This militarization contrasts sharply with the U.S. border with Canada, which is relatively open and unpoliced. The physical border is a concrete illustration of the less visible, socially constructed borders that divide "us" from "them" within the United States.

International human rights bodies have sharply criticized U.S. deportation policy. Despite this, the country has expanded its use of deportation. In his book *Deportation Nation*, Daniel Kanstroom argues that "we need an understanding of sovereignty, membership, citizenship, and government power that is 'supple and flexible' and more functionally reflective of reality as it is experienced by those who have faced this kind of state power."[26] My hope is that this book will contribute to this effort by moving the legal discourse on the topic—which has historically treated the consequences of the law on people's lives as irrelevant—toward a framework where the trauma and suffering people experience when they are deported matter more in the eyes of the law.

ONE IN THE SHADOW OF DUE PROCESS

In the exercise of its broad power over immigration
and naturalization, Congress regularly makes rules that
would be unacceptable if applied to citizens.
—*Fiallo v. Bell* (1977)

The first time she was deported, Gina was apprehended after a traffic stop. She was taken to jail and deported without setting foot in court, even though she had been a lawful permanent resident for over twenty years. Normally, a lawful permanent resident would be entitled to a court hearing to determine her deportability. However, Gina was subject to one of five major exceptions to the right to appear in immigration court—exceptions that now result in over 80 percent of the deported population being removed without a judicial hearing.[1]

She had missed a previous immigration court date, at which time she was ordered removed in absentia—in her absence. At the time, Gina had moved from Los Angeles to Colorado to join her parents because her children's father had become abusive. When she missed her court date in Los Angeles, the judge issued a removal order. She had been in the process of applying for relief from deportation based on the hardships her children would face—an option available to her because she had not been convicted of an aggravated felony. Her lawful permanent resident status was revoked. Under an administrative process called reinstatement of removal, immigration officials were allowed to deport Gina again without allowing her to appear in court.[2] She was taken into immigration custody and dropped off in Tijuana.

Shocked and alone, she immediately tried to come back to the United States. Gina walked across the border at the port of entry and presented her Colorado driver's license. Customs and Border Protection officers realized she had previously been deported; she was detained and deported again. A few weeks later, in a state of desperation, Gina tried to run across the border. She explains,

> I knew I would get caught. But I didn't care because I just wanted to talk to a judge—to explain how this was just a mistake and that my kids need me. Everybody kept telling me that I couldn't go to court because they already deported me. But that wasn't fair because I never got to explain my problems to a judge. I thought, "I'd rather be in jail over there than be stuck over here."

Gina's instinct that she should be able to appear in court to present the hardships deportation would cause for her and her children is consistent with the procedural due process protections that would generally apply in other legal proceedings—protections most Americans expect from the legal system, like the right to a fair trial. However, she lost this right when she missed her court date. During the deportation process, Gina recalls meeting with an immigration agent who told her "that [she] had to sign the paper." Rather than sign the document, Gina asked to go to court. "You lost that right," the agent replied. Once the deportation order had been issued in absentia, it could be reinstated outside of court. The only court she was likely to get taken to was criminal court, where she could be prosecuted for the federal crime of illegal reentry. Relatively speaking, she was lucky. She was dropped off back in Tijuana rather than being sentenced to serve time in federal prison.

Gina's children were two, five, and seven years old at the time of our first interview six years ago. The two oldest were going to therapy on a weekly basis due to emotional and behavioral issues stemming from their separation from their mother. Gina was reluctant to bring them to Mexico because, she said, "I'm not even stable. I don't have money. I don't have a place, nothing. So what am I going to do with my kids over here?" Toward the end of our first interview, she asked, "Do you know how I can get to court? They're telling me I have to wait twenty years to go back. Is that true? My kids can't wait that long."

If she had understood the serious consequences of missing her court appearance, Gina undoubtedly would have gone to court. However, under the severe stress of being embroiled in a physically abusive relationship and raising young children—one of whom had special needs—she didn't realize how crucial this court date was. Losing the opportunity to appear in court before a judge who could consider the negative toll her deportation would take on her and her children is an extreme sanction. However, in deportation cases, judicial efficiency and finality are often prioritized over people's well-being.

In addition to highlighting the human toll of legal policies that value finality over humanity, Gina's case illustrates the cost of eliminating courtroom appearances for so many people, combined with a lack of access to quality legal representation. Gina may have qualified to file a motion to reopen the original removal order that had been issued in her absence. This is essentially what she wanted to do when she said "I was asking everyone to take me to court" while in immigration custody. However, she did not have an attorney and did not know how to obtain one while in custody. She tried making phone calls but to no avail. She did not know how to file a motion to reopen, or even that such a motion existed. Thus her previous removal order was reinstated, and she was dropped off in Tijuana without seeing a judge. If she had been taken to court—even if she had not filed a motion to reopen—a judge might have advised her that this was an option and could have scheduled a future court appearance, giving her some additional time to seek the assistance of an attorney. However, without this procedural protection in place, Gina lost that opportunity.

Once deported, she dug herself deeper into a hole. Her impulsive efforts to reunite with her children made a lawful return even more unlikely. When Gina was first deported, she was barred from returning to the U.S. lawfully for a period of ten years. She might have qualified to file a waiver to request permission to return through the U.S. consulate, but she didn't realize that. Instead, she tried to walk across the border. The government asserts that when she did so, she claimed she was a U.S. citizen. Making a false claim to citizenship triggers a permanent bar, with no waiver available—ever. Gina has now been in Mexico for over seven years and might have been able to return to her children if she had not tried to walk across the border in a state of desperation. Instead, she recently consulted an immigration attorney who told her she had no hope of ever lawfully returning because of the false claim to citizenship she made that day.

Standard constitutional protections that apply in almost every other area of the law systematically underprotect people in immigration cases. Due process protections that Americans expect in the legal system—hearings before judges, access to attorneys, and the right to appeal—are frequently unavailable to people facing deportation. Lawyers who are unfamiliar with immigration law are often shocked when they hear about the practices courts allow in the immigration realm because the rules deviate so sharply from the standards that exist in the rest of the legal system. History explains how this has come to be.

HISTORICAL CONTEXT OF EXCLUSION

The systematic lack of protection for noncitizens facing deportation is the current manifestation of a long history of demonizing and excluding racialized "others" in the United States. Citizenship has been an exclusive category in the U.S. since its inception.[3] In the past, the terms employed were more explicit—African Americans, Native Americans, Asians, anyone else courts categorized as nonwhite, and women were excluded from full citizenship. The United States exterminated and isolated Native Americans onto reservations. African American slaves were so dehumanized and excluded from membership in U.S. society that they did not even qualify as people under the law.[4] Now, although overt racial restrictions are no longer a part of the law, this exclusionary framework continues to govern both legal and social constructions of citizenship and membership in society. Deportation is the most overt manifestation of these roots.

The United States has historically employed its immigration laws specifically to exclude people of color. The 1790 Uniform Rule of Naturalization specified that only "free white men" could naturalize to become U.S. citizens. The Chinese Exclusion Act—which was in effect from 1882 until 1943—explicitly prohibited Chinese people from migrating to the United States. In 1924, the United States passed its first comprehensive immigration bill, which further institutionalized white privilege by specifically barring immigrants deemed nonwhite, such as people of Chinese, Japanese, and Indian descent, from becoming citizens.[5] The Supreme Court maintained the whiteness requirements in immigration law throughout the 1920s.[6]

The roots of modern deportation law can be traced back to two cases that upheld the government's decision to exclude or deport long-term residents because they were Chinese.[7] In the 1889 case of *Chae Chan Ping v. United States*, a long-term Chinese resident of the United States traveled to China. While he was there, Congress changed the law. Previously, Chinese residents had been allowed to reenter the country as long as they had a residency certificate, but the Scott Act of 1888 barred reentry for Chinese residents even if they had this certificate. Chae Chan Ping argued that he should be able to return because the change in the law violated his constitutional rights.

The Supreme Court's decision focused on the larger question of whether the judicial branch had authority to review acts of Congress that regulate immigration. It decided that it did not have such authority, justifying its deference to Congress's plenary power to regulate immigration as "an incident of sovereignty" essential to the country's ability "to preserve its independence, and give security against foreign aggression and encroachment." It concluded that foreign aggression can come not only in the form of a "foreign nation acting in its national character" but also "from vast hordes of its people crowding in upon us."[8] Therefore, the Court found that excluding Chinese migrants because they were Chinese was perfectly constitutional.[9] This rule of judicial deference to congressional authority in immigration matters became known as the plenary power doctrine. In the 1893 case of *Fong Yue Ting*, the Supreme Court extended the plenary power doctrine to apply to people facing deportation from within the United States.[10] It held that the right to deport people "is as absolute and unqualified, as the right to prohibit and prevent their entrance into the country."[11]

The decision to exempt long-term residents facing exclusion or deportation from standard constitutional protections was not clear cut. Vehement dissents argued that noncitizen residents "are within the protection of the Constitution, and secured by its guarantees against oppression and wrong," and that "arbitrary and despotic power can no more be exercised over [foreign resident] persons and property than over the persons and property of native-born citizens. . . . As men having our common humanity, they are protected by all the guaranties of the Constitution."[12] However, the majority's exclusionary approach won out because the residents in question were perceived as "vast hordes of . . . people crowding in upon us."[13] At the time, President Theodore Roosevelt praised the United States for acting "with the clear instinct of race selfishness" when it "kept out the dangerous alien"—the Chinese—whom he also called "the race foe."[14]

Limited Protections in Deportation Cases

Paradoxically, around the same time that the Supreme Court decided to allow overt racial discrimination in immigration cases, it held that racial discrimination against people who were not citizens violated the Constitution in non-immigration-related cases. In *Yick Wo v. Hopkins*, the Court held that noncitizen Chinese laundry owners were entitled to equal protection under the Fourteenth Amendment. The city of San Francisco had passed an ordinance that had a disparate impact on the operation of Chinese-owned laundries. The Court ruled that the Constitution protected citizens and noncitizens alike from racial discrimination.[15] Combined, the *Yick Wo*, *Chae Chan Ping*, and *Fong Yue Ting* cases set up a contradictory legal framework that imbues noncitizens with constitutional protections in some cases but not in others.[16]

In 1903, the Supreme Court narrowed its decision in *Fong Yue Ting* by holding that noncitizens facing deportation from the United States were at least entitled to procedural due process protections.[17] Yet despite the fact that procedural due process limits formally apply to deportation proceedings, courts have generally been "unwilling[] to give the procedural due process requirement any real content."[18] As the Supreme Court stated in the 1977 case *Fiallo v. Bell*, "In the exercise of its broad power over immigration and national security, Congress regularly makes rules that would be unacceptable if applied to citizens."[19] Deportees do not have the right to a jury trial in removal proceedings, the right to appointed counsel, the right to bail, the right to standard Fourth Amendment protections preventing the use of illegally obtained evidence, and the right to protection from ex post facto laws.[20] In the words of deportation scholars Daniel Kanstroom and M. Brinton Lykes, "Indeed, much of the late twentieth and early twenty-first century story of deportation is a story of de-formalization in which even certain very basic procedural rights recognized by courts— such as the right to be heard by a judge—have been severely restricted."[21]

Given the underprotection of people's rights in immigration-related cases that has emerged from this history, the Constitution has not functioned as a shield against the harsh immigration laws that have emerged in the past quarter century, driven in large part by anti-Mexican sentiment.

THE SOCIAL CONSTRUCTION OF MEXICANS AS "THE OTHER"

Like the Chinese, Mexicans were framed as "the other" in the nineteenth and early twentieth centuries. The rhetoric of Manifest Destiny was employed to frame Native Americans and Mexicans as inferior "savages" and "imbeciles" in order to justify taking their land.[22] Between 1880 and 1930, Mexicans were widely depicted as "inferior beings" in popular publications, and Mexico was presented as a "social problem."[23] In the early 1800s, a politician asserted that Texas was "redeemed by Anglo-American blood and enterprise" from Mexicans, whom he characterized as "savages . . . benighted by . . . ignorance and superstition."[24] A widely read 1845 publication reported that Mexico's "incorporation into the Union was not only inevitable, but the most natural, right and proper thing in the world. . . . Imbecile and distracted, Mexico never can exert any real governmental authority over such a country."[25] Mexicans continued to be characterized as "underdeveloped," "unambitious," and "uncivilized" in popular discourse in the United States at the beginning of the twentieth century.[26]

At the same time that these racist and derogatory attitudes were directed toward them, Mexicans were privileged under U.S. immigration law because they were largely exempt from the whiteness requirement governing access to citizenship in the late 1800s and early 1900s. They occupied a unique position because the Treaty of Guadalupe Hidalgo authorized Mexicans to obtain citizenship after the U.S. took over much of Mexico's land. Despite several notable exceptions wherein Mexicans were barred from naturalizing because they had "a strain of Indian blood," federal law generally allowed Mexicans to become citizens during a time when other immigrants of color—Asians and Native Americans—were not.[27] Notably, people of African descent were also exempted from the whiteness requirement as a result of the legal reforms that abolished slavery.

Despite the fact that they were allowed to naturalize, Mexican Americans were quite clearly treated as racialized "others" in the social sphere. They were subject to Jim Crow segregation across the Southwest and attended segregated schools; children were routinely beaten if they were heard speaking Spanish in school. Texas Rangers killed migrants at the border with legal impunity, and hundreds of Mexicans and Mexican Americans were publicly lynched across the Southwest between 1850 and 1935.[28] The discrimination and marginalization Mexican Americans experienced during this period contributed to the social construction of Mexican as a subordinated racial group in the United States.[29]

Large-scale deportation campaigns targeting people of Mexican descent demonstrate the extent to which Mexicans—and Mexican Americans—have been treated as socially expendable "others" in the United States. During the Depression era, when the need for Mexican labor shrank due to the country's struggling economy, an estimated one million people were removed to Mexico. Historian Mae Ngai refers to these "repatriations" as "a racial expulsion program exceeded in scale only by the Native American Indian removals of the nineteenth century."[30] Local police conducted raids of Mexican communities, workplaces, and public parks where people of Mexican origin were indiscriminately rounded up and detained without bail. Twenty years later, the United States embarked on another wave of mass deportations targeting people of Mexican descent. Between 1954 and 1959, an estimated 3.7 million Latinos were deported, the majority to Mexico.[31] Over a million were deported through Operation Wetback at that time, a program that was explicitly labeled with racially derogatory language.

Now, Mexican immigrants continue to be framed as "the other." Latinos occupy such a marginalized status that scholars have developed the term "citizen aliens"—citizens who are treated as aliens because they are perceived as "different than the 'typical' American" based on their Latino origins.[32] Anthropologist Leo Chavez attributes anti-immigrant laws and policies to the "Latino Threat Narrative," which he argues is "pervasive when not explicitly mentioned."[33] According to Chavez, this dominant depiction of Latinos as a threat is "the cultural dark matter filling space with taken-for-granted truths in debates over immigration on radio and TV talk shows."[34]

Two major myths about Mexican immigrants have gained traction in the popular consciousness and have influenced immigration law: (1) immigrants as invaders, and (2) immigrants as criminal aliens.[35]

Invasion Rhetoric

As of 2015, more Mexicans were leaving the United States than were coming into the country.[36] Yet rhetoric expressing fear that Mexicans are invading the United States continues to be pervasive.[37] In 2000, political scientist Samuel P. Huntington alleged that "the invasion of over one million Mexican civilians" was "a comparable threat" to an invasion by one million Mexican soldiers. According to Huntington, "Mexican immigration looms as a unique and disturbing challenge to our cultural integrity, national identity, and potentially to our future as a country."[38] Ann Coulter's 2014 best seller ¡Adios, America! argues that Americans should "fear immigrants" from Mexico "more than ISIS."[39] And similar rhetoric drives support for President Donald Trump's plans to build an "impenetrable wall" to keep Mexican migrants from "pouring through our borders."[40]

The Supreme Court has incorporated the fear of invasion from Mexico into its reasoning as well. In 1975, the Court wrote of the "silent invasion of illegal aliens from Mexico," and in 2000, an opinion expressed concern about the "northbound tide of illegal entrants into the United States."[41] When migration from Mexico is framed as a threat, harsher laws and more militarized enforcement practices seem more legitimate. Similar rhetoric was used to justify mass deportation efforts in the 1950s, which one government official argued were necessary because Mexican migration amounted to "an actual invasion of the United States."[42] Comparing Mexicans to threatening invaders is reminiscent of the reasoning the Supreme Court used to uphold the Chinese Exclusion Act, a parallel that demonstrates how invasion rhetoric is employed to perpetuate racial subordination.

Criminal Alien Rhetoric

The term "criminal alien" evokes images of dangerous "others"—inhuman monsters or violent predators. It also serves as a proxy for race. Policies are designed to discriminate against this population, but they appear legitimate (rather than racially discriminatory) because the "criminal alien" label implies that these people deserve to be treated more harshly than the rest of the population. The term manipulates the public's understanding of immigrants—particularly immigrants from Mexico—by framing them as dangerous threats when in fact most are not.

Language informs subconscious beliefs, and labels applied to immigrants shape how people are treated. Referring to an "immigrant" corresponds to a more inclusive approach to immigration, while using terminology like "illegal," "alien," and "criminal alien" evokes the politics of exclusion that characterize much of U.S. immigration law.[43] D. Carolina Nuñez conducted a content analysis of the use of "alien," "immigrant," and "citizen" in mainstream media and academic writings, concluding that the term "alien" corresponds to "non-human invaders or, at best, criminals" who are lowest on the hierarchy of societal membership, while "immigrants are persons, but they are still outside the majority," and "citizens" are "upstanding and law abiding members of the community."[44] Once people have been framed as aliens, and especially criminal aliens, harsh deportation practices appear more legitimate. Equating Mexicans with criminals dates back to the U.S.-Mexican war, when Mexicans attempting to defend their land were commonly depicted as lawless bandits.[45] The image of a Mexican bandito—bandit—is a racialized trope that has now become a familiar U.S. stereotype of Mexicans. The institutionalization of "criminal aliens" as a category of people combines the historical racialized depictions of Mexicans as violent and as invaders.

The "criminal alien" label specifically manipulates the public's perception of Mexican immigrants by (1) expanding the definition of who qualifies as a "criminal alien" to include many who have not been convicted for activities that would typically be understood as crime, (2) conflating the existence of a criminal conviction with dangerousness, and (3) erasing empathy for people categorized under this label.

Expanding Definitions

The "criminal alien" construct first emerged in 1956 as part of an effort to shift public sympathies away from Mexican migrants. The Border Patrol's chief enforcement officer for the Southwest Region informed his officers that they should no longer refer to migrants as "wetbacks" because the term "'creates a picture in the minds of the public and the courts of a poor, emaciated, Mexican worker, entering the United States illegally to feed a starving family at home.'"[46] Instead, he advised, "whenever a criminal record exists, we use the words, 'criminal alien,' and when no criminal record exists, the words, 'deportable alien.' I feel this change will have a psychological effect on the public and courts that will benefit the Service."[47] Following this announcement, the Border Patrol deliberately inserted this new terminology into popular discourse through a concerted effort using public information officers.[48] Then, much like now, the number of Mexican immigrants who were engaged in crime was grossly inflated for political purposes. In 1957, only three people who were apprehended each day qualified to be prosecuted for crimes. However, the next year, Immigration and

Naturalization Service Commissioner Joseph Swing argued in the House of Representatives that "of the aliens currently apprehended, over 50 percent have been previously arrested for various crimes." Before making these remarks, he specified, "I am still talking about Mexicans, Mr. Chairman."[49]

U.S. immigration law has included exclusions for people with criminal convictions for hundreds of years, but the exclusion (and ejection) of people with criminal records now affects much broader segments of the population, and the label carries harsher consequences. What began as a narrow exception has evolved into the norm. The expansion of the "criminal alien" category threatens to remove protections that apply to other immigrants from a sizeable segment of the immigrant population—primarily Latinos. In the 1980s and '90s, punitive deportation policies were enacted alongside the criminal laws that fueled mass incarceration. Fears of immigrants as violent criminals gained traction despite widely accepted social science research documenting that immigrants in the United States are less likely to engage in crime than nonimmigrants.[50] This unsubstantiated fear of immigrants as criminals was then incorporated into the law.

The largest category of "criminal aliens" deported in 2015—33 percent— were defined as "criminal aliens" because they had been convicted of an immigration-related crime.[51] The most common crimes were entering or reentering the country.[52] Prosecutions for these offenses have skyrocketed in the past fifteen years, increasing by 1,420 percent between 1993 and 2013. Notably, this greater focus on prosecuting immigration transgressions as crimes has come about during a time when migration to the United States has actually decreased. In recent years, around 30 percent of all federal criminal convictions are for immigration-related offenses.[53] According to law professor Ingrid Eagly, "Not since the Prohibition has a single category of crime been prosecuted in such record numbers by the federal government."[54] These prosecutions mostly target Latino immigrants. According to the U.S. Sentencing Commission, 95.7 percent of the people convicted of these crimes were Hispanic in 2015.[55] Labeling immigrants criminal aliens based on convictions for immigration offenses renders all immigrants who entered without permission vulnerable to being defined as criminals and treated accordingly.

The definitions ICE employs further demonstrate how the label has expanded.[56] Forty-six percent of the "criminal aliens" deported in 2015 had only been convicted of immigration or traffic offenses. The most serious convictions of another 17.3 percent were drug related. Most of the people deported through ICE's Criminal Alien Program (CAP)—a specialized enforcement program—either have no criminal convictions or have been convicted only of nonviolent offenses.[57] In contrast, 0.5 percent of the people deported through CAP had been convicted of a homicide offense.[58] While the rhetoric surrounding "criminal aliens" focuses on murderers and rapists, 98 percent of the people who are treated as "criminal aliens" are neither.[59] Lumping more and more people into the category reinforces the myth that most immigrants are criminals and expands the population of noncitizens who are excluded from basic protections under immigration law.

Equating Criminal Convictions with Dangerousness

Popular discourse frames "criminal aliens" as dangerous, but the fact that one has been convicted of a crime—even a violent crime—does not mean that the individual poses a present danger to society. Crime-based deportations can be based on very old convictions. Many deportees' convictions occurred over twenty years ago. Some U.S. veterans reported being deported on the basis of convictions they obtained before they enlisted. They were not deportable when they entered the military, but the law later changed, rendering them deportable based on their previous conduct. The fact that someone committed a crime years ago—even a violent crime—does not mean that the individual is currently dangerous. Laws governing parole from prison recognize that the facts surrounding an old conviction—even in the most heinous cases—cannot by themeselves demonstrate current dangerousness.[60] For instance, in California, the recidivism rate for people who have been convicted of murder and have been released on parole is 1 percent, including convictions of any crimes—even minor ones—in the calculation of recidivism.[61]

In addition, given that racial bias pervades the criminal justice system, the fact that one has been convicted of a crime often has more to do with race than criminality. Communities of color are more heavily policed, making people in these areas more likely to be arrested for violations of the law that go undetected in areas that are less monitored. As Michelle Alexander explores in The New Jim Crow, "Although the majority of illegal drug users and dealers nationwide are white, three-fourths of all people imprisoned for drug offenses have been Black or Latino."[62]

Border regions are also more heavily policed, resulting in more arrests of immigrants because of the higher levels of enforcement in areas that tend to have higher concentrations of immigrants. In a study that compared prosecution practices among different federal districts, Mona Lynch documented how people charged with drug offenses along the southern border of the United States are treated differently than drug offenders in other areas of the country. She found that in a federal district court in the northeastern U.S., "a paternalistic logic undergirds drug prosecutions" whereby a defendant is typically perceived as "a troublemaker . . . but also vulnerable because of his lifetime exposure to the impoverished, degraded conditions" that characterize "neighborhoods targeted for enforcement." This contrasted sharply with her observations in a federal district court located near the U.S-Mexico border in the Southwest. There, 80 percent of those convicted were not U.S. citizens, and "those worthy of prosecution were less likely to be constructed as broken or damaged and more simply as dangerous people who had no respect for the law." Targeted border enforcement in the region increased the likelihood of arrest and prosecution of noncitizens; 83 percent of the federal drug possession cases during the time of this study occurred in the southernmost region of the southwestern district Lynch observed.[63]

Immigration enforcement efforts directed toward "criminal" aliens reinforce the racial inequality that permeates the criminal justice system. A study of CAP concluded that the program "appears to be biased against Mexican and Central American nationals" given that people from these countries "accounted for 92.5 percent of all CAP removals between FY 2010 and FY 2013, even though, collectively, nationals of said countries account for 48 percent of the noncitizen population in the United States."[64]

Erasing Context and Empathy

Perhaps most perniciously, the "criminal alien" label dehumanizes people by obscuring the complex details that generally surround participation in crime. People tend to be more forgiving—and less punitive—when they hear more details about the circumstances surrounding the commission of an offense.[65] The popularization of the "criminal alien" construct strips away the potential for promoting empathy or understanding and helps to legitimize deportation practices that contradict fundamental notions of fairness. Juliet Stumpf explains, "This extraordinary focus on the moment of the crime conflicts with the fundamental notion of the individual as a collection of many moments composing our experiences, relationships, and circumstances. It frames our circumstances, conduct, experiences, or relationships that tell a different story about the individual, closing off the potential for redemption and disregarding the collective effects on the people and communities with ties to the noncitizen."[66] In the words of a U.S. veteran facing deportation, "I am not a national security threat. What I am is a son, a father, a friend, and a brother." However, the law erases these other aspects of his identity, including the fact that he served in the U.S. military in Afghanistan, earning commendations and, in his words, "defend[ing] democracy, our people, and our American way of life."

Over time and in various societies, deportation has been employed as a mechanism for excluding people deemed socially undesirable, a tool for "dividing insiders from outsiders, the wanted from the unwanted, the deserving from the undeserving."[67] "Criminal aliens" are perhaps the most demonized socially undesirable group in the United States today. This perception has driven the massive increase of deportation efforts in the past decade, to the extent that legal scholar Ingrid Eagly observes, "The deportation of 'criminal aliens' is now the driving force in American immigration enforcement."[68]

During the late nineteenth and early twentieth centuries, "states increasingly used deportation as a way of governing the welfare of their populations, both by excluding the socially 'undesirable' (paupers, prostitutes, anarchists, criminals, the insane, excludable races, etc.) and by removing foreign labor . . . during periods of economic recession."[69] Contemporary U.S. deportation policy similarly targets those who are deemed "socially undesirable" by targeting Latinos and Blacks from less economically prosperous countries and calling them criminal aliens even when they have not been convicted of crimes.[70] Policies directed at deporting so-called criminal aliens receive bipartisan support. According to President Obama, his administration targeted "criminals, gang bangers, people who are hurting the community, not . . . folks who are here just because they're trying to figure out how to feed their families." In another speech, Obama pledged to continue to focus immigration enforcement "on actual threats to our security. Felons, not families. Criminals, not children. Gang members, not a mom who's working hard to provide for her kids." Trump appropriated this rhetoric and escalated it, going so far as to describe immigrant gang members as "animals" who target "young, beautiful girls" and "slice them and dice them with a knife because they want them to go through excruciating pain before they die."[71]

The widespread exclusion of people with criminal convictions from proposals for immigration reform, even in progressive circles, points to the possibility that people deemed "criminal aliens" will become solidified into a permanently marginalized category. Nowhere is this more apparent than in the laws that apply to people who have been convicted of crimes categorized as aggravated felonies, whose rights were severely limited by reforms Congress passed in 1996.

1996 IMMIGRATION REFORMS

In 1996, Congress passed two sweeping bills that dramatically restricted the rights of noncitizens facing removal. At the time, Lucas Guttentag criticized "the provisions in the Senate and House bills that abrogate procedural protections and deny meaningful judicial review" as a "thinly-veiled attack on the courts themselves" that "attempt[ed] to prohibit the courts from enforcing individual rights and civil liberties guaranteed by the Constitution and our laws."[72] The 1996 reforms were far-reaching, limiting refugees' access to protection, authorizing state and local officials to participate in enforcing immigration laws, and limiting access to public benefits for immigrants.[73] The reforms were so broad that Professor Anil Kalhan describes them as "a far-reaching experiment in what may be described as comprehensive immigration severity."[74] The harshest reforms apply to people convicted of crimes defined as aggravated felonies, a term that is misleading because it includes misdemeanors as well as felonies, nonviolent as well as violent offenses. Under the 1996 reforms, even lawful permanent residents are subject to virtually automatic deportation (after they complete their criminal sentences) if they are convicted of a qualifying crime.

The aggravated felony category initially applied only to a handful of crimes: murder, drug trafficking, and firearms trafficking cases. It was created in the Anti–Drug Abuse Act of 1988, which was a cornerstone of the Reagan administration's War on Drugs. Although the deportation consequences were severe at the time, courts still had the authority to stay deportations in cases where the individual had strong connections to the United States.[75] A series of bills in the early 1990s expanded the list of crimes that qualified as aggravated felonies and stripped those labeled as aggravated felons of more and more rights.[76] The Immigration Act of 1990 expanded the list to include "crimes of violence" punished by at least five years in prison. In 1994, an administrative removal process was created for those without lawful permanent resident status who were convicted of aggravated felonies—they no longer had the right to contest their removal in immigration court.

Then, in 1996, the Illegal Immigration Reform and Immigrant Responsibility Act (IIRIRA) and the Antiterrorism and Effective Death Penalty Act (AEDPA) greatly expanded the list of crimes defined as aggravated felonies. Whereas in 1988 only five crimes qualified, after 1996 over twenty crimes were defined as aggravated felonies, including nonviolent offenses such as failure to appear in court (under some circumstances), fraud, receiving stolen property, and drug offenses.[77] The IIRIRA also eliminated judges' discretion to balance the harm an individual's deportation would cause against the government's interest in deportation.

What began as a narrow exception is now widely used to deport people—especially people with long-term ties to the United States.[78] Most people deported under the aggravated felony provisions have lived in the U.S. for extended periods of time. Between 1997 and 2006, a quarter of all those deported for aggravated felonies had lived in the U.S. for twenty years or more.[79] On average, they had been in the U.S. for fifteen years.[80]

Taken together, the underprotection of constitutional rights that has characterized immigration law since its inception and the restriction of rights brought about by the 1996 reforms contribute to a legal regime that routinely violates people's fundamental rights. The remainder of this chapter explores three key areas in U.S. deportation law where due process protections are particularly lacking: (1) out-of-court removal orders, (2) lack of judicial discretion, and (3) absence of appointed counsel.

NO DAY IN COURT

Jose was deported through an administrative process with no right to appear in immigration court. He had lived in the U.S. since he was four years old and had acquired lawful status before his criminal conviction. He was not entitled to a hearing because people with conditional permanent resident status (as opposed to lawful permanent resident status) may be deported through the administrative removal process. His father had acquired a green card in the 1986 amnesty and had applied for lawful status for his children. Jose was on track to become a lawful permanent resident, but he had not yet become one. As a teenager, he had been able to work lawfully as a conditional resident, taking after-school jobs to help his family financially. Although he had lawful status and had spent most of his life in the United States, he did not qualify to appear before a judge to dispute his removal.

"It didn't feel right," he recalls, "that they could just stamp a paper and say you're banned for the rest of your life without even taking me to court. I feel like if they're going to take people to court before making them pay a fine or putting them in jail for a few days, they should at least take me to court before they tell me I can never come back. They just took me into an office and gave me a paper that said I'm banned for life."

Similarly, Luis was lawfully in the United States but was not a citizen. He recalls, "I was already kicked out before I even got a chance to speak up to the judge. I never got a chance to see the judge." He thought he had requested asylum, but that claim was either denied or lost. "I had put in some paperwork . . . for a political asylum [because] I don't think at the time it was safe for me to go over there [to Nicaragua]." However, he continues, "When I got deported in '08, it was never mentioned or anything. I never got to see a judge. I just had an automatic deportation." Court appearances can provide an important check in the system—a chance to make sure legitimate legal claims are appropriately processed and considered. In Luis's case, a judge might have looked into whether his asylum claim had been considered and rejected or merely fell through the cracks. Instead, Luis had to flee Nicaragua to escape from the death threats he had anticipated.

Now, most people the United States deports are not entitled to appear in court to contest their deportation.[81] Whereas only 3 percent of removals prior to 1996 occurred through such procedures, 75 percent of removals post-1996 have occurred outside the judicial process.[82] These out-of-court removal procedures include expedited removal, administrative removal for people with aggravated felony convictions, reinstatement of a prior removal order, and stipulated removal, where people sign away their rights and agree to their deportation—though often under confusing or coercive circumstances. In addition, judges may order people deported in absentia—in their absence—if they miss a court hearing. And, even for people who are entitled to court hearings, these proceedings are increasingly conducted using videoconferencing.

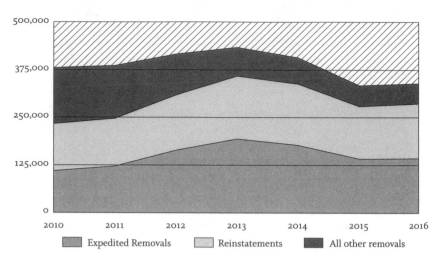

FIGURE 1.1. Expedited Removals and Reinstatements, 2010–16. Source: Department of Homeland Security, *Immigration Enforcement Actions: 2016* (Washington, DC: U.S. Department of Homeland Security, 2017), table 6.

In 2016, 83.6 percent of the 340,056 people removed from the United States were deported via expedited removal or reinstatement (see figure 1.1).[83] This does not include others who were deported through administrative or stipulated removal, or those whose removal orders were issued in absentia when they missed their court appearances. According to the Executive Office for Immigration Review, 25 percent of all cases completed in immigration court were terminated through in absentia orders in 2016.[84]

Gina's case involved several of these procedures. She was initially ordered deported in absentia when she missed her court date. When she was apprehended by police, she never set foot in court because the order that had been issued when she missed her court date was administratively reinstated. After she tried to reenter the U.S. by walking across the border, she was deported through the expedited removal process that applies to people apprehended near the border.

The expedited removal process was created to quickly process people who are apprehended while trying to enter the United States and has generally been used to remove people who have been in the country fourteen days or less. In expedited removal, immigration officers may issue a removal order with no formal hearing if an individual either lacks proper documents or has fraudulent documents. The order is not subject to judicial review unless the person (1) alleges she is actually a citizen; (2) is a returning lawful permanent resident, asylee, or refugee; or (3) asserts a credible fear of persecution, thus triggering the process of submitting an asylum petition. In recent years, over 40 percent of all removals have occurred through the expedited removal process, with 75 percent to Mexico.[85]

In contrast to expedited removal, which applies to people who have been in the U.S. for short periods of time, the Immigration Act of 1990 created an out-of-court administrative removal process for those convicted of aggravated felonies, many of whom have lived in the U.S. for many years. The 1996 reforms expanded the scope of this administrative removal procedure.[86] Under current law, the attorney general may "issue an order of removal" against those who are not lawful permanent residents if the individual has been convicted of an aggravated felony offense.[87] Thus, people who have lived in the U.S. for many years—including people who had permission to be in the country, like Jose and Luis—can be summarily deported with no right to appear in court. Lawful permanent residents maintain the right to challenge their removal in front of an immigration judge, but others with lawful status do not. This mechanism is now widely used to deport people with criminal convictions.

Still others are deported via stipulated removal, wherein people purportedly agree that they should be deported. However, many deportees report being pressured into agreeing to their deportation through stipulated removal orders. A survey of deported people in Mexico found that 33 percent of those who had signed a removal order reported feeling pressured into signing the order.[88] Twenty-seven percent reported they did not know what they had signed.[89] This does not surprise me, given the general confusion many deportees expressed in their interviews regarding the deportation process. Under the stress of being detained and facing removal, the experience is a blur for many. Some people reported that they were willing to sign anything in order to be released, not realizing that they were signing away their rights to challenge their deportation in the process.

Finally, through the reinstatement of removal process, people like Gina who have been previously deported are kept out of court. Over 40 percent of all people deported from the United States are deported via reinstatements of previous removal orders.[90] But it hasn't always been this way. Deportation expert Daniel Kanstroom explains, "Prior to 1996, most recidivists were placed in deportation proceedings before an immigration judge. They had the opportunity to explain why a previous order was erroneous" and could potentially apply for discretionary relief.[91] The 1996 reforms greatly expanded the scope of people who would be subject to reinstatement orders. Now, more people are deported under reinstatement of removal orders than by immigration judges.

Gina did not know it, but she could have appealed the reinstatement order. However, she had limited access to legal counsel because she was in custody and then was in Mexico. She missed the deadline to file an appeal in circuit court because there is a thirty-day time limit.[92] She also could have challenged the initial order that had been issued in absentia. Generally, removal orders issued in absentia are final and may not be revisited. However, it is possible to file a motion to reopen the case either (1) within 180 days of the order, if one can show "exceptional circumstances" such as "serious illness of the alien or death of an immediate relative of the alien"; or (2) at any time if the person can establish he did not receive notice or was in custody and therefore was not at fault for failing to appear.[93] Notably, eligibility for discretionary relief is not subject to judicial review after an order in absentia is issued. This means that Gina lost the opportunity to apply for cancellation of removal—to argue that she should be able to stay in the U.S. because deporting her would result in extreme hardship to her U.S. citizen children—when she missed her court date. As her story highlights, these procedures overlap and intersect to create a web that keeps noncitizens from the possibility of obtaining judicial relief from deportation.

When people are kept out of court, they lose the opportunity to mount a defense, and people with legitimate defenses fall through the cracks.[94] Keeping people out of court also obscures the pain and harm people experience as a result of deportation—it sanitizes the process by hiding the suffering in administrative offices rather than public courtrooms. The public nature of courtrooms is a fundamental aspect of U.S. democracy, meant to promote transparency and accountability in the adminstration of justice. Making the bulk of these decisions behind closed doors contradicts the country's democratic ideals.

THE LACK OF JUDICIAL DISCRETION

Frank might have qualified to remain in the United States under the pre-1996 standards. A veteran of the U.S. Marines who had been diagnosed with posttraumatic stress, he was deported based on a conviction for cashing a fraudulent check after leaving the military. While in the Marines, he deployed to Kosovo. Upon his return, he was honorably discharged, got married, and had a baby. He got his contractor's license and started a business. To his son, he was Daddy. To his fellow soldiers, he had been a brother. But to the U.S. government he once served, he became a "criminal alien" when he was convicted. His green card was revoked, and he was ordered deported—permanently—because the conviction qualified as an aggravated felony.

When he was deported, he left behind his U.S.-citizen wife and son. He had struggled with an alcohol problem, receiving a disciplinary write-up for alcohol use while he was enlisted, and was convicted on two occasions for driving under the influence. Nonetheless, his service in the U.S. military, coupled with his family ties to the United States, might have convinced a judge to allow him to stay in the country. He could have become a citizen while in the military if he had filled out the proper paperwork, but since he didn't, he was deportable. He says, "Ultimately it was the failure to fill out a form and get a couple of signatures that had the powers that be kicking me out of the U.S." But his aggravated felony conviction rendered him ineligible for relief; the judge who heard his case had no lawful authority to allow him to stay. Frank reports that his son's performance in school has suffered greatly since his deportation. When they speak on the phone, his son begs him to come home.

Although appearing in court gives people access to the possibility of mounting a defense, even those who are entitled to go before a judge face limited options. Lawful permanent residents like Frank who have been convicted of aggravated felonies, while entitled to court hearings, face extremely limited prospects for relief. The 1996 reforms stripped judges of the power to consider individual circumstances such as ties to the United States and the length of time the individual has spent in the country in these cases. Judges must order deportation if they conclude that the individual was convicted of an aggravated felony unless they are convinced the person subject to deportation will be tortured once removed. The bar for establishing torture is set very high. For example, one court found that "indefinite detention in a Haitian prison, under inhumane conditions" does not amount to torture.[95]

People who have not been convicted of an aggravated felony and who are entitled to court hearings may qualify for cancellation of removal—a judge can decide to allow the individual to stay in the United States. The rules are different depending on the noncitizen's immigration status. Lawful permanent residents—green card holders—who have been in the U.S. for seven years and have had green cards for five years can qualify for relief if a judge decides that the humanitarian concerns their deportation would raise outweigh the negative factors in the case. Judges engage in balancing tests on a case-by-case basis to determine whether an individual qualifies to stay. People who are not permanent residents may qualify for relief if they have been residing in the U.S. for ten years, have not been convicted of certain crimes, have "good moral character," and can establish that their removal would cause "exceptional and extremely unusual hardship" for specific citizen or lawful permanent resident relatives. This form of relief may only be granted to four thousand people per year, so even people who qualify must often wait quite a while for an opportunity to become available. People with aggravated felony convictions are excluded from applying for cancellation of removal.

Excluding people convicted of aggravated felonies from this kind of relief marks a dramatic change from the past. From 1976 to 1996, judges could weigh the danger an individual posed to society against the potential harm that would be caused by deporting him or her even if the individual had been convicted of an aggravated felony, with some limits.[96] The non-citizen facing deportation had to establish that, on balance, it would be "in the best interests of this country" to allow him to stay, based on the following factors:

- Family ties to the United States
- Long duration of residence in the United States, "particularly when the inception of residence occurred while the respondent was of young age"
- Hardship to the individual and his or her family if the deportation occurred
- Military service
- Employment history
- Business or property ties
- Community service or other evidence of value to the community
- Evidence of "genuine rehabilitation if a criminal record exists"
- Other evidence of good character[97]

These factors were to be balanced against "the presence of additional significant violations of this country's immigration laws," evidence of poor moral character, and "the existence of a criminal record." When weighing an individual's criminal record, however, "its nature, recency and serious-ness" were considered.[98]

Allowing judges to exercise their discretion in this way did not prevent all deportations. In fact, many people were ordered deported after judges balanced these factors in individual cases. For example, Byron Paredes-Urrestarazu was removed although he had lived in the U.S. since he was twelve years old and had an American wife and children. His participation in gang-related robberies, misconduct while in the military, false testi-mony, a history of drug abuse, and an arrest for drug possession convinced judges that his deportation would be in the best interest of the country.[99] However, judges could waive deportation in cases where the harm the in-dividual's deportation would cause outweighed the government's interest in deporting the individual, as in the case of Benedictor Diaz-Resendez. He was convicted for possession of a large quantity of marijuana with intent to distribute, had been a lawful resident for twenty-nine years, and had an American wife and children who were dependent on him.[100] He was allowed to stay. Bill Ong Hing, an immigration law professor with an ex-tensive practice background, explains that prior to 1996, "the immigration judge would pay close attention to the testimony or statements from family members, friends, employers, parole or probation officers, counselors in or outside prison, and psychiatrists" in order to "discern whether the ap-plicant would engage in criminal activity again."[101]

In contrast, the current law allows judges to consider only two issues: (1) whether the criminal conviction qualifies as a deportable offense (for example, a Supreme Court case examined whether hiding drugs in a sock qualified as an aggravated felony), and (2) whether a defense against de-portation is available (which, in aggravated felony cases, would be limited to cases where people can prove they would be tortured if deported).[102] As Justice John Paul Stevens explained in Padilla v. Kentucky, "While once there was only a narrow class of deportable offenses and judges wielded broad dis-cretionary authority to prevent deportation, immigration reforms over time have expanded the class of deportable offenses and limited the authority of judges to alleviate the harsh consequences of deportation. The 'drastic measure' of deportation or removal is now virtually inevitable for a vast num-ber of noncitizens convicted of crimes."[103]

Immigration judges express concerns with a legal system that does not allow them to make individualized determinations about whether people should be deported. Retired immigration court judge Paul Grussendorf has been a vocal advocate for restoring judicial discretion "to grant relief from deportation in deserving cases" by "revisit[ing] these harsh provisions and restor[ing] fairness and flexibility . . . by expanding the authority of immigration judges."[104] In the midst of immigration reform debates in 2013, Judge Dana Leigh Marks, then president of the National Association of Immigration Judges, publicly criticized the 1996 reforms that "curtailed the discretion of immigration judges," lamenting that "judges are no longer allowed to grant most forms of relief for individuals with an aggravated felony on their record, no matter how minor or old the conviction."[105] Judge Zsa Zsa DePaolo echoed this sentiment, explaining that she often has to tell people who appear before her, "If I had the authority to do that, I would. But I don't. . . . The law doesn't give me any other option."[106] Similarly, according to Judge James P. Vandello, "Each case I hear is a life story. . . . I have been able to unite or re-unite families. On the other hand, in many cases I have had to deal with the frustration of not being able to grant relief to someone because of the precise requirements of the statute, even though on a personal level he appears to be worthy of some immigration benefit."[107]

Only three years after the 1996 reforms went into effect, legal scholar Nancy Morawetz concluded that the reforms devalued family unity: "By eliminating (in most cases) the system of relief hearings that allowed family members to testify about the consequences of family separation, the laws operate as a statement that the effects of deportation on family members do not matter. This result is highly incongruous with both existing immigration laws and general values that permeate our legal system."[108] As Morawetz predicted, eliminating judicial discretion in cases involving aggravated felonies has undercut the possibility of deportation relief based on family unity in many cases. Eighty-six percent of the parents of U.S. citizen children removed in 2013 were deported due to criminal convictions, meaning that the harms U.S. citizen children face as a result of a parent's deportation are legally irrelevant most of the time.[109]

The Inter-American Commission on Human Rights has found that the lack of judicial discretion available in aggravated felony cases violates multiple articles contained in the American Declaration of Human Rights, including the rights to family unity and the best interest of the child.[110] The Inter-American Commission determined that even in cases involving aggravated felonies, the government should use a balancing test to weigh its right to deport against an individual's right to remain in the country, considering (1) the person's age of entry and length of time in the United States; (2) family, social, and other ties to the U.S.; (3) the severity of the crime, the time elapsed, and evidence of rehabilitation; and (4) possible hardship for U.S. citizen children, spouse, and other family members.

It is no surprise that families are routinely separated by a system that does not allow judges to balance whether deporting people will cause more harm than good. Although he signed the AEDPA, President Clinton expressed concern that "this bill . . . makes a number of major, ill-advised changes in our immigration laws having nothing to do with fighting terrorism. These provisions eliminate most remedial relief for long-term legal residents."[111] The human toll of these policies is high.

Under the old standards, Edgar—a father of two U.S. citizen teenagers who was deported for making verbal threats—may well have qualified to stay in the United States with his wife and children. Under the current law, however, he was permanently deported with no hope of lawfully returning. Edgar had been a green card holder but was deported for a conviction arising out of an incident that occurred nearly twenty years ago. According to Edgar, he and his wife were at a carnival; she was six months pregnant at the time.

> I was with a group of people and they got into a fight with some other people. So then with my wife being pregnant I told her, let's go. And we were leaving but there was this guy who followed us to the parking lot. . . . He pulled out his gun, and he told us to lay on the floor. And I told him I would, but my wife can't because she's pregnant . . . and me and him got into a—not a physical confrontation at all, but we just started arguing.

Edgar was eighteen or nineteen years old when this incident occurred; he is in his forties now. "I ended up doing about six months for it, but I took a deal. That's another thing that gets me is I should have fought it." The crime is an aggravated felony because it is categorized as a crime of violence under federal law.

Before 1996, Edgar would have had a strong argument that he should stay. His mother brought him to the U.S. when he was a young child, and he grew up attending public school in Southern California. All of his immediate family members lived in the United States, and none in Mexico. Further, his U.S. citizen wife and children would be negatively affected by his deportation. However, the law prohibited the judge from balancing these factors. In a sentencing motion filed when Edgar was charged in criminal court with illegal reentry after returning to the U.S. to reunite with his family five years after he was deported, his lawyer made the case for a sentencing reduction:

> When [Edgar] married his wife of 16 years, he underwent a remarkable transformation. He left behind his friends from the violent public housing project that he lived in for 14 years; and instead went to work every day to provide for his wife and children. He became a dedicated father, driving his children to and from school, helping with homework, and coaching sports teams. He also became a supportive husband, encouraging his wife to attend college and financially supporting her while she attended college.[112]

However, none of this was relevant in immigration court. The judge's authority was limited to analyzing whether Edgar's offense qualified as an aggravated felony.

Edgar and Frank are the kind of people who may have qualified to stay in the United States with their families before the 1996 reforms. In fact, the reforms were motivated by concerns among some members of Congress that over half of those with criminal convictions who applied for discretionary relief from deportation were allowed to stay. However, deportation has become virtually automatic for people convicted of crimes categorized as aggravated felonies.[113] Once deported, most are permanently barred from legally returning to the United States.[114]

LACK OF APPOINTED COUNSEL

Only a handful of the people I interviewed were represented by immigration attorneys before they were deported, partly because many were expelled through administrative proceedings. Others reported their families had consulted with attorneys but were told they had no chance of obtaining relief. Some had hoped to hire attorneys but could not afford to do so. Although people have the right to hire attorneys to represent them in deportation proceedings, the government does not provide a lawyer to those who cannot afford to hire one. Thus, only 14 percent of detained people in immigration proceedings (and 37 percent of all people who appeared in immigration courts) had attorneys between 2007 and 2012.[115]

Legal representation greatly impacts one's chances of success in immigration court. A study of deportation proceedings in Northern California found that detained people prevailed in their immigration cases 33 percent of the time if they had a lawyer, compared with a success rate of 11 percent for those without an attorney.[116] A national study similarly found that those represented by attorneys fared better in immigration court. For example, 21 percent of detained migrants represented by attorneys had successful outcomes, in contrast to only 2 percent of those without attorneys.[117] Nonetheless, courts have held that the government is not obligated to provide appointed counsel for indigent noncitizens because legal representation is not necessary for "fundamental fairness."[118]

For years, advocates, scholars, and judges have argued that fairness requires government-appointed counsel in deportation proceedings. In 1975, Judge DeMascio argued in a dissenting opinion that "a resident alien has an unqualified right to the appointed counsel" because "it is unconscionable for the government to unilaterally terminate" one's lawful permanent resident status without legal representation.[119] According to the judge, "Expulsion is such lasting punishment that meaningful due process can require no less," and "our country's constitutional dedication to freedom is thwarted by a watered-down version of due process on a case-by-case basis." If Gina had been provided with an attorney before she was deported, she might have been able to reopen her case to continue with the claim for cancellation of removal she had initiated, or she might have discussed strategies for petitioning to return after she was deported. Her conviction was not an aggravated felony, so she had some options for lawfully returning. Those options evaporated when she walked across the border and claimed to be a citizen. A consultation with an attorney might have helped her to understand this before it was too late.[120]

THE CURRENT DEPORTATION WAVE

The year after the 1996 reforms, removal numbers began to increase. Now, the United States deports significantly more people than it did in the past—six to seven times the number of people it deported just twenty years ago. Whereas the United States deported 50,924 people in 1995, it deported 333,341 in 2015.[121] The differences in these numbers cannot be attributed to migration patterns. While only half the number of unauthorized migrants

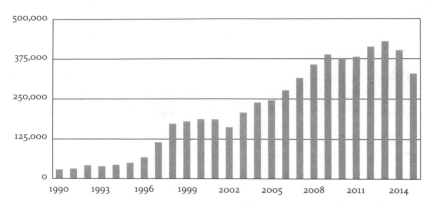

FIGURE 1.2. Removals from the United States, 1990–2015. Source: Department of Homeland Security, *Yearbook of Immigration Statistics 2016* (Washington, DC: U.S. Department of Homeland Security, 2017), table 39.

entered the United States in 2015 compared to 1995, six times the number of people were deported that year. President Donald Trump's efforts to deport more immigrants began at a time when deportation numbers had already reached unprecedented heights (see figure 1.2).[122] Between 1997 and 2012, the United States removed or returned 127 immigrants for every 100 immigrants who were granted admission, up from three deportations per 100 admissions in 1920.[123]

The United States now deports so many people that scholars characterize the current policy as a mass deportation campaign. Over three million people were removed during Barack Obama's presidency alone. In the past decade, Mexican nationals have consistently constituted over 70 percent of the population the United States deports. Mexican nationals have historically been—and will likely continue to be—the population most affected by U.S. deportation policies.[124]

The United States breaks actions to eject people from its territorial boundaries into two categories: removals and returns. When I use the term "deportation," I am referring to removals. Returns occur when people apprehended at the border are processed informally and are essentially turned around. When people are returned, they generally are not barred from coming into the United States, nor are they subject to enhanced punishments if they are apprehended in the future. In contrast, removals occur through formal processes—both in and out of court, as previously described. The crucial distinction is that removals trigger more serious consequences, such

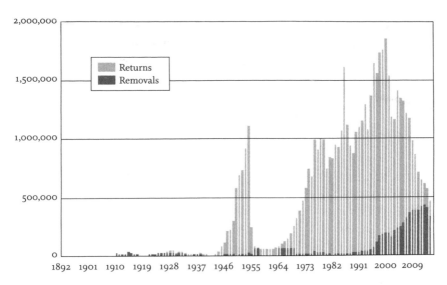

FIGURE 1.3. Removals and Returns, 1892–2015. Source: Department
of Homeland Security, *Yearbook of Immigration Statistics 2016* (Washington, DC:
U.S. Department of Homeland Security, 2017), table 39.

as prohibitions against returning to the country, ranging from three years to lifetime bars, and enhanced criminal sentences if people are apprehended returning without official authorization. The proportion of removals—formal deportations—has increased markedly from the past (see figure 1.3).

While returns primarily affect migrants entering the country for the first time, removals often target people with longer ties to the United States. Under President Obama, the U.S. increased its immigration enforcement efforts directed at people residing within the United States (as opposed to entering at the border). By expanding federal cooperation with local law enforcement agencies in order to identify people who could be deported, Obama's administration shifted the focus of deportation onto people living in the country; more resources were thus directed toward deporting people who had lived in the U.S. for long periods of time and whose lives were therefore deeply tied to the United States.[125]

Some deportees previously lived in the United States without lawful status—they were part of the population of 11.3 million people referred to as undocumented, irregular, or unauthorized. Despite their lack of legal status, this population is deeply tied to the United States. Two-thirds have lived in the country for more than ten years, and around half have U.S.

citizen children.[126] But, surprisingly to many, not all deportees were undocumented in the United States. A sizeable population had lawful status, including lawful permanent resident status; many had been green card holders. More than thirteen million lawful permanent residents reside in the United States.[127] Over 60 percent of this population is eligible to become citizens, which would free them from the specter of deportability. But until they go through the naturalization process, they too face the prospect of being deported if they are convicted of breaking the law.

The move toward enhanced immigration enforcement within the country has changed the population of deportees the United States sends to Mexico. Whereas in the past, most deportees had only recently migrated and had families or homes to return to in Mexico, there is a growing segment of the deported population with nowhere to go because their extended families now live in the United States. Approximately one-third of the people deported to Mexico consider the U.S. their home. This marks a dramatic change from the deported population in the past. In 2000, only 4.4 percent of deportees surveyed in Tijuana reported that the United States was their country of residence. A decade later, that number increased to 33.15 percent.[128] Another study of deportees in Mexico similarly found that 28 percent "stated their current home is located in the United States."[129] For people with long-term ties to the United States, deportation is experienced as an ejection from home, rather than a return to it.

The history of racial exclusion within the United States shaped a legal framework that has allowed discrimination under immigration law that would be prohibited in virtually all other contexts.[130] The decision to exclude deportation cases from the same constitutional protections that normally apply was highly contested in 1893, when the Supreme Court ruled in the case of *Fong Yue Ting* that courts should defer to Congress's plenary power. At the time, Justice Field's dissent expressed concern that exempting deportation cases from judicial review would bring "brutality, inhumanity and cruelty" into deportation cases.[131] This is precisely why the United Nations Office of the High Commissioner for Human Rights recommends an immigration system imbued with due process protections "of all migrants regardless of their status, including: the right to an individual examination, the right to a judicial and effective remedy, and the right to appeal."[132] The current deportation regime in the United States stands in stark contrast to this model, as evidenced by the U.S. Commission on Civil Rights' 2015 critique of the immigration detention system—the deportation pipeline—for violating due process protections and "threatening American values."[133] The "brutality, inhumanity and cruelty" Justice Field worried about in 1893 now characterize the U.S. deportation system.

The United States Supreme Court has been more willing to apply constitutional protections to immigration cases recently, but immigrants' rights continue to be underprotected in deportation cases.[134] The historical evolution of deportation law has undermined the Constitution's ability to protect immigrants and their family members from harsh policies enacted due to unfounded racialized fears. Courts' systemic underprotection of noncitizens' rights in deportation cases corresponds to a more widespread devaluation of immigrants—particularly immigrants of color. The persistence over two decades of the reforms enacted in 1996—laws that have been criticized by international human rights bodies as violations of fundamental human rights—is a strong indication of the depth to which (Mexican) immigrants have been socially excluded from becoming full members of U.S. society.[135] Even lawful residents who migrated as children and have lived in the country for decades—people who are integral members of American families and communities—can be permanently ejected with virtually no legal recourse.

Although many deportees perceive themselves to be American, the law treats them as outsiders by withholding standard constitutional protections in removal cases. Absent these protections, the law then converts them from members of U.S. society to outsiders by physically ejecting them from the boundaries of the country. The consequences of removing people from the place they consider home are quite severe. Although the law renders them irrelevant in many cases, these consequences are essential to understanding the true nature of U.S. deportation practices.

TWO RETURN TO A FOREIGN LAND

Many deported Americans recall the moment they realized they could be deported as a traumatic loss—a challenge to their very existence.[1] The sense of loss is most profound among those who had been lawful permanent residents, because they had not experienced this vulnerability vis-à-vis their immigration status before. One young man recalls, "When they told me I was being deported I was like, 'No. I'm from here. You can't deport me.'" Another reported that before he was put into removal proceedings, he "didn't feel any different than anyone else." Later, he says, "I saw they could just throw me out like I'm nothing." In a short amount of time, people are transformed from being Americans to being deportees.

Those who had been living without lawful status in the United States—a minority of the people I interviewed—describe a similar sense of loss when they recall the moment when they learned of their tenuous immigration status. They describe that as children, they felt like they were "the same" as their siblings or classmates who were citizens, or that they "did not know there was anything different" about them when they were younger. According to a security guard in Tijuana who had been undocumented before he was deported:

My brother had papers. My mom did too. . . . She had me over here [in Mexico]. My mom crossed me with my cousin's papers [at the age of four]. . . . I never knew about papers, anything like that until I told my mom, I don't want to go to school—I want to go to work.

She's like, "Oh, you can't." "Why?" "There's things about you." I'm like, "What's wrong with me? I'm not deformed, am I? I'm not rare."[2]

Through this conversation with his mother in his teenage years, he found out that he *was* different, according to the law. This difference became even more tangible after he was deported and was barred from ever returning to the United States. However, regardless of the fact that the law defines them as different, even those who grew up without lawful status in the United States develop such attachments to the people, places, and institutions that surrounded them in their childhood years that they too identify as Americans.

The labels that are employed to signal people's social exclusion sting, not only because they are demeaning, but also because they challenge people's sense of place in the world. "I hate when they call us aliens," Joe says. "We're people just like you. I've never been to outer space."[3] The demonization of so-called criminal aliens is so powerful that people go to great lengths to distance themselves from this identity. According to one deportee, "Just by saying I'm deported, they assume I'm a criminal. I mean, I guess you could say I am, but not like they're thinking. I'm a good person, you know?" "I don't even like being called a deportee," another says. "It's humiliating. It's like telling the world that I was kicked out, rejected. It's like walking around saying 'I'm a reject.'" A pensive young woman compared her experiences as a deportee in Tijuana to the experiences of Hester Prynne in Nathaniel Hawthorne's novel *The Scarlet Letter*: "I walk around with this mark on me telling the world that I'm different or like that something's wrong with me."

In addition to the labels that are used to convert people from members of society to outsiders, the process of being deported functions to strip people of their sense of belonging in U.S. society. Deportees regularly report being insulted with racial slurs by U.S. immigration officials.[4] They report being called a "fucking wetback," a "dirty little Mexican woman," and "Mexican pieces of shit."[5] Physical abuse and medical neglect in immigration detention facilities is common. In addition, people are detained in temporary holding tanks that are made to be so cold that they are regularly referred to as *hieleras*—ice chests.

Those who are responsible for deporting people seem to purposefully make the process more painful. People frequently report being dropped off in Mexican border towns in the middle of the night—20 percent in a recent survey were deported between 10 PM and 5 AM.[6] That same study found that 34 percent of deportees indicated that at least one of their belongings was taken from them during the detention and deportation process—U.S. officials routinely keep people's ID cards when deporting them.[7] This is particularly problematic because "widespread extortion and harassment by Mexican officials has been linked to lack of identification," and functioning without an ID is virtually impossible because "one cannot receive a wire transfer, get a job, board an airplane or access certain state services without official documents."[8] Those in deportation proceedings are treated as if their rights do not deserve protection, a clear indication that they are no longer being treated as members of U.S. society.

Anthropologist Deborah Boehm documented the courtroom proceedings of Operation Streamline, a fast-track process designed to sentence migrants for the crime of illegal entry quickly and efficiently. She remarks on the dehumanizing function of the proceedings: "Each day, these groups of migrants are alienated quite literally . . . constructed as 'aliens' and thus as different from and defined against those who are perceived as authentic and deserving members of the nation. . . . The migrants are collectively shamed, ostracized, othered."[9] Boehm observed that "witnessing these mass deportations, one also witnesses the formal conversion of migrants to 'aliens,' the legal category used by the state."[10]

The process of moving someone who has been lawfully present in the United States from the category of lawful immigrant to deportee highlights the liminal nature of immigration status.[11] Categories are not fixed. Rather, they are fluid and can change at any moment. When people who think of themselves as Americans arrive in Mexico after being deported, they widely report that they do not feel like they belong. They experience their arrival as an ejection from their homes rather than a return to them, feeling like strangers in a strange land.

ARRIVAL STORIES

Arriving from the United States

After Victor was dropped off in San Luis Colorado, a town just south of the Arizona border, the soles of his shoes flapped open as he walked because Border Patrol had cut them open to look for contraband. They kept his ID, his money, his wedding ring—all of his belongings. The money and ID presented a particular problem because he could not even pick up money from Western Union without a government-issued identification. He was able to call his wife from a migrant shelter. "I'm cold . . . and hungry," she remembers him telling her. He met another deportee whose family lived in the border region. Victor asked his wife to wire some money to this new acquaintance, who was able to pick it up for him. "A risky move," his wife recalls, given the recency of this friendship. He bought a bus ticket to head south toward Playa del Carmen, where a cousin lived. En route, the bus was in a major accident. He was injured. Others died.

Farther east, David was dropped off in Juárez, right across the border from El Paso, Texas. While he was in immigration detention, he learned that he would be deported to Juárez. He was lucky because at least he knew in advance where he would be dropped off. Most people don't. He was also unlucky because his destination was Juárez—a border town with an infamous reputation for violence. His wife booked him a hotel room for one night and paid in advance, knowing that he would probably not have access to cash once deported. She also used an internet program to create a detailed map showing him the path to take from the border directly to the hotel. She mailed it to him while he was still in the detention facility so that he would know where to go. He would stay the night in the hotel and would make his way to the bus station the next day to travel to a safer part of the country. Another deportee tears up recalling the day that his wife traveled from their home in Utah to meet him in Juárez. "She had never been to Mexico," he recalls, "and there she was standing out on the street in the most dangerous city in the country, holding our baby just waiting for me all day in the sun." In Reynoso, a government-funded group greets deportees with a sandwich and a ride to the closest bus station. Rumor has it that cartels recruit recent deportees, so the government has a vested interest in helping them to get out of town. "They don't care where you go—they just want you out of there," explains one deportee.

People deported to Mexico usually arrive on foot, as in the cases described above. Border Patrol officials watch them walk through the pedestrian gates that lead into the country. The United States also deports some people on planes to Mexico City, which is 1,700 miles from the U.S. border, in an effort to reduce the likelihood that deportees will immediately return. Once in Mexico, people struggle to accept the reality that they have been deported. "I keep looking across," a deportee in Tijuana told me, referring to the fence that separates Tijuana from San Diego. "Like I can't believe I'm really here." From the hills of Tijuana, people look down into a large outlet mall that sits a few feet from the last row of barbed wire–lined fencing on the U.S. side of the border.

Jose was deported after living in the United States for twenty-three of his twenty-eight years. As a child in Mexico, Jose recalls regularly being hungry because the family did not have enough money for food. His mother brought him across the border when he was four. Although he struggled to learn English at first, it quickly became his primary language. He spoke Spanish at home with his parents and older relatives, but his siblings communicated with one another, and with their friends, in English. The stress of his family's poverty combined with physical and emotional abuse he experienced at the hands of his stepfather propelled Jose into joining a gang. The gang became his refuge; it gave him shelter when he ran away to escape the turmoil at home and became his support system when he felt rejected by his parents. He was arrested at the age of sixteen for participating in a robbery and served twelve years in adult prison. During this time, he maintained strong relationships with his siblings, who visited him regularly. He earned his GED and then an associate of arts degree. He cut ties with the gang that had meant so much to him as a child, and he looked forward to finishing college and spending time with his brothers, sisters, nephews, and cousins when released. His siblings were by now all U.S. citizens. Some had been born in California, while others became citizens when his mother naturalized, and the oldest obtained her citizenship after becoming a lawful permanent resident through her father. He no longer had any family in Mexico.

Like other noncitizens, he served his criminal sentence in the United States before immigration consequences were levied as a result of the conviction. At the end of his prison term, Jose was transferred to immigration custody instead of being released. He was taken to the Mexican border and dropped off in Mexicali, a border town. Prior to his arrest, he had been on track to become a lawful permanent resident; the family qualified through his stepfather. However, his conviction derailed this process. Before he was deported, he consulted with immigration attorneys and was told that he had no hope in immigration court and that his deportation was inevitable.

He was deported at the same time as five others. They figured it would be safer to stick together, so they walked as a group from the border to a bus station, carrying all of their earthly possessions in paper grocery bags with their names and prison ID numbers on them. These paper bags were the obvious sign that this was the newest group of deportees to arrive in Mexico. One of the members of this group of six was from Tijuana. He had been to Mexicali before, so he became the guide, leading the way to the bus station. There they pooled their money to buy bus tickets to Tijuana, those with a little extra covering the tickets for those without enough. Once Jose arrived at the Tijuana bus station, he was the lucky one. His family was en route from Los Angeles to pick him up to take him to a beach house they had rented for a family reunion. Waiting there at the bus station though, he felt unspeakably nervous. His palms were sweating, his heart racing. He was on high alert, concerned that any number of suspicious-looking people were ready to rob him or forcibly recruit him to get involved with criminal activity. Back in prison, he had heard stories of drug cartels recruiting deportees using strong-arm tactics, staking out the places where ICE deposits people every day to tap into this desperate labor pool. His fear was not unfounded. Some deportees have been kidnapped immediately upon their arrival to Mexico, targeted based on the assumption that their family members in the United States have access to ransom money.[12]

Even once he got into the car with his family, his heart kept beating quickly. When they decided to stop for tacos, he didn't want to get out of the car. "I'll just wait here," he said. He felt scared, threatened, and uncomfortable. He had long dreamed of coming home to his mother's house in Los Angeles—to eating at his favorite childhood restaurant and then stopping by his aunt's house to say hello before taking his nephews to eat ice cream at his favorite spot. This was different than what he had imagined. "I felt panicked. Scared. No one could have any idea how panicked I felt that day unless they have gone through it themselves," he recalls.

The challenges with Jose's adjustment can be attributed not just to culture shock but also to his transitioning to the free world after spending so much time in prison. But this shock, fear, and struggle to adjust is echoed by many other deportees who have not spent time in custody—or who have spent much less time behind bars. Most American deportees speak of feeling fear and alienation when they arrive in Mexico. They also struggle to adjust to day-to-day life. One deportee explained his challenges with transitioning from using dollars to pesos, saying, "When I got here, I had no idea what all the different bills and coins were. The money is all different colors and everything. I would just hold out my money and have people take what I owed."

Arriving from Central America

A subgroup of deportees who have settled in Mexico are originally from Central American countries. They navigate a more complicated path to arriving in Mexico. Luis was born in Nicaragua. He grew up in Los Angeles and now lives in Tijuana. He got involved with a gang at a young age, was convicted of assault in his early twenties, served time in prison, and was deported upon his release. His wife, Sara, is from Los Angeles; they were high school sweethearts. Their first son was born when they were teenagers. He is now nineteen. They also have a six-year-old daughter who was born in Mexico several years after Luis was deported. The family settled in Tijuana so Sara could work in San Diego. However, Luis's journey to Tijuana was more difficult than for Mexican deportees. "I'm a survivor," he said. "Otherwise I wouldn't have made it here [to Mexico]."

His deportation came as a shock. He recounts, "I was never really warned, 'You're about to go to a whole other country. You're not going to have no means of getting no money. You're not going to have no career. . . . We have no plans to help you.'" His father and grandfather left Nicaragua in the aftermath of the civil war. "We all went with papers," he says. He remembers getting his green card in 1990. However, he got into trouble with the law in his early twenties. According to Luis, an undercover police officer attacked him, and, not knowing that the person attacking him was a police officer, Luis reacted by shooting him. He was convicted of assault and was deported after serving twelve years in prison. According to Luis, "[Deportation] never crossed my mind. I didn't even feel like I was not from the U.S. I mean, why would I be deported if I'm from the U.S.?"

Luis's family warned him his life would be in danger in Nicaragua because of his family's political history. While in Nicaragua, he recalls being in a park with a cousin when someone recognized his family name. "He actually drew down a gun on me and he said he would kill me if it wasn't for my cousin . . . because they really hated . . . the Sandinista[s]. They didn't like them." He stayed in Nicaragua for three months, waiting for a passport so that he could leave the country.

In order to get to Mexico, he had to pass through Honduras and Guatemala. He had decided to circumvent El Salvador because of its notorious gang problem and the militarized police response to gang members. "I didn't want to go because of the tattoos," he says, referring to the tattoos that cover most of his body. "In Honduras about twice I was pulled over, taken off the bus in the middle of the road, got stripped naked because of my tattoos," he recalls. While he was crossing a river to enter Honduras, a scorpion bit him. He stayed in Honduras for nearly two weeks while he recovered and then boarded a bus that took him to Guatemala. From there, he paid Mexican authorities to allow him safe passage into the country.

Luis had grown up in the U.S. and was accustomed to dressing in an urban American style—he usually wears a T-shirt, baseball hat, and loose pants. For his journey through Mexico, he bought clothes that he thought would help him to look more stereotypically Mexican in the hopes of avoiding apprehension. "My outfit consisted of some white alligator boots, right? . . . I had some dark blue Wranglers; I'm talking about butt tight, really tight. I had a white alligator belt with button Wranglers, double-pocketed shirt tucked in with about a ten-gallon hat on. And I had to let my moustache, just my moustache, grow." In recounting the story, he uses humor to minimize the fear he obviously felt, but it is clear that he went to great pains to try to disguise his identity as a deportee from the United States, as well as his Nicaraguan citizenship. His family in the United States had sent him some money, so he was able to pay for bus tickets rather than riding the infamous train—La Bestia (the Beast)—that Central American migrants with fewer resources ride through Mexico toward the U.S. border.

He followed a clandestine route from safe house to safe house. He describes an underground railroad of sorts, where migrants pass along information about where to stop for food and shelter as they travel north. Along the way, he had to overcome numerous obstacles—a soldier took all of his clothes and money at one stop; at another, he had to convince a local bus driver to allow him to hide under the bus to make it past an immigration checkpoint. He also recounts stories of community—families who offered him food and shelter despite their limited economic resources, and a farmer who gave him a job so that he could earn money to continue his journey after the soldier robbed him. Two months after departing Nicaragua, Luis arrived in Tijuana. His wife and son still laugh remembering what he looked like that day when they reunited on Avenida Revolución, Tijuana's downtown tourist strip, dressed in the outfit he selected to help him fit in as a stereotypical Mexican cowboy. Luis says, "When they pulled up to Revolución, I was standing in front of a hip-hop club and I was dancing in the boots and they were just laughing because I couldn't stop dancing." Since coming to Tijuana over ten years ago, Luis has been able to build a stable life in Mexico. He obtained lawful status and now runs a small business.

COMMON EXPERIENCES WITH ARRIVAL TO MEXICO

Although everyone's experience with arriving in Mexico is different, common themes emerge in people's narratives. Deportees' arrival stories highlight the myriad ways in which those with long-term ties to the United States experience the return to their country of birth more like arriving in a foreign country than returning home. Deported Americans report (1) experiencing culture shock and fear immediately upon their arrival; (2) lacking family ties, housing, and support systems in Mexico; (3) facing barriers to education and employment due to their lack of cultural familiarity; and (4) confronting stigma and rejection in Mexico.

Culture Shock and Fear

Anthropologist Kalvervo Oberg coined the term "culture shock" to refer to "how people react to strange or unfamiliar places."[13] Generally, it is "a feeling of confusion, doubt, or nervousness caused by being in a place (such as a foreign country) that is very different from what you are used to."[14] The culture shock that deportees who grew up in the United States experience upon their arrival in Mexico demonstrates the depth of their immersion in American culture.[15]

Like Jose, most of the people I interviewed reported feeling shocked, scared, and/or disoriented when they first arrived in Mexico.[16] Many also brought up how different the quality of life is in Mexico from what they were accustomed to in the United States. Gina—the mother of three whose story begins the book—was struck by "the houses on the hills." She also expressed fear upon her arrival, reporting, "I feel like someone is going to rape me or rob me. You walk and all the guys [are] staring at you like if they wanna do something or they're planning to do something to you." Another deportee refused to take public transportation because, he said, "I don't know about all that here. . . . Someone could try to do something." His fear stood out to me because he had grown up in a notoriously violent area of Los Angeles and had served time in maximum-security prisons. His unfamiliarity with his new environment made it more intimidating. Edgar—who was deported based on the threat he made at a carnival twenty years ago—was struck by the enormous potholes in the streets. In his words, "I'm always complaining about the streets. Like if this was a U.S. city, the streets would be really nice. Look at San Diego—it's right there. Look at how much nicer it is 'cause their government really takes care of that stuff. Ours, I don't know." Observations about hygiene, the extreme poverty, and the state of disrepair of buildings, homes, and streets are common in deportee narratives. One woman recounts visiting a government-funded medical clinic where there was no soap for patients or doctors to wash their hands. She reports being asked to leave the clinic after creating a scene because she was so upset.

The differences are more extreme for those who move to rural areas, where some homes lack indoor plumbing and, in some cases, even electricity. A deportee who moved to a rural community explains, "I'm used to taking hot showers. Inside a bathroom [laughs]. I can't believe I even have to say that. Inside . . . I grew up in the projects but we all had bathrooms. But yeah, this is where I shower." He shows me a bucket. "I fill it up with water. If I have time I can heat some up on the stove over there. Otherwise, it's just cold water in a bucket. That's how we do it here." Far from returning home, this group of deportees experiences their return to Mexico as if they were arriving in a foreign country.

Lack of Family Ties to Mexico

Most deportees who came to the U.S. as children no longer have family residing in Mexico. If they do, their family ties are to distant relatives rather than to immediate family members. Their close family members are generally rooted in the United States. This complicates the adjustment to living in Mexico. Most of the people I interviewed did not have family homes to return to, and they lacked guidance from relatives who could otherwise help them to acclimate. One deportee whose entire family resides in the U.S. recounts, "It would be different if I had family here to give me a place to stay, or to guide me about basic things. Like how to open a bank account. Or what is a CURP."[17]

Only four of the 112 deportees I interviewed reported that they had immediate family members living in Mexico when they were deported. Twenty-five had extended family members with whom they had some contact in Mexico, but the majority could not identify any family members who resided in Mexico. My findings are consistent with a qualitative study of deported women living in a migrant shelter in Tijuana, each of whom had spent between eight and thirty-eight years in the United States. Only one of the twenty-one women in the study indicated a desire to return to the state where she had been born.[18] She ultimately decided to try to return to the U.S. instead. According to the authors of this study, most of the women who reside in this shelter do not return to their communities of origin because "they have lost contact with these places for many years, and their networks of family and friends are found in the United States."[19]

Responding to concerns from border towns about the concentration of deportees in their cities, the Mexican government subsidizes bus tickets for those who wish to return to their communities of origin after they are dropped off in the border region by U.S. authorities. Residents and government officials in border cities express concern about being inundated with deportees because of the widespread perception that they are likely to engage in crime. However, given the lack of family ties that many deportees have to their birthplaces and the substantial ties they tend to have with the U.S., many opt to reside along the border, where it is closer for their families to visit or where they can attempt to return to the United States. A 2012 survey found that deportees who lived in the United States for more than five years are more likely to stay in the border region or to attempt to reenter the United States soon after their deportation than those who have spent less time there.[20]

Although his family all lives in the United States now, Jose—who was panicked when he was released from prison and deported to Mexico—tried to go back to the town in central Mexico where he was born. His mother's great-aunt lived in the town, as did his brother-in-law's parents. He had never met these extended family members before, but they were all he had. He only lasted a year because the way of life there felt so foreign to him. "I didn't fit in there—I just couldn't adjust." He eventually moved back to the border region. Edgar, whose mother brought him to the U.S. when he was four, similarly settled in the Tijuana area. He explains why: "I do have family here [in Mexico]. I was born in a place called Guerrero. I don't know them though. I think it's like my mom's family, grandparents. I don't know them at all. That's why I'd rather be here." Edgar's immediate family members—his mother, siblings, wife, and teenage children—are all U.S. citizens and live in Southern California. He lives in a beach community on the outskirts of Tijuana that is populated by wealthy Mexican families, retired Americans, and deported people like himself who identify as American. He chose to live here because, in his words, "It's the closest thing to living in the U.S. Everyone speaks English."

Lacking family homes to return to, deportees with fewer financial resources seek shelter in makeshift homeless camps that have sprouted up in border towns. Tijuana's riverbed runs parallel to the border with San Diego and has been home to between seven hundred and one thousand homeless deportees at any given time.[21] A middle-aged man who had been living there for five months explained that he was there because his entire family was in the United States, and he wanted to stay close so that he could try to go back. He grew up in the United States, where he had worked in construction since turning eighteen. He went through a rough patch in his early twenties and started using drugs; he was convicted of possession of methamphetamines for the purpose of sale, although he maintains that he never sold drugs but had them for his own use. Years after this conviction, when he went to renew his green card, immigration officials detained and deported him. He left behind two daughters under the age of ten. He had been sober for ten years, but he relapsed upon his deportation. In his words:

> I felt like my whole world collapsed. Like I'm never going to see my girls again 'cause who's going to bring them over here? I can't work because I don't speak Spanish and I'm dirty from sleeping out here on the streets. I would just sit here and stare across [the border], wishing I could just fly over that fence. . . . I took my first hit three weeks after I got deported.

Over half of the homeless people who populate the area surrounding the Tijuana riverbed speak English, and nearly 60 percent had lived in the U.S. between six and twenty-five years, indicating that many deportees with strong ties to the U.S. find themselves homeless after deportation, living literally next to the barbed-wire fence that divides Mexico from the United States.[22]

Barriers to Education and Employment

Deportees who migrated to the U.S. as children face many barriers to working or enrolling in school in Mexico because they attended school and established their work histories in the United States. The process of applying for a Mexican identification card is time consuming and challenging, often involving trips to multiple government offices and sometimes to one's birthplace hundreds of miles away. Even once the paperwork is in order, the language barrier can be a problem. Although many are accustomed to speaking Spanish at home with family members, it is quite different to attempt to communicate in a professional context. According to Gina:

> Being here is so complicated too because if you want to look for a job it's hard because they ask you for your high school diploma, your ID. They want a new birth certificate. . . . I can't do nothing here. They ask me for a bunch of things. A CURP and what, I don't even know. All the doors are closed to me. I don't see a future here. I don't know what to do.

In order to work in Mexico, people must provide their employers, at a minimum, a government-issued identification card called a *credencial elector*, issued by the Instituto Federal de Elecciones, and a Clave Única de Registro de Población (CURP), which is a federal identification number. The credencial is the most widely accepted form of identification and requires a birth certificate and a photo ID. Obtaining a birth certificate can be a complicated process, particularly for those who are not familiar with Mexican procedures. Many towns maintain their birth and death records in noncomputerized ledgers, and some find that traveling to their birthplace is the only way to get a copy of their birth certificate.

Edgar sums up his experience with obtaining Mexican identification documents as a "pain in the butt." "I had to go all the way to [southern] Mexico to where my mom registered me and do all that, find my birth certificate." Communicating in Spanish with government representatives was another challenging part of this process for Edgar. He explains that his Spanish was "really bad" when he first arrived in Mexico, but it has improved. However, he said, "It's still hard. I could carry [on] a conversation with somebody but as far as going to city hall and asking for a paper or once they start using them long words, you know."

For Jose, obtaining a birth certificate was not the only challenging part of applying for a credencial. He also had to figure out how to obtain a photo ID. He had been incarcerated since he was sixteen years old and was deported without any identification. He figured out that he could obtain a driver's license, but in order to apply, he needed to show proof of residence in the form of utility bills in his name from the past two months. However, he was staying in a short-term rental and the utilities were not in his name. Time was of the essence because he had been stopped at a routine military checkpoint and asked for his credencial; when he explained he did not have one, the soldiers informed him that Mexico required everyone to carry identification, and he could be sent to jail for not having one. He went through a stressful process of visiting one government agency after another to try to find a solution to this problem. "I was freaked out. I just got out. I didn't want to go back to jail just because I didn't have an ID. . . . I kept going to different offices, trying to find a way to get an ID, and people were rude. I would try to explain myself in my Americanized Spanish—I don't think that helped my cause."

Ultimately, he found a helpful person who issued him a Certificate of Residence, which he could use along with his birth certificate to obtain a driver's license. However, in order to take the driving test, he had to report to the test center with a car registered in Mexico; his sister's car would not work because it was registered in California. He didn't know anyone who lived in Mexico, much less anyone who would lend him a car. Jose was creative, and he paid a taxi driver to use the taxi to take his driving test. He successfully obtained his driver's license, which he then used to obtain his credencial. Each step in this process costs money, and Jose was lucky to have financial support from his family members in the U.S. Without it, obtaining official identification would have been virtually impossible. Getting a job would have been too.

In addition to the challenges surrounding obtaining proper identification, deportees face barriers to employment because their education and work experience have all been in the United States. Edgar explains, "All my training was in the U.S. All the experience we had is over there, so it's kind of like we gotta start over here, so we gotta find something to do that we can do long-term." It can be difficult to enter the workforce in Mexico with Spanish language skills that do not rise to professional standards. Further, the pay differential is extreme. It is typical to earn 1,200 pesos a week for full-time employment, which generally requires fifty to sixty hours of work. Depending on the exchange rate, this is about sixty to one hundred U.S. dollars per week, which is under two dollars per hour. This is a dramatic pay decrease, and the adjustment is challenging. According to Edgar:

> For about eighteen or twenty years I worked warehouse in the U.S. And I went everywhere from the entry-level positions to supervisor.

I was getting paid good over there. I left making a little over thirty bucks an hour. So from that to this, you know, it's . . . I did apply for—I seen some big warehouses like Sharp and I figured they're, you know, big warehouses, known brands, they're gonna pay you good. But damn, they pay like sixty bucks a week, six days a week.

The dramatically lower wages people earn in Mexico come up in almost every interview with deportees who have been accustomed to working in the United States. Many point out that what they earn in a week equates to what they used to earn in a day. Although the cost of living is lower in Mexico, it is not proportionally equivalent.

Low wages affect a much broader segment of the Mexican population than deportees—limited economic prospects have motivated migration from Mexico to the United States for years. In 2016, protests erupted across Mexico in response to a projected increase in the cost of gas brought about by the government's decision to stop subsidizing gas prices. However, the adjustment from being a member of the working class in the United States to trying to survive as a member of the working class in Mexico presents a unique challenge for people who have become accustomed to life in the United States.

Many deportees express dreams of enrolling in school in Mexico. This is complicated, however, for those unfamiliar with the process of applying to a university in Mexico. Further, having graduated from high school in another country is an obstacle to gaining admission to public universities.[23] Nancy Landa experienced these challenges firsthand after her deportation to Mexico. She had graduated from California State University, Northridge, where she had been the president of the student body. She decided to enroll in a master's degree program. She explains:

It was five years ago when I encountered a bureaucratic nightmare that I did not know existed. Upon returning to Mexico due to a deportation, I learned that my entire academic and professional career I built in the U.S. as an undocumented student would not be recognized in the country where I could prove to be a citizen. It has already been difficult to survive one of the worst type [sic] of rejection I had experienced—the expulsion from the country that I lived most of my life. Even more painful was to arrive to a country which I am told is supposed to be "my home" and where I "belong" simply because I was born there, but where I could also encounter countless obstacles when I attempt to use the education and knowledge I had acquired "abroad." In other words, according to government agencies like the Secretariat of Public Education (SEP) in Mexico, my education from the U.S. is worthless.

She found it easier to enroll in a master's degree program in the U.K. than in Mexico and returned to Mexico after completing the degree.

Mexican universities require applicants to obtain their transcripts from the United States and have them apostilled, which entails obtaining verification from the state or federal government that the document is valid. Once they obtain the apostilled transcripts, they must then have them translated by a certified translator in Mexico in order to apply for admission. This process is complicated for people who cannot enter the United States to obtain the necessary documents, and each step can be costly. In addition, applicants to public universities must take an entrance exam that is administered in Spanish and is particularly challenging for those whose education has been completed in English. While high school transcripts will generally be accepted after they have been apostilled and translated, college is more complicated because the degree requirements must be 75 percent the same as the equivalent degree in Mexico in order to qualify; this is the problem Nancy ran into when trying to use her BA degree from the United States to qualify for entrance to a master's program in Mexico. The process of enrolling in a private university is easier, but the cost is prohibitive for many.

Language barriers present another challenge to deportees' pursuing education. One deportee who was attending university in Mexico reported that it was very challenging to adjust to learning in Spanish, even though he speaks conversational Spanish with ease.

> It's so different, trying to speak formal Spanish, reading all the books in Spanish. The worst is when I have to give presentations in class. I stumble over my words because my brain is jumping back and forth between English and Spanish. The other students laugh at me—even the teachers laugh at me and mock me. One teacher said I should go back to the other side. I don't tell them I can't go back. It's embarrassing.

The economic challenges deportees face are the primary obstacle to pursuing higher education in Mexico. Most work fifty to sixty hours per week just to pay for food and shelter; this does not leave time or financial resources for school. Having attended school in the United States, they face distinct challenges with integrating into schools or careers in Mexico.

Stigma and Rejection

Rather than being accepted upon their return, deportees who grew up in the United States face stigmatization and rejection in Mexico. They are caught in between two cultures and feel rejected by both. Just as the term "immigrant" has been conflated with "criminal" on the U.S. side of the border, people in Mexico tend to view deportees as criminals as well. Although most people who have been deported to Mexico have never been convicted of a crime, many of those who are most recognizable as deportees—people who prefer to speak English and are more culturally American than Mexican—have been deported due to criminal convictions. This is because but for their criminal conviction, they would probably have been allowed to stay in the U.S., either because they were lawful permanent residents or because their strong ties to American citizen family members would have allowed them to qualify for relief from removal. Thus, deportees who identify as American—and who are easily recognizable as deportees—often have criminal convictions. This stigma is exacerbated by the fact that some of the deported, particularly those without family support, make up a large portion of the homeless population in the border region. One deportee explains, "When I talk with Mexican people, I just pretend that I moved over here because I wanted to. Because if I say I'm deported, they assume the worst."

It is painful to feel simultaneously rejected in both the United States and Mexico. In a conversation between two deportees, one said, "The United States says we're not American, but Mexicans say we're not Mexican. So what are we?" The other replied, "People don't look at us like real Mexicans. So we're screwed on both sides." Deportees report being frequently asked in Mexico, "Qué eres?" or "De dónde eres?"—"What are you?" or "Where are you from?" If they say they are Mexican, this is met with laughter, as if to say, "No you're not." Some even voice their disbelief. "No, but where are you really from? I can tell you're not Mexican," one deportee recalls being told. According to one deportee, "They call me a *gabacho* here—that means a white guy—I guess because of how I dress and my accent when I talk in Spanish. Look at me—I'm dark! No one ever called me a gabacho in L.A."

Another deportee explained, "Over there, they call me a wetback because I'm Mexican. Here, they call me a *pocho* [a derogatory term for a Mexican American] because I'm American. So I'm caught in between. No one wants me." The stress that deportees report when asked to identify who they are, or where they are from, signals the profound identity crisis people experience when they are rejected by both the country they consider their homeland and their country of origin. A young woman shared a strategy she developed: "Now, I just say I was born here, but I grew up on the other side. They seem to get that, and it explains who I am better than saying I'm either Mexican or American, because I guess I'm neither one."

The rejection people who have been socialized in the United States report upon their return to Mexico reveals that the American identities they feel internally are also observed by outsiders. They are not perceived as Mexicans by people in Mexico. Understanding the unique experiences of this population opens the door to a more realistic assessment of the harms caused by their ejection from the boundaries of the United States. The rigid boundaries the law draws to divide citizens from noncitizens do not capture people like Gina, Luis, Jose, and Edgar, who identify as American in every respect, from language to family ties to cultural familiarity to social upbringing, but who have been excluded from formal citizenship. Once removed from the United States, they experience Mexico as a foreign country, facing language and cultural barriers, stigma, and intense feelings of homesickness and alienation.[24]

THREE LIFE AFTER DEPORTATION

Deportation affects people's lives so completely that over half of the people I interviewed compared the experience to death. A forty-two-year-old man in Tijuana said, "When I first got deported—that first year—I felt like I literally died. I lost everything that had meant something to me, you know?" The Supreme Court has acknowledged that deportation "may result . . . in loss of both property and life; or of all that makes life worth living."[1] This is certainly the case for people whose lives are deeply tied to the United States. People recount stories of losing their homes, cars, and personal belongings. Many lose their marriages and even their children. They experience rejection in both the United States and Mexico, threatening their identities and internal sense of self.

Given the extent of the loss that accompanies deportation, it is not surprising that a sizeable population of deportees—especially those who had lived in the United States for longer periods of time—experience depression, anxiety, and suicidal thoughts. Some turn to substance abuse to cope with the loss. And, without family in Mexico, many become homeless. Many deportees respond to this loss by going back to their homes and families in the United States. They risk lengthy prison sentences and death to do so, but the pull to return is so strong that people are willing to risk everything for the possibility of going home. Given the mountain of obstacles that people face when they are deported, it is remarkable that a sizeable number of deportees are overcoming all odds and are rebuilding their lives in Mexico.

This chapter describes the three most common trajectories deported Americans' lives follow after deportation to Mexico: (1) experiencing homelessness and/or addiction, (2) rebuilding lives in Mexico, and (3) returning to the U.S. It is common for people to cycle through each of these categories in the years following their deportation. Notably, even the most socially integrated deportees I interviewed reported persistent struggles with the desire to go back to the United States despite the substantial risks this would pose.

MENTAL HEALTH AND DESPAIR

Deportation can be so traumatic that it threatens people's mental health and stability, as in the case of Giancarlo Sarabia, who committed suicide by jumping off an electrical tower in Tijuana on Valentine's Day in 2014. He had been deported from Los Angeles and was separated from his children. While standing on the side of the tower—before gathering the nerve to jump—he shouted to the crowd of onlookers that his children had been taken into foster care in the United States, presumably when he was ejected from the country.

Suicidal ideation was frequently reported by the people I interviewed, who often said they had "lost everything" as a result of their removal from the United States. While some internalize the pain of deportation by becoming depressed and suicidal, others externalize their hopelessness by engaging in high-risk behaviors such as jeopardizing their lives in attempts to return to the U.S. Losing one's home, family, career, and stability are virtually inevitable consequences of deportation, at least temporarily. Not surprisingly, losses this profound can trigger a downward spiral of depression, anxiety, drug addiction, homelessness, and despair.

A study in Mexico's border region found that deportation is "a particularly traumatic experience" for "people already settled in the United States [who] . . . have established a life there."[2] Recall Gina—the mother who was separated from her three children when she was deported. In the years since her initial deportation, Gina has cycled through periods of depression and contentment. She attempted to return to the U.S. twice, but was caught both times. She refers to the time she spent in jail following her apprehension as "one of the worst things that ever happened to me." Despite this, she has seriously considered going back, even looking into hiring a smuggler at several points. Seven years have passed since her last attempt.

Four years into her life in exile, Gina became pregnant. Overwhelmed by the prospect of raising the child on her own in Mexico, she contemplated having an abortion. Instead, she decided to allow an American couple to informally adopt the child. Gina's primary concern was about raising a child "without papers." "All my other kids are citizens," she said, "so what would happen to her if I go back [without permission]?" Gina's experience of not having papers was so negative that she did not want to put her child in the same position. "That way she has all the opportunities she deserves," she explained. "It's not her fault she was born over here." The opinion that it would be better to give up her daughter than to have her live without American citizenship indicates the depth of Gina's despair about her deported status.

Soon after the baby's birth, Gina changed her mind. After the adoptive couple took the baby to the United States, Gina could not stop crying. "I need my baby," she said tearfully. "I love her. I miss her so much. I don't think I can live without her." This loss seemed to bring up raw feelings about her separation from her other children, especially her daughter, who was only one year old when Gina was deported. In the intervening years, her daughter had grown from a baby into a child of elementary school age, but Gina still pictured her as the one-year-old she had left behind. She embarked on an extensive legal battle for the baby she had given up for adoption, invoking the Hague Convention to fight for her parental rights. Her experience with deportation has unfolded as a series of traumas, each one making the others exponentially more painful.[3] Some days, she says, she understands why her former roommate—also a deportee who had grown up in the U.S.— tried to kill herself.

Gina won her battle for her daughter, and she now lives with her two children who were born in Mexico and her partner in a modest home in Tijuana. She says, "I'm so happy to have my daughter," but quickly qualifies this statement about her happiness with a reminder of the pain of being separated from the children she left behind in the U.S. "My oldest is gonna be thirteen now," she says, "and he's done with me. He doesn't even want to talk to me on the phone." Whereas a couple of years into her deportation, Gina reported that she did not feel like she could take care of her children in Mexico because she did not have a stable residence or an income, she now feels up to the task. However, when she saved up enough money to invite her three children to come visit her during their summer vacations, only one decided to come. "The other ones didn't want to come see me," she said through her tears. "They don't even know me and I'm their mother." This kind of emotional pain contributes to mental health issues, particularly among deportees with strong ties to the United States.

Deportees in Mexico experience depression, anxiety, and suicidal ideation at significantly higher rates than the rest of the Mexican population.[4] The most comprehensive study of deportee mental health in Mexico found that 16 percent of deportees experienced mental disorders immediately upon their arrival in Mexico.[5] Those with strong ties to the U.S. fare even worse. People who have spent more time in the United States report more symptoms of mental and emotional distress. Further, people with a spouse in the United States, people who had been returned to Mexico multiple times, and people with lower levels of social support all reported more symptoms indicative of common mental health disorders. Notably, 39.8 percent of women surveyed demonstrated a mental health disorder immediately following their deportation. The most common symptoms were feeling nervous/tense, feeling sad, experiencing sleep problems, and having thoughts of suicide. At the time the questionnaire was administered, 1.7 percent of men and 7.6 percent of women surveyed reported thoughts of suicide.[6]

I believe these numbers likely underrepresent the extent of mental health issues among deportees who are members of the 1.5 generation—those who migrated to the U.S. as children. This survey tracked all deportees, but the experience of deportation is especially traumatic for people who grew up in the United States. In addition, the survey was administered at the moment when people arrived in Mexico, and the challenges associated with deportation often increase over time as people struggle to adjust to their new status and new lives. As the American Psychological Association reports, "Immediately after the [traumatic] event, shock and denial are typical."[7] People are unlikely to process the emotional toll of their deportations while in a state of shock or denial, and the true numbers of deportees experiencing mental health issues are likely higher.

Dr. Tonatiuh Guillén López, president of El Colegio de la Frontera Norte, the foremost research institution focused on migration issues in Mexico, argues that the move to deport more people with long-term ties to the U.S. marks a "radical modification in the social composition of deportations," which has rendered "the human cost [of deportation] much more elevated and severe."[8] A Tijuana psychologist who works with deportees observes that depression and anxiety are most common among those whose families remain in the United States. "They feel completely lost in Mexico," she says, "and they become focused on how they can go back." When they cannot return—or when they try and fail—people often spiral deeper into depression.

This phenomenon is not unique to Mexico. Based on extensive fieldwork with deportees with strong ties to the U.S. in the Dominican Republic, sociologists David Brotherton and Luis Barrios found that "feeling abandoned, depressed, and estranged in their homeland, the totality of their social and cultural displacement often makes deportees suicidal."[9] Mental health professionals who work with deportees from the United States in Jamaica also note the presence of anxiety, depression, and posttraumatic stress among the population.[10] "I would say all the deportees come back here with adjustment disorder," reports Dr. Myo Oo, a psychiatrist in Jamaica. "You don't know what to eat; you don't know where to sleep. I could almost say 100 percent of deportees deal with depression and anxiety." According to Dr. Oo, "Deportees feel marginalized, because nobody is here for them. Often everyone in their family is abroad."[11]

Homelessness, Substance Abuse, and Despair in Tijuana

Located just across the border from San Diego, Tijuana received almost sixty thousand deportees from the United States in 2013 alone.[12] That equates to over 3 percent of the city's population—a substantial influx of people. And while some of those being deported assimilate easily into Tijuana, deportees who have strong ties to the United States have evolved into a distinct cultural group in Mexico; they are widely perceived as foreigners, and they are looked down upon. Without social support in Mexico, a sizeable portion of the deported population slides into homelessness and despair.

A major highway in Tijuana runs parallel to the border with San Diego. Tijuana's trash-filled, concrete riverbed sits next to the highway, followed by a series of fences marking the divide between Mexico and the United States. A typical American outlet mall lies just past the fences on the U.S. side. Until 2015, the Tijuana riverbed—commonly referred to as El Bordo—was a makeshift homeless encampment for hundreds of deportees with nowhere else to go. They lived in shelters pieced together with boxes or in holes they dug out of the dirt that flanks the riverbed. It was a skid row of international dimensions, where people the U.S. had banished gazed out at the country they used to call home. The Tijuana government has disbanded the encampments on the riverbed itself, but a large number of homeless deportees populate the surrounding neighborhood.

The area is a haven for people with serious drug addictions; it is common to see people injecting themselves with needles in plain view. Deportees whose lives are centered in the United States sometimes get stuck there because they feel they have nowhere else to go, and the separation from their families and lives in the U.S. can become overwhelming. A 2013 study of El Bordo found data that support the proposition that people with extensive ties to the United States are disproportionately represented in the homeless population of Tijuana. Of the homeless population that resided in El Bordo, 91 percent had previously lived in the United States; 67.3 percent of them had children in the United States, and 52.4 percent spoke English.[13] Similarly, a 2013 study of people who received free breakfast at a program in the El Bordo area found that 70 percent of the participants had been deported; 62 percent had lived in the U.S. for over ten years, with 35 percent having lived in the U.S. for over twenty years.[14] Among this population, the majority of those under sixty years of age reported experiencing symptoms of anxiety, depression, or both.[15]

Without accessible mental health support, some deportees self-medicate by using alcohol or drugs. Martha Romero Alvarez, who worked at a residential substance abuse treatment center in Tijuana for six years, says, "Many of the men in the center were deported. And in many cases they were not drug addicts when they arrived [in Mexico]." Alvarez reports that her clients turned to drugs to numb the pain of being separated from their families in the U.S. In addition, the poor living conditions people without financial support face after deportation threaten their stability. Alvarez asks, "What is their quality of life? Living in a canal? There are people who live in holes in the ground, and they eat from the trash. They feel insecure and live in fear of what will happen to them." The social disruption associated with deportation for people who identify as American, and the challenges they face upon arriving in an unfamiliar country, "can influence engagement in risky activities as a form of coping mechanism," according to scholars who study the health implications of deportation.[16] According to a qualitative study of injection drug users in Tijuana, "Deportees perceived changes in their drug use following deportation."[17] For example, several had not been injection drug users prior to their deportation and attributed their use of injection drugs to "post-deportation stressors," such as "lack of money, shelter, [and] social networks."[18] Others saw an increase in their drug use following deportation "as one mechanism for dealing with the emotional consequences of deportation (e.g. feelings of shame and resentment, trauma, loneliness, and separation from spouses/partners, parents, siblings, and children)."[19]

A study focused on deported female injection drug users in Tijuana similarly found increased drug dependence after deportation. Many reported using methamphetamine for the first time after being deported, and several who had previously used drugs but had not injected began injection drug use once deported to Tijuana. Women in this study attributed their elevated drug use to the widespread availability of drugs in Tijuana's Zona Norte neighborhood that encompasses El Bordo and a "lack of control over their lives."[20] Further, depression and family separation contribute to increased substance abuse among deported women.[21] As one woman explains, "I felt alone. I felt abandoned. . . . Before my deportation, I did use drugs, but not like right now. . . . I had my house, my children. . . . Well, the deportation affected me a lot since in the past, I did not use drugs on the street. I feel humiliated." She was deported ten years before this interview, and her children grew up in her absence. Another study found that 16 percent of deported injection drug users in Tijuana started using new drugs (most often, methamphetamine) following their deportation.[22] Trying a new drug following deportation was found to be more common among drug users who felt sad following their deportation and among those who had been deported more times.[23]

One deportee who had been diagnosed with bipolar disorder reported that he was treating his symptoms with alcohol since he could not afford the psychiatric medication he used to take in the United States. He said the alcohol helped to minimize his hallucinations if he drank enough. A 2016 study of deported injection drug users in Tijuana found that 45 percent reported symptoms of depression.[24] Researchers attribute higher rates of substance abuse among the deported population to their displacement, the discrimination and human rights abuses many experience once they arrive in Mexico, and their lack of social networks in Mexico.[25] Access to treatment is also more difficult for deportees who lack cultural familiarity with Mexican institutions. It is not surprising that a survey of injection drug users in Tijuana found that those who had been deported were less likely than other study participants to receive drug treatment or medical care.[26]

Deportation contributes to crimogenic conditions in that people are removed from their social attachments and often land in areas with high concentrations of drug use and crime. One deportee compares the practice of leaving people with histories of substance abuse in Tijuana to "dropping someone with a gambling addiction off in the middle of Las Vegas and saying, 'Good luck!'" It's a "city of vices," he says. A team of researchers from the University of California at San Diego found that deported injection drug users in Tijuana feel similarly—they "frequently indicated that the post-deportation social, drug, and economic climates of Tijuana facilitated their drug use behaviors."[27] Tijuana government officials attribute a rise in the city's crime rates to deportees with substance abuse problems. In a 2013 interview, Tijuana mayor Kurt Honald blamed deportees for a 300 percent rise in petty crime.[28] Local residents are concerned as well. When the Obama administration announced plans to release six thousand drug offenders from federal prisons in 2015, a Tijuana newspaper ran a front-page story focused on concerns about the potential influx of people with substance abuse problems to Tijuana because a third of this total were noncitizens slated for deportation. Despite his concerns about the deportees' involvement in crime in Tijuana, Mayor Honald maintains, "They're mostly good, honest people who were going to seek the American dream." However, in the words of Tijuana's minister of public security, deportation is "turning good people into bad ones."[29]

Scholars have found that banishing people—restricting them from certain geographic areas within the United States—is generally "counterproductive because it imperils efforts by the socially marginal to integrate with mainstream society."[30] Displacing people undermines their stability while doing "nothing to resolve any of the underlying conditions that generate social marginality, such as poor employment prospects, inadequate affordable housing, or the challenges of addiction." The experiences of deportees in Tijuana demonstrate that, like banishment, deportation is counterproductive.

Deporting People with Preexisting Mental Health Issues

While many who are deported develop mental health issues as a result of their deportation, others have a history of mental health problems prior to deportation. The father of a deportee in his early twenties explained his son's intensive treatment regimen for schizophrenia before he was deported. Once in Mexico, access to psychiatric services was limited. Although this young man's family attempted to visit him in Mexico and encouraged him to get help, his mental health deteriorated rapidly in the six months following his deportation. During our first interview, only two months after his deportation, he was able to articulate the things he missed about the United States and expressed his grief over being separated from his family. One month later, he demonstrated paranoid thought patterns, accusing me of working with the CIA and of reading his mind.

In 2010, the Ninth Circuit Court of Appeals held that people with mental disabilities—at least those whose mental health issues are so severe that they were deemed mentally incompetent—are entitled to government-appointed attorneys in deportation proceedings. This ruling was the result of a class action case the ACLU filed on behalf of Jose Antonio Franco Gonzalez, a Mexican citizen facing deportation who had the cognitive functioning of a two-year-old and had been diagnosed with moderate mental retardation. The ACLU argued, and the court agreed, that he and other members of the class—those with mental disabilities—are entitled to representation at the government's expense as an accommodation of their disabilities under the federal Rehabilitation Act. As a result of this case, the federal government adopted a policy that would provide legal representation to people with "serious mental disorder[s] or conditions that may render them mentally incompetent to represent themselves in immigration proceedings."[31] Appointing counsel in these cases is an important step toward protecting the rights of people with mental health issues in removal proceedings, but many problems remain.

Even when people have attorneys, the law may not protect them from eventual deportation. Once deported to Mexico, many will not be able to access needed medications and treatment. The Mexican government launched a program in Tijuana to attempt to coordinate treatment with U.S. authorities in order to connect deportees to mental health resources immediately upon their deportation so that people do not experience a lapse in access to needed psychiatric medications. However, many people fall through the cracks.

The influx of deportees with mental health issues to Mexican border communities represents a major challenge to mental health delivery systems that are already stretched thin. In 2012, an average of four hundred migrants each month—mostly deportees from the United States—received mental health treatment at Tijuana's Hospital de Salud Mental, the city's only mental health hospital.[32] According to one study, an estimated 9,247 people in need of mental health support are deported to Tijuana every three months.[33] Their needs often go unmet.

U.S. veterans who suffer from posttraumatic stress face limited access to mental health services once deported. At a meeting of Banished Veterans—a support group for deported veterans in Tijuana—ten veterans of the U.S. armed forces gathered in a courtyard outside of an apartment that also functioned as the makeshift office of the organization. All ten were green card holders who got into trouble with the law at some point after their military service. Some wore their old uniforms, while others wore T-shirts with the Banished Veterans logo. A popping sound emitted by a passing car clearly startled many in the group. "PTSD," joked one of the vets. "We're taking small arms fire," said another, followed by a chorus of nervous laughter.

But posttraumatic stress is a serious problem for many of them, including Frank, a forty-year-old veteran who served in the Kosovo conflict in the late 1990s, whose story was introduced in chapter 1. He was ordered deported as a result of a conviction for cashing a fraudulent check years after he had been discharged from the military. At the time of his deportation, he was getting treatment for posttraumatic stress through the Department of Veterans Affairs (VA) in California. However, he has been unable to access these services since his deportation to Mexico. At first, his wife would send him his prescription medications, which the VA continued to ship to his family's home in the United States, but eventually they stopped sending the medication. In Mexico, Frank does not have health insurance and lives on a tight budget; he cannot afford to see a psychiatrist or to pay for medication out of pocket. His symptoms of posttraumatic stress persist.

To Frank, being in the conflict in Kosovo seemed worse than being at war. He explains, "In a war, you know who is the enemy. . . . When doing peacekeeping, you don't know who the enemy is. . . . You're talking to someone who you think is on your side, and then suddenly he appears with C-4s ready to blow." Shortly after his return from Kosovo, Frank remembers hiding behind the sofa in his living room one night. He thought he was in battle. His behavior startled his wife; she locked herself in the bedroom with her then newborn son. More than fifteen years later, he still experiences flashbacks. He says, "I just want it out of my head."

According to Dr. Ietza Bojorquez, deportees face numerous obstacles to receiving mental health treatment in Mexico. "First," she explains, "they need to know that a mental health hospital exists. Then they need to find the hospital." Even if they make it to the hospital, they are often denied treatment. In Mexico, basic health services are covered by a national medical insurance program, but people must go through an enrollment process.

The Mexican government established a new program for deportees in Tijuana. Somos Paisanos—We Are Countrymen—aims to help connect deportees to needed resources. It provides recent arrivals with a thirty-day temporary insurance enrollment document that should allow them to access necessary medical and mental health treatment while they go through the enrollment process required for more long-term coverage. However, the mental health hospital is notorious for refusing to treat people with this temporary insurance status.

Efforts to screen recent arrivals for their health needs fall short. In Tijuana, a receiving center for deportees has been set up at the location where ICE has deportees enter Mexico. A doctor is on site to provide medical referrals. While those with apparent needs, such as broken bones, are often identified and referred for medical services, those with less visible problems such as diabetes, hypertension, or mental health problems often go untreated. Dr. Bojorquez recalls seeing a man just outside the receiving center screaming uncontrollably, obviously in a psychotic state, and nobody did anything to attempt to connect him to mental health services.

Substance abuse and mental health issues are a predictable consequence of current deportation policies. Yet even though these problems are pervasive, they are only one side of the coin. Many deportees who grew up in the United States are forging new paths in Mexico, using their American upbringings, English language fluency, and cultural familiarity to cultivate job opportunities and to launch small businesses.

REBUILDING LIVES

A sizeable population of deportees who grew up in the United States are adapting to life in Mexico, working to overcome the pain and trauma that deportation brings. The more socially integrated people become—either into Mexican society or into American enclaves within Mexico—the more they are able to move on with their lives. People do not follow one singular path, but many tap into their familiarity with the United States in order to succeed in Mexico. Some are employed to recruit English-speaking tourists to sign up for tours, come into restaurants, or buy time-shares. Others find work in hotels or restaurants that cater to travelers from the U.S. and Canada. Some use their language skills to teach English in language schools. Call centers serving people in the U.S. are one of the largest employers of recently arrived deportees. In addition, a growing number of deportees with some financial resources use their American cultural familiarity to start small businesses that cater to American tourists or expats.

In contrast to countries like the Dominican Republic where deportees with criminal convictions are housed in prisons upon their arrival, criminal records from the U.S. do not follow people to Mexico. As it stands right now, people deported to Mexico have a chance to start over without their past mistakes hanging over them. Jobs and schools typically require applicants to submit a document that certifies they do not have criminal convictions, but this document (*la carta de antecedentes penales*) only reflects convictions from Mexico. For people with felony convictions in the United States, in some respects Mexico can offer more opportunities than the United States. The following pages explore some of the common career paths deportees take once returned to Mexico. In telling the stories of deportees who have followed each of these paths, this analysis delves deep into individuals' experiences to highlight both the breadth and commonalities in the experiences of deportees in Mexico.

Teaching English

One of the most obvious ways that deported Americans draw upon their unique cultural backgrounds is by working as English teachers in Mexico. Speaking English is an important skill for people of all socioeconomic statuses in Mexico. It opens doors for those seeking to work in the multibillion-dollar tourist industry, and business deals are routinely made with foreigners in English. Further, professionals consider English essential to keeping up with developments in their fields given that academic articles and books are often not translated into Spanish. While a teaching certification is required for many teaching jobs, some private schools will hire people based on the fact that they speak English alone.

Teaching English is a viable career path for people who have spent many years in the U.S.[34] When Jorge appeared at his parole hearing in a California prison, the members of the parole board responsible for deciding whether he should be released asked him what plans he had for working if released and deported to Mexico. Jorge replied that he planned to teach English at a language school. The members of the board called this plan "pie in the sky" because he did not have any formal training in teaching English as a second language. However, people with native speaking capabilities can find employment as teachers fairly easily, even if they have a criminal record from the United States. In the words of a young woman who grew up in the U.S. but returned to Mexico to take care of a family member and now cannot return to the U.S., "Mexico is like a no-man's land. Everything they [deportees with criminal records] did [in the U.S.], it goes back into neutral."[35]

"I didn't know much about grammar when I started doing this," reports a deported English teacher in the border region, "but they hired me because I speak better English than all of their other teachers. I watched one class, and the teacher was working on pronunciation. She was telling them the right way to pronounce avocado was avocãdo. And I had to tell them, no, no, no. Avocado is not the same as tomãto-tomato. So I have the advantage of knowing how to pronounce things in English." Although the wages are low, he enjoys working in a professional role. "I'm treated with a level of respect because I'm the teacher. It feels good," he says.

While teaching can provide stable employment, even the most prestigious language schools in Mexico do not pay much. Demonstrating resourcefulness, some deportees transcend borders by teaching online. Before he was deported, Erick was trained and certified to teach English as a second language through a prison education project offered by a state university. Because of this background, he is qualified to teach English classes online to students in Asia. This allows him to earn higher wages than he could if he were teaching within Mexico.

Call Centers

Foreign companies capitalize on the availability of the native English-speaking workforce in Mexico, hiring English-speaking deportees to handle customer service calls, or to collect debts, from offices in Mexico. Major call center operations in Tijuana, Mexico City, Monterrey, Puebla, and Guadalajara primarily employ deportees.

"I like taking the calls," reports a deportee from California, "because it makes me feel like I'm home. . . . We talk to people over there and it reminds me of what my life was like." Major call centers operate out of two of the most luxurious office buildings in the city of Tijuana, in suites outfitted with computers and telephone headsets. Employees are expected to dress in business attire. One call center employee told me, "I wear a tie to work every day. It feels good to be in a job where you gotta dress nice. You got a bunch of guys who knew each other in prison over there, and now we all work together wearing ties. You don't see that over there [in the U.S.]."

Call centers draw upon the large labor pool of deportees who not only speak English but also understand American culture. Call Center Services International, which operates call centers in Tijuana, advertises, "Our agents are fully bilingual [and] bi-cultural."[36] Bill Colton, the president of Global Telesourcing, which operates a call center in Monterrey, Mexico, reports that 95 percent of their employees grew up in the U.S. "Our employees speak English not just well, but they speak it natively."[37] He believes they can provide better service "because they are essentially Americans and understand the way American consumers think."[38]

Jill Anderson, who has interviewed call center employees in Mexico City, has found that most of the employees of call centers are deportees who grew up in the United States.[39] She believes the sense of community among coworkers in call centers is one of the appeals of working there, a community she refers to as "a critical mass of other people who have lived in the United States for many years, if not most of their lives."[40] According to Anderson, "Speaking English with coworkers comes as a relief. They get the same jokes. They are dealing with the same things."[41] In Tijuana call centers, work schedules honor U.S. holidays like the Fourth of July and Thanksgiving, and managers bring fast food from the U.S. as a reward for employees.[42] A sense of camaraderie develops among coworkers who feel more at home speaking English than Spanish, and who consider the U.S. home although they have been deported to Mexico. "While you're at work, you still get a sense that you're back home, which I like very much," reports Henry Monterroso, who grew up in California from the age of five, was deported in his early thirties, and now works as a supervisor at a Tijuana call center.[43] In the words of a deported employee of a Tijuana-based collections agency, "Even though I feel bad sometimes trying to make people pay, I like talking to people over there. . . . I feel closer to home."

While these jobs pay more than other entry-level positions in Mexico, they are far from ideal. Jill Anderson found the turnover at one call center in Mexico City was nearly 100 percent. A thirty-something man I interviewed described feeling "exploited" in his position at a Tijuana call center. He quit after working there for several weeks. "They're making all this money off of us, and they treat us like shit," he explained. Others report leaving because they are bored or because they are not earning enough money. A deported call center employee in Mexico City says, "This job is very tedious. You feel like you're getting nowhere. It doesn't make me feel very successful or proud of myself, to be honest with you. I want to do something more."[44] Wages vary, but reports range from salaries of $60 to $300 USD per week. A typical work week is fifty to fifty-five hours, over the course of six days.

In Mexico alone, call centers are a $6 billion industry.[45] In 2014, corporate consulting firm Frost and Sullivan estimated that Mexico had over 85,000 outsourced call center workstations, each staffed by two or three shifts a day. In the state of Baja California, nearly ten thousand people are employed in call centers; nearly half are deportees.[46] TeleTech, one of the world's largest global outsourcing firms with an annual revenue of $1.2 billion, operates three call centers in Mexico, where it employs thousands of people to handle customer service calls for American companies like Time Warner, AT&T, and Dish TV.[47] This billion-dollar industry's dependence on a steady stream of deportees is cause for concern. Jill Anderson argues, "Transnational call centers that serve U.S. clients have a vested interest in the current numbers and nature of deportations by the U.S. Department of Homeland Security."[48]

Sociologist Tanya Golash-Boza links the rise in deportation to the global economic crisis.[49] Although she admits that "it is difficult to substantiate the claim that corporate profit is the primary reason for mass incarceration or mass deportation," she notes that deportation has "fueled the growth" of call center industries in countries that receive high numbers of deportees.[50] It is not difficult to imagine a future where industries dependent on a labor supply of native English speakers willing to work for low wages in the countries to which they are deported begin to lobby for immigration policies that will ensure a continued labor pool, in the same way that private prison industry leader Corrections Corporation of America has lobbied heavily for increases in immigration detention, spending $10 billion between 2008 and 2014 on immigration-related lobbying.[51] With billions of dollars at stake, corporate interests in ensuring high rates of deportation could shape future immigration reforms.

Tourist Industry

Tourism is one of Mexico's largest industries, employing approximately seven million people per year.[52] Deportees are a logical fit for many tourism-related jobs. American and Canadian tourists are targeted for time-share presentations and tours in resort cities along Mexico's beaches. Some report that working as waiters in restaurants that cater to foreign tourists allows them to earn more than other jobs. According to a deported waiter who had worked in the food services industry in the U.S., "I make more tips than the other guys because I can talk to the Americans."

Security Jobs

Many deportees find work as security guards for gated, upscale residential communities. Their English skills are desirable for communicating with American retirees who live in these communities, and there are virtually no prerequisites for employment.

Alfredo works as a security guard in a residential community in Rosarito Beach, where he earns 1,500 pesos per six-day week, which equates to less than 100 U.S. dollars, depending on the exchange rate. He was raised in Los Angeles, where his parents, sisters, and children still live. When he was nineteen, he had a drug problem—meth, specifically. To support his habit, he started to sell small quantities, ultimately leading to a conviction for possession for sale of methamphetamine. He got clean and hadn't used drugs in over ten years when his conviction caught up to him and he was deported. "I have my good days and bad days," he says. He has a daughter in the U.S. whom he rarely sees because her mother does not like her to come to Mexico. He lives alone in a small apartment, surrounded by photos of his family back home. One time, he caught someone trying to break into one of the homes in the residential community where he works security. He chased him down and held him while he waited for the police to arrive. Later, he questioned the wisdom of this choice. "I risked my life, and I get paid less than $20 a day. I don't know if that was the best decision when I think about it now." Although he struggles to make ends meet, he lives a relatively comfortable life. He recently started dating a local woman, which he says helps him to feel less lonely than before. "It's not like I'm used to it," he says, "but every day I try to make it the best day I can." This positive attitude and his resilient spirit may be the key to his survival post-deportation. He hasn't used drugs since 1998.

Manny's life after deportation unfolded more tragically. He was deported following a short stint in prison as a result of drug possession. He found a job as a security guard in a residential community near the beach on the outskirts of Tijuana. He worked there for three years before befriending one of the residents, a Mexican American woman who had moved there to live near the beach for a fraction of the cost of living in California. They were around the same age, and they found they had a lot in common. Manny moved in with her, and they adopted a dog together—Tyson—a boxer with lots of energy. Things seemed to be looking up for Manny, but his substance abuse issues haunted him. Following a drug binge, he hanged himself.

Small Businesses

Once he arrived safely in Tijuana from Nicaragua, Luis—whose journey through Mexico was described in chapter 2—set out in search of work. Over the ten years that he has lived in Tijuana, Luis has worked in three of the most common deportee career paths. He started out recruiting people to come into Señor Frogs, a club popular with tourists. "Since I could speak English . . . I would approach them [tourists] in a way that they felt comfortable." He then started working for Verizon, providing technical support in a call center before moving on to another call center that focused on bill collections. He was successful there and moved up, eventually convincing a California-based company to outsource their collections work to his employer. He earned a bonus, which he used to open his own business—a tattoo shop. "Now I just tattoo, tattoo everyday. And take care of my kids. . . . My daughter was born this year [in 2012] so I have a chance to take care of my kids and do what I love and still be myself." His daughter sat in an infant carrier next to him as he tattooed. He would stop to give her a bottle or burp her as needed.

Deportees who can gather the financial capital to launch a small business often move in this direction. Even in small or informal businesses, people find they can generally earn more working for themselves than as employees. "Everybody says we're bringing problems here," one deportee says, "but when you look at it, we're helping the economy. There are a lot of new businesses in town because of us."

Pollos Deportados—Deported Chickens—embraces the owner's identity. Alejandro (Alex) Carrera migrated to the U.S. when he was two years old. He opened Pollos Deportados in the tourist district of Rosarito, blocks away from the historic Rosarito Beach Hotel (which opened in 1924 and became a popular destination for Hollywood celebrities in the Prohibition era). American customers remark not only on the quality of the roasted chicken, but also on the owner's ability to "speak perfect English." According to Alex, when people are deported they can "feel like their lives are over because their lifestyle changes—the plans they had—change overnight." However, he says, "Here [in Mexico] we can succeed too—there, money is easier to earn, but here, we can regain our dignity."[53]

Deportation can open opportunities under the right circumstances. "If I had never been deported," reports a deportee who opened a tattoo shop in Tijuana, "I would have never done this." He follows up quickly with, "Don't get me wrong—I still think about going back every day. But my life is turning out all right over here." With hourly wages in Mexico so low, many people who are accustomed to U.S. wages feel that starting a small business or being self-employed is the only path that makes economic sense. "It's not like over there where you can get a job and live good," explained a deportee who works for himself washing cars. "I could either get a job and earn a couple dollars an hour or I can do this and keep all my profits."

People with access to some financial capital can start a small business in Mexico with far less money than in the U.S. Rent is relatively inexpensive, and overhead costs are low, as are wages if the business ultimately hires employees. Some people who had worked for years in the U.S. report cashing in their 401K retirement accounts to start businesses. Others rely on their family members in the U.S. for financial capital.

Mark was deported for the second time three months before we spoke. He served time in federal prison for the crime of illegal reentry and was then deported again. This time he was trying to make things work in Mexico. He started out by getting a job at a call center, but that did not last long. "They wanted me to dress in expensive clothes. That's not really my get down." He continued, "They were paying me crap, but they wanted me to wear a tie. I couldn't buy expensive clothes with the money they were paying me." So he launched Stufft Burgers, a hamburger stand that he set up just down the street from where he lives. He got a business license from the city and, he boasts, "I'm legit." Six days a week, he sets up a large barbecue, a deep fryer, and a cooler on the side of the road. He has a sign that advertises the "best ribs ever." He sells burgers, hotdogs, ribs, and chicken skewers with sides of fries, coleslaw, and potato salad. He even has cheesecake for dessert. On a hot summer weekend afternoon, his stand is busy. Most people order in English, although there are a few people speaking Spanish. A middle-aged white woman in conservative dress slows her Honda Accord as she drives by. She asks the cook—wearing a blue bandanna on his head, his face covered in tattoos—"How's business?" "It's good," he says with a smile. "I'll be back later," she replies. "You close at five, right?" Mark says, "People always like the underdog. They see me out here struggling, and they want to help."

Café Miguel, located in a coastal suburb of Tijuana, is named after its founder, who was barred from returning to the U.S. for twenty years because he had entered without permission on two occasions. He had worked as a cook at Marie Callender's in Utah, where he and his American wife and two children lived in a house they owned. Once in Mexico, the family tried to rent the house out so they could continue making the mortgage payments, but it was difficult to manage from Mexico. They eventually lost the house. Miguel had a hunch that a café that served food like the menu at Marie Callender's, including pies, would be a draw for Americans who lived in the area. He started on a shoestring budget, acquiring a loan and moving the refrigerator out of his family's kitchen and into the small space he rented to convert into a café. At first, he only offered breakfast, in order to limit the number of ingredients he had to keep stocked in the kitchen. He gained a good reputation with the locals and soon became the most popular neighborhood restaurant for breakfast. He's now been in business for six years and has expanded the restaurant to include an upstairs deck with an ocean view. He employs a staff of eight cooks and servers, many of whom are deportees.

Miguel credits his wife for the success of their business. "It's really because of her that we were able to do this," he says. If it had been up to him, he would have tried to return to the U.S. to rejoin his family in their home in Utah. "But my wife told me, 'No. We have the chance to be together in Mexico. Don't give that up.'" She gave him an ultimatum—"If you try to come back and make it, great. But if you get caught and go to jail, I'm leaving you," he recalls her saying. He decided to give their life in Mexico a try. Now, nearly ten years later, he would be happy to stay in Mexico. "I want my papers because it would make my wife's life easier," he says. "She has a lot of stress. She has to leave the house at five to cross the border to get to work. She homeschools the kids three days a week and takes them to school in San Diego twice a week." Normally, she buys the groceries for the restaurant in the U.S. She's pregnant now, though, and is supposed to be on bed rest. She still drives the kids across the border to school twice a week. But she's had to enlist the help of her father to do the shopping and load the ingredients into her car. "If I could get my papers," he says, "it would help her a lot."

Although deportees have limited social capital given their expulsion from the United States and stigmatization in Mexico, they are finding innovative ways to tap into the financial and cultural capital they built in the United States in order to succeed in Mexico. Sociologists have documented a broader pattern of Mexican migrants bringing skills they developed in the United States back with them when they return to Mexico.[54] These skills include both technical, job-related skills (such as American-style construction and cooking) and softer skills like social and language skills.[55] As I have found with deportees, a study of return migrants in central Mexico, including people who returned voluntarily and involuntarily, found that a high percentage of return migrants were self-employed. Most drew upon skills they obtained while working in the United States to launch their businesses. The marginalized status of deportees in Mexico was evident in this study as well; deportees were less likely to launch businesses with employees than people who returned voluntarily, partially due to the stigma attached to being deported and partially because voluntary returnees could set themselves up to succeed because they anticipated returning to Mexico.[56]

Research on deportees in El Salvador who had migrated to the United States as children has similarly found that, despite their "antipathic societal reception that subjects them to social and economic marginalization" in El Salvador, there is also great potential for deportees to draw upon "social remittances"—"'ideas, behaviors, identities, and social capital' learned in their former host countries."[57] In Mexico, although deportees face stigmatization and rejection by the dominant culture, it is not as extreme as in El Salvador. Thus, people in Mexico have more opportunities to draw on their social remittances—their language, skills, and ability to relate to people from the U.S.—to rebuild prosocial lives in Mexico.

Educational Opportunities

Some deportees attended college in the U.S. and hope to continue their education in Mexico. Others develop educational aspirations after deportation. As they consider how to start their lives over in a new country, many turn their thoughts to careers they had not considered in the United States. However, people whose schooling took place in the United States face bureaucratic obstacles in Mexico that make higher education unattainable for some. Advocacy groups have started to raise awareness about the barriers faced by people whose primary education was in the U.S. when trying to enroll in higher education in Mexico, and soon after Donald Trump's election in 2016, the Mexican Congress passed a bill that would ease some of the bureaucratic restrictions.

Lisa grew up in Los Angeles, where she earned her GED rather than graduating from high school. After her deportation to Tijuana, she decided to study law. She went through the cumbersome process of requesting her records from the U.S., having them apostilled by the state of California to certify their validity, paying to have them translated by an approved translator in Mexico, and taking the entrance exam for the college she hoped to attend. She envisioned being a lawyer, helping people more than the lawyers she had interacted with had ever helped her. Sadly, halfway through her first semester, she was pulled out of class and informed that she would not be able to continue because the school did not accept the GED. Only a high school diploma would be accepted. She became overwhelmed by the process and gave up, but two years later she figured out an alternative and reenrolled. She took advantage of a program offered by the Mexican government called Prepa Abierta—open high school—designed to help adults who have not completed high school to do so in an abbreviated amount of time. She is on track to become an attorney in Mexico.

Dream in Mexico is a nonprofit organization founded with the purpose of helping deportees and voluntary returnees to Mexico to navigate the vexing process of enrolling in Mexican universities. Daniel Arenas, one of the organization's founders, acknowledges that for those with serious criminal records in the U.S., coming to Mexico provides a "clean slate"—a chance to start over. His organization seeks to help people overcome the bureaucracy that prevents some who grew up in the U.S. from attending college in Mexico. According to Arenas, universities can be "nitpicky about many things, and things are very formal. They ask for very special requirements and sometimes are very rigid. But they are only rigid when they want to be, and they make exceptions when they want to. That can be very frustrating."

Although it was not common among the people I interviewed, a handful had overcome these obstacles and were attending or had graduated from colleges or professional degree programs.

Rural Life

The families of most deported Americans originated from poor, rural areas before they migrated to the United States. "Our people cross because they're poor," a deportee from a rural part of the state of Guanajuato explains. Once deported, some return to the rural communities where they were born. The transition from living in the U.S. to living in a rural community in Mexico is extreme. As one woman explained, "The poorest people over there [in the U.S.] live better than the richest people here." Many homes in her *rancho*—the rural community where she was born—do not have plumbing, and people try to avoid using electricity because money is tight. The transition appears to be easier for people who migrated to the U.S. as adults. For them, returning to their ranchos represents a homecoming of sorts, a return to a slower pace of life. But for those who spent their formative years in the U.S., the transition is more challenging. "I feel like I traveled back in time. We shower with water in a bucket. . . . I feel dirty. There's nothing to do here. People just sit around and talk about each other. There's no work."

With the loss of an estimated two million agricultural jobs in Mexico after NAFTA—the North American Free Trade Agreement—went into effect, people living in rural communities that used to subsist on farming have become increasingly dependent on remittances sent by family members who work in the United States. Thus, many of these communities have become more desolate. A deportee who returned briefly to live in the community where he grew up in Michoacán reports, "I remember when I was a kid, people had animals. They grew corn in the fields. People got up and went to work. But now, it's just sad. People wait for their families to send money [from the U.S.]. It's not the same."

The differences in the quality of life are more pronounced for people moving to rural areas than to cities. Some are able to adjust to the different standards of living and can adapt to the slower pace of life. However, many deported Americans are more comfortable living in urban environments and move away from the communities where they were born.

Adapting to Life in Mexico

In light of the increasingly interconnected nature of the world, some argue that borders and territory are becoming less salient than cultural ties and identities.[58] People do not lose their cultures and identities when they are deported in part because "places are not only located—they are constructed."[59] In Mexico, deportees are reconstructing places that feel like home, incorporating tastes in food, dress, and style that they developed in the United States. American-style restaurants like Stufft Burgers and Miguel's Café, tattoo shops, and barbershops specializing in "fades" or American-style haircuts are some examples of how people use their social remittances in positive ways. Re-creating a sense of national community across the border seems to help many deportees to manage the stigma and marginalization they face due to their deported status.

People who become integrated into supportive social networks seem better adjusted and more able to work toward building stable lives in Mexico than those who remain detached from social networks in Mexico. Some find a sense of community in school or at work. Others get married or have children in Mexico. Many people I interviewed became active in English-speaking churches, participating in social activities, worship services, and community service activities, and even finding employment at the church in some cases. "We're like a family, you know?" said one deportee while describing his involvement in church outreach and social events. According to Daniel Arenas of Dream in Mexico, "There are so many difficulties that face people when they return. One thing that has helped is that people need a support system here in Mexico—in life in general whether it's in a university or a work environment or a social environment. A support system is very important." Arenas continues, "The hope is that over time, people feel more accepted [in Mexico]."

The integration process unfolds over time. Mexico slowly becomes less foreign and more familiar. Jose explains, "I think about how I spoke Spanish when I first got here, and it makes me laugh. Now, I still mess up sometimes and pronounce things with an English accent, but a lot of times I think in Spanish. I dream in Spanish now." A study of a group of Mexican college students who had grown up in the United States confirms my findings, tracing how the subjects identified more as Mexican as time went on. In the words of one of the study's participants, "Five years ago I would say English 100 percent, I thought [of] myself as American . . . I mean, I enjoy baseball games, I love barbecues, barbecue sauce, I mean, I like American culture a lot and uh . . . but then little by little as the years have gone by and I'm in Mexico I feel a lot more Mexican now."[60] This study assessed a group of college students studying teaching English as a second language in an undergraduate degree program at the University of Guanajuato.[61] The researchers noted that students in the program who had grown up in the United States gravitated toward one another and created friendships with one another more than with other students in the program due to their shared experiences and acculturation in the U.S.

The ability to adapt to life in Mexico is also closely related to family relationships. Generally, people whose family members moved to Mexico with them following their deportation were more integrated into Mexican society than those whose family members stayed in the U.S. In family situations where relatives remained in the United States, deportees who essentially cut ties with their families and started over in Mexico by creating new families or relationships were better able to adapt. Those who maintained close relationships with family members who stayed in the United States had a more difficult time building their lives in Mexico. It is as if moving on would be a betrayal of their hopes of going home to their families.

The pull to return continues to threaten deportees who successfully adjust to their new lives in Mexico. "I *hated* it when I first got here," a waiter at a Rosarito hotel reported, "but once I got used to it and made my home here, I realized it's better than being in the U.S. I never want to go back. I bought my house here. I got married here, and I'm happy." He explains that he was lucky because he had worked in the U.S. for many years before he started to use drugs. After serving prison time and being deported for a drug-related charge, he was able to cash in his retirement savings to buy a house in Mexico. "Without that," he says, "it would have been real hard." Although happy in Mexico, he is not sure what he'll do when his parents' health deteriorates. They live in Los Angeles, and he worries that he'll feel compelled to cross the border to help them if they need him in the future.

Although a significant number of deportees have built successful lives in Mexico, many are still foreclosed from obtaining permission to return to the United States even after many years because their deportation orders are permanent and do not allow for waivers or exceptions. They are clearly rehabilitated, but in many cases this is irrelevant under current law.

GOING BACK

From Tijuana, the skyline of downtown San Diego is visible in the distance. On the beach, a metal fence extends along the sand and into the ocean, ending just past the shore break. The U.S. is so close you can reach your hand through the fence and extend it into American airspace. "Every time I walk on the beach and I see the border, I just want to jump over there and I just want to go," says Gina, whose story began this book. She contemplates trying to swim across, although she does not know how to swim. "I even thought of signing up for swimming lessons," she confides.

The two most common motivating factors driving people to return to the United States after deportation are (1) the desire for family unity and (2) the pull to go home. The director of a shelter that serves deported women and children in Tijuana estimates that 90 percent of the women she sees at the shelter attempt to return to the United States to reunite with their children. She says, "The United States is separating these women from their children, often permanently. We see two responses: some women become depressed and suicidal. Others will stop at nothing, including dangerous journeys through the ocean or desert, to try to return to their children." Fathers who go back are also motivated by the desire to reunite with their families. A study of deportees in El Salvador similarly found a link between return migration and having family members in the U.S. Deportees with children in the U.S. were 2.6 times more likely to plan to return; those with a spouse in the U.S. were 2.7 times more likely, and those with a spouse and children were 3.8 times more likely to plan to return.[62]

Thirty to 70 percent of all deportees to Mexico report plans to return to the U.S., but planning to return is clearly more common among people who consider the United States home.[63] One study found that 88 percent of those "who stated that their home is in the United States" planned to return someday.[64] The study concluded, "Nothing affects the decision to cross again as much as stating that one's home is in the United States."[65]

Even for those who have built stable lives or careers in Mexico, the pull to go back to the U.S. is always there. According to the wife of a deportee whose husband runs a successful small business in Tijuana, "Some days he'll just tell me, 'That's it. We're going back.'" She explained, "We're pretty happy here. We have our house, our kids. I'm used to crossing [the border] every day [to go to work]. But all it takes is one thing, and he's like, 'I'm tired. We're going home.'" Home, to them, is Los Angeles.

Over half of the people I interviewed had tried to return to the U.S. on at least one occasion following their initial deportation. Most who had attempted to return had subsequently been sentenced to serve time in federal prison for the crime of illegal reentry. People generally attempted to return within several months of being deported or in response to a traumatic event that affected a close family member in the United States. For example, a forty-four-year-old deportee had lived in the border region of Mexico for five years and had resolved not to go back to the U.S. One evening, he got the news that his mother was in critical condition in the hospital. "I had to see her," he said, "so I decided to try." He attempted to enter the United States by walking through the San Ysidro port of entry using another person's identification. He was apprehended and prosecuted for the crime of illegal reentry. His mother died while he was in custody. "It wasn't a rational decision," he recalls years later, "but it was just this feeling that 'I gotta go.'"

Another expressed plans to settle down in Mexico permanently. His wife and children moved from Oregon to join him. They enrolled the children in school, and his wife started looking for work. Several months after she arrived, she got pregnant. "I have high-risk pregnancies," she said, so she was looking into options for good prenatal care. She was considering finding a doctor in Mexico, but was also looking into the option of crossing the border to obtain care in San Diego. She was concerned about the possibility of going into labor and having to make her way across the border. At the same time, she was told that Mexican hospitals were not equipped with the same technology as most American hospitals, and she worried about what would happen if there were complications with the birth. Halfway through her pregnancy, she decided to return to Oregon until the baby was born. The week after she left, her husband abandoned his plans to stay in Mexico. He was apprehended while trying to join his wife and kids and was prosecuted in criminal court for the crime of illegal reentry. He was in prison for the birth of the baby and will be deported again after he completes his criminal sentence.

Robert Lopez, who came to the United States at the age of three, was deported due to an assault conviction.[66] He stayed in Tijuana for several years until he found out that his wife, the mother of his four American citizen children, had developed a drug addiction. Stuck in Tijuana, he felt helpless. He explains, "You hear all this bad news [in Tijuana], and you feel like you're in jail because you're incapable of doing anything." Concerned for his children, he returned to the U.S., where his wife reported him to immigration authorities after he was granted emergency custody of their children. Although he is serving a four-and-a-half-year federal prison sentence for reentering the country, he reports, "Even though I'm in jail here, I feel closer to my kids than I did there, free."

Gina and Edgar—whose immediate family members stayed in the United States after they were deported—both attempted to return to the U.S. on two occasions. Gina's motivation was to return to her three children. She explains, "Just because you're Mexican, they throw you away. They don't even care about your family." The second time she tried to return, Gina literally tried to run across the border. She climbed a fence, started running, and then got tired and had to take a break; while resting, she was apprehended by a Border Patrol officer who reported that he saw her climbing the fence. She recalls, "All of a sudden I saw a shadow, and the guy was like, 'Hey kid, get up.' I said, 'Please let me go. I'll jump back.' He said, 'Why are you doing that?' "Cause I want to go back with my kids.'" She adds, "They don't even care if your kids need you." Gina was not prosecuted for illegal reentry, although she did serve some time in custody due to an outstanding warrant. Edgar, on the other hand, made it across the border without being apprehended. He returned to his life prior to deportation, living with his wife, their children, and their dog in a suburb of Los Angeles until one day—several months after his return—ICE agents raided his home and took him into custody. He was prosecuted for the crime of illegal reentry and served time in federal prison before being deported again.

After Edgar's most recent deportation, he and his wife separated. His children stopped coming to visit as regularly as they had in the past. He gave up hope of returning and refocused his energy on creating a sustainable life in Mexico. Five years later, he is married to a woman who lives with him in Mexico. They have become very involved in a local church, and they run a small business together. Now, he sees his future in Mexico. "I don't want to risk going back," he says.

The United Nations' special rapporteur on the human rights of migrants instructs that "irregular entry or stay should never be considered criminal offences: they are not per se crimes against persons, property, or national security."[67] However, immigration crimes are the most-prosecuted crimes in the U.S. federal criminal justice system. In fiscal year 2015, 39 percent of all federal criminal cases prosecuted involved immigration-related crimes—nearly double the number of criminal cases filed in federal court for drug-related crimes.[68] Entering the United States without permission has been defined as a misdemeanor crime punishable by up to six months in jail. Reentering the country after being deported is a felony and may be punished by up to twenty years in prison. The United States has dramatically increased its efforts to prosecute people for immigration-related crimes. Whereas only 3,900 people were convicted of illegal entry in 2000, 92,215 were convicted of this offense in 2013.[69] Prosecutions for illegal reentry also skyrocketed in this time period, going from 6,513 annually in 2000 to 19,463 in 2012.[70] Over sixteen thousand people were serving time in federal prison for an immigration-related crime in August 2016, at an estimated cost of $1 billion annually.[71]

Many of those incarcerated for illegal reentry have strong ties to the U.S. In 2010, the federal Sentencing Commission recognized "cultural assimilation" as a valid reason for imposing a shorter sentence when "those cultural ties provided the primary motivation for the defendant's illegal reentry or continued presence in the United States."[72] However, so many defendants meet this criteria that judges shy away from using it as a reason to reduce sentences.[73] According to one judge who expressed reluctance to reduce sentences due to cultural assimilation, "Unfortunately, the Court sees a number of illegal aliens who come into the United States around age 10, and the Court has trouble distinguishing [the defendant in the present case] from the many others before the Court."[74]

Returning to the U.S. is not just punished with prison. Some people die while trying to come home. The number of people who have died attempting to enter the United States from Mexico has skyrocketed in the past twenty years due to increased border militarization, which has pushed people to cross through the most precarious desert terrain. The risk of dying was seventeen times greater in 2009 than in 1998.[75] Following his deportation from California, Jose Segura—who had grown up in Los Angeles and graduated from high school there—was so desperate to reunite with his family that he attempted to swim across the Rio Grande. He drowned in the process, leaving his three American children without a father and his wife without a husband. His sister now warns the families of other deportees to encourage them to stay in Mexico so they do not meet the same fate as her brother. But people with strong ties to the United States will continue to risk death and incarceration to return because the pull to come back is so strong.

In Mexico's border region, crossing the border is an integral part of life. The San Ysidro port of entry joining Tijuana and San Diego is the world's busiest border crossing on land. People from Mexico go to the United States to work, to shop, and even to have lunch. The frequency with which people cross the border makes the prohibition against crossing particularly salient in the lives of deportees. "I asked my coworker where a good Chinese restaurant is around here," says one deportee, "and he told me to go to P. F.

Chang's in San Diego. It just makes it feel worse that I'm from over there and I can't go." The border is also home to a transient population. People move there temporarily to wait for a visa to come through, or they give up and decide to return without permission. "I feel like every time I get comfortable with someone, they leave," says one deportee. In this context, the choice of whether to stay or go is constantly present. "I look over there and I see the buildings in San Diego," one deportee says, referencing San Diego's downtown skyline, which is visible from Tijuana, "and I just wonder when I'll give up and just try to run across."

LIVING IN LIMBO

For some, the passage of time helps people to adjust. Most often, deport-ees socialized in the United States occupy an in-between space—a limbo, where they oscillate between the pull to go back and the push to move on. This makes adjustment to life in Mexico even more challenging because people who are seriously considering returning to the U.S. cannot move forward with making long-term plans for life in Mexico.

Saul stands out for the educational success, family ties, and financial sta-bility he has achieved in the decade since he was deported. He enrolled in medical school and completed the six-year program, graduating as a doc-tor. He lives in Cancun, where he purchased a home in a community popu-lated by American retirees and Mexican professionals. But, he reports, the path was not easy. He rotated through several of the typical jobs available to English-speaking deportees, working in the tourist industry, at a call center, and teaching English in a private language school before deciding to go back to school. And he continues to experience stigma and rejection, due to either his deported status or to the fact that people perceive him as American.

Although the challenges of deportation are more severe for those with fewer resources, the emotional difficulties associated with deportation af-fect people across socioeconomic levels. "It's harder for the people with nothing," a deportee who lives in a relatively affluent community explains. "But deep down, we're all going through it. There's not much that separates me from the guys you see out there on the streets. . . . I feel their pain." Ines Hasselberg documents similar struggles with identity among people facing deportation from the U.K. and finds that "this identity—as one who is rejected, undesirable and unwanted—is experienced as an assault on the sense of self."[76]

Many people I spoke to struggled with a fundamental tension between holding onto hope of returning to the U.S. and accepting the idea of spending the rest of their lives in Mexico. Focusing on going back to the U.S. often prevents people from moving on with their lives in Mexico because their plans revolve around returning to the lifestyles they had known. People fantasize about ways they might be able to cross the border—from climbing through holes in the border fence to using someone else's passport to walk through the port of entry to riding a jet ski through the ocean, people think incessantly about how to make it home. They meet with lawyers, spending the little money they have on legal consultations even when they have been told many times that their immigration cases are hopeless. Every day, people sit and stare through the fence that marks the U.S.-Mexico border, imagining a return to their lives on the other side—to the sounds, sights, food, and people they grew up with.

As painful as waiting to return can be, moving on is painful too. Those who accept the fact that they will not be able to go back to the U.S. face the difficult task of rebuilding virtually every aspect of their lives in a new country. Like moving on from the death of a loved one, in order to fully embrace their new lives, they must start to let go of the past. This is particularly painful when this past includes one's family. "At first, I used to see my daughter every few months," a deportee who had been in Tijuana for twelve years reported. "But her mom got tired of bringing her, and I haven't seen her for years. It hurts. It hurts a lot." Later in the conversation, he added, "It's not that I'm used to it, but it's not as bad as it was at first." Little by little, people are forced to let go of their former lives in order to endure the pain of their separation. This means loosening, if not severing, family ties.

As people adjust to the idea of starting over in Mexico, the prospect can open new opportunities. Many rise to the challenge, imagining opportunities for themselves in this process of rebirth. "I miss my kids [who live in the U.S.], but I have my life here now too," one middle-aged man explained. He married a Mexican woman and adjusted to life there. In his words, "I get to look at the ocean every day, see the dolphins, watch the whales. So hey, it's not so bad." Being able to transition from the loss of deportation to seeing the positive side is a critical step in the process of adjustment.

When Maggie first returned to Mexico after growing up in the U.S., she experienced a profound sense of loss. "It was like if somebody had died inside of me, because it was like, OK, bye, house, bye, church, bye, friends, bye, school, bye, dog. I mean, I wasn't prepared."[77] But after seven years in Mexico, she has a more positive attitude about life here. She teaches English and attends college, with aspirations to work in the tourism industry. "I want to travel more in this country. I know it's beautiful. I know it has many positive things. And I'm starting to see that beautiful side of Mexico."[78]

Mike, who had a heart attack several years after his deportation, has lived in Mexico for eleven years, trying to make things work. Although he has resisted the temptation to go back for so long, he is now making plans to return. After he was deported, Mike lived in Guadalajara in Central Mexico for several years. There, he explains, the temptation to go back was not as strong as it is in the border region. "Here," he says, standing outside his home in Rosarito Beach, about twenty minutes south of the Mexican border, "you think about it every day. Everybody's constantly coming and going." He moved closer to the border because he only got to see his family once a year when he lived in Guadalajara. The distance took a toll on his thirty-year marriage, and he had an affair that led to the birth of a child. He moved closer to the border to try to repair his marriage. Since moving closer, he sees his family more often. They are all U.S. citizens—his wife and four children, who are now young adults. One is an accountant, another a teacher, and one is a chef. "He went to the Culinary Institute," Mike boasts. "My kids all did real good." None got involved with gangs, although Mike himself was one of the founders of a neighborhood gang when he was young.

It is clear that Mike grew up speaking English. He uses colloquial expressions indicative of a native speaker. "I went to the U.S. when I was two years old," he says. "I had the wife, the kids, a business, a house, the whole shebang. There are a lot of hard things about being deported, but being away from the family is the worst." Standing in the living room of the home he rents for $500 per month with help from family members in the U.S., he points to the bedroom and says, "What kills you is the call you get from the family, when you're lying in bed at night. When you get off the phone, you're here alone. . . . That's what kills you."

Although Mike sees his wife and kids more often since moving closer to the border two years ago, he still feels a profound sense of loneliness.

> They come for the weekend, and we have a good time. We go to the beach, we go to the water park. . . . I always plan activities for them to do when they come because I want them to have a good time when

they're here. . . . I stock up on groceries, I take care of them, and they have a ball . . . but then they leave. They're over there and I'm stuck right here. That's no way to live. That's not a life.

To cope with the loneliness, he runs, works out in the gym, and sometimes, he says, "I scream into the pillow really loud, just to let it out. . . . That's what you gotta do sometimes." Mike says that although he does not use drugs, he understands why many deportees do. It's a way to forget the pain that, he says, is still there even when you are better off than others. Mike's pain manifested itself physically several years earlier when he had a heart attack. "The doctors said it was my stress," he said. "I've always worked out, stayed healthy, but this stress was eating me up inside."

He lives in a clean two-bedroom home not far from the beach. He has a plasma TV, a garden, a dog, and a car. He has more than most. But, he says, "It still hurts." It hurts so much that he has decided to return. "I'm looking for a coyote right now," he says. His wife asked him if he was sure he wanted to go back. "I'm sure," he says with confidence. "I'd rather be in prison than be here."

Although deportation is framed as a solution to crime on the U.S. side of the border, in actuality it places people in contexts that are known to contribute to criminality. Removing people from their families, jobs, and communities puts them in positions where they are more likely to engage in crime. Emerging research indicates that deportees who spent signficant periods of time in the United States are more likely to experience mental health issues and substance abuse upon their deportation. This raises serious humanitarian and public policy concerns. Although many deportees are resilient and have found ways to thrive in Mexico, even those who are most successful by outward appearances report depression, anxiety, and the pull to go home to the United States. This is an important finding because it indicates that the consequences of deportation are not fleeting, but persist over time. Higher rates of mental health issues among deported Americans highlight the need for a legal framework that considers the unique position of people who grew up in the United States and are functionally and culturally American.

This chapter has presented a comprehensive picture of the varying trajectories of deportees in Mexico. The narratives raise questions about the legitimacy of deportation laws that (1) ignore the strong ties people feel to U.S. society and the serious harms people face as a result of being separated from the people, places, and experiences that have given their lives meaning; and (2) prohibit decision makers from considering people's rehabilitation in determining whether they should be deported or readmitted. In some respects, people are able to break free of the labels of criminality that originated in the United States by starting over in Mexico without the obstacles their criminal backgrounds would pose in the U.S. At the same time, the long arm of the U.S. criminal justice system captures them indefinitely via the permanent (or very long-term) bars to the United States effectuated by their deportation orders.

Almost without exception, people I interviewed who returned to the U.S. without permission did so in order to reunite with their family members in the United States. Many times, the decision to return was not planned but arose when a family member faced some kind of crisis. In these cases, people were willing to risk their lives and freedom for a chance of being with their families. This pattern has important policy implications because it demonstrates the limited deterrent value of long prison sentences for the "crime" of reentering the country. People also report with some frequency that they would rather be in prison in the U.S. than live as deportees in Mexico because they would be geographically closer to their families. This too speaks to the limited deterrent value of prison sentences for people considering returning after deportation.

In spite of their challenging circumstances, many deportees demonstrate remarkable resilience and, over time, have become more socially integrated into Mexican society. They have started businesses, returned to school, and established new careers. These stories of rehabilitation and redemption reveal the misguided approach of deportation laws that permanently bar people from coming back. Why should people who are contributing members of society be permanently barred from returning?

This chapter has only peripherally considered the experiences of the family members of deportees. Children, spouses, parents, siblings, and extended family members are deeply affected when a family member is forced out of the country. The two chapters that follow focus on the families of deportees, presenting information about their experiences and exploring how current laws fail to protect the rights of the spouses and children of deportees.

FOUR Deported by Marriage

"When ICE detained my husband, it felt violating. Like a rape. Like something had been snatched out of my body. That's the best way I can describe it," says Stephanie with tears in her eyes. She had been living in Mexico for seven months and was still raw from the trauma of her husband's deportation. "I miss our life," she laments. "We owned our own home. We had a dog, two vehicles. I was happy."

Almost a year before this interview, Stephanie's husband had been apprehended by ICE while driving to work. They lived in Georgia—her husband had been in the U.S. for seventeen years. Before her husband was detained, Stephanie had been privileged enough to be unaware of the complexities of immigration law. When she found out he had been arrested, she grabbed her marriage certificate and headed directly to the jail where he was housed. "I thought I could take my marriage certificate to the detention center and show them he was my husband, and that would be the end of it," she says. When she presented the officials with the marriage certificate, she recalls, "they laughed and told me to come back during visiting hours." Two months later, her husband was ordered deported. He was flown to Mexico City and given a bus ticket to Chiapas, where he had been born. A few months later, he tried to return to the U.S. He was caught at the border and was deported a second time. This time Border Patrol had him walk across the border into Mexico. When she found out he had been caught, Stephanie was despondent. She couldn't believe that her husband would not be able to return to their home. "I couldn't sleep," she recalls.

"I never slept in our bed again after he was deported. I was ready to end it when he didn't make it back. I took an overdose of pills." She recovered and decided to join her husband in Mexico—she might not be comfortable, but at least they could be together.

Once she decided to move, she began the process of giving up everything that meant something to her—their home, their cars, even their dog. "I could only bring what would fit in two suitcases," she recalls. "I felt like a failure. To be forty-two years old and have nothing. I remember buying a lasagna at Walmart before I left and having to eat it with my fingers. And I realized I don't even own a fork." She gave their dog to a neighbor because she couldn't afford the $60 fee to bring him on the plane. Between hiring an immigration attorney, paying a coyote to help her husband return (which was unsuccessful), and losing his income for nearly a year, the couple was out of money. They went from living a comfortable life in a home they owned to not being able to afford to rent an apartment in Mexico for 100 U.S. dollars per month.

Stephanie had never been to Mexico before. She moved into a residential neighborhood on the outskirts of Playa del Carmen, where the couple lived with her husband's cousin. Although Playa del Carmen is a major tourist destination, and the tourist district was only a fifteen-minute bus ride from where she lived, it felt like a world away. According to Stephanie, "I feel like a fish out of water. I very rarely leave the house. I'm the only white person wherever I go." She doesn't speak Spanish, and she worried about venturing out alone. "I'm still in shock that this even happened." She felt paralyzed and wasn't sure how to move forward. "I want to find a job," she says, "but I'm still shell-shocked. . . . I lost faith in the American government, in God, in pretty much everything. . . . This is my legal husband. You send him to Mexico, and where does that leave me?"

As a result of the recent trend of deporting people with long-term ties to the United States, many American citizens' marriages have been fundamentally undermined.[1] People whose spouses are deported must choose between staying in the United States without their life partners or leaving the United States in order to stay together. Either way, they experience financial, psychological, and emotional hardships.

Those who leave the U.S. are uprooted, losing proximity to family and friends, access to their property, and professional opportunities they trained for in the U.S. They face cultural and language barriers once they move abroad. Most importantly, they miss the intangible things—the smells, the sounds, and the incomparable feeling of home. Their experiences parallel those of their deported spouses. Some scholars refer to the family members of deportees as de facto or constructive deportees—people who are effectively deported even though they are not technically deported under the law.[2] In Mexico, many binational couples choose to live in close proximity to the border so the spouse with lawful status in the United States can commute to work on the other side. At an earnings ratio of roughly five to one, this makes economic sense, although the daily struggle of waiting two to three hours to cross the border takes a toll. Those who stay in the United States lose the companionship of their spouses and, with international borders between them, their marriages are often pushed beyond their limits.[3]

In other legal contexts, the Supreme Court has said that forcing people to choose between two fundamental rights violates the Constitution. However, up until now, courts have routinely said that deporting the spouses of U.S. citizens—or keeping them out of the country—does not violate the Constitution.[4] According to these decisions, the right to marriage is not infringed upon because the citizen "remains free to live with her husband anywhere in the world that both individuals are permitted to reside."[5] Alternatively, the citizen spouse could decide to stay in the United States without the deported spouse.[6] Thus, courts have concluded, the citizen has no right to challenge a spouse's deportation as a constitutional violation because this choice of which constitutionally protected right to give up cures any potential constitutional issue.[7] According to a U.S. citizen whose husband was deported, "When he was deported, I lost everything. In a lot of ways, it feels like I was deported too, but no one seems to care that I'm American too." The limited constitutional protections that apply to immigrants seem to spill over to their citizen spouses; their marriages are underprotected because they chose to marry noncitizens.

Two recent Supreme Court decisions signal an opening to reconsider the legal fiction that deporting a citizen's spouse does not infringe upon the citizen's rights. In *Obergefell v. Hodges*, which extended the right to marriage to same-sex couples, the Court emphasized the fundamental importance of marriage.[8] *Obergefell*'s recitation of the various reasons the Constitution must protect the right to marriage highlights the importance of protecting marriages from the interferences posed by deportation. In *Kerry v. Din*, decided in the same term as *Obergefell*, a U.S. citizen argued that her right to marriage implied the right to live with her husband in the United States.[9] There was no majority opinion in the case, but the tie-breaking opinion in the plurality rested on the assumption that the citizen's marital rights were affected by the denial of her husband's visa.[10] Four dissenting justices clearly concluded that citizens should be able to challenge decisions to exclude their spouses from the country.[11]

The day-to-day lives of married couples change dramatically when the partners live across international borders. Yet immigration law renders "the compelling narratives of loss and separation that accompany the enforcement of immigration law . . . largely irrelevant," particularly under the 1996 reforms that stripped judges of the discretion to consider the effects of deportation on family members in so many cases.[12] Although courts have historically framed deportation as causing merely "incidental impacts" on the lives of U.S. citizen family members, this reasoning does not hold up when considered in light of deportation's real-world effects on families.[13] This chapter offers a closer examination of the lives of U.S. citizens whose spouses have been excluded or deported, revealing that the consequences of spousal deportation are far more profound than courts have recognized them to be.

There is an important gender dynamic at play in spousal deportation cases. Most U.S. citizens affected by spousal deportation are women—primarily, but certainly not exclusively, Latina women.[14] Same-sex couples have suffered more under immigration law because marriage prohibitions prevented them from accessing the same immigration benefits as heterosexual couples for decades. Here, I focus on heterosexual marriages because those are the relationships I found to be most commonly affected by spousal deportation in my research, much of which took place before the legalization of same-sex marriages across the United States. With the Supreme Court's 2015 recognition that the right to marriage is fundamental and applies to same-sex relationships, the effects of deportation on same-sex couples warrant further examination.

Courts' decisions that the deportation of a spouse does not implicate a citizen's rights flow from a history of undervaluing and marginalizing women's citizenship, manifested most overtly in denying women the right to vote until 1920 and divesting women of their citizenship when they married foreign nationals in the early 1900s. The effects of current practices are quite similar to the effects of divestment of citizenship in the past. This chapter delves into this history, comparing the current experiences of women whose spouses are deported to the history of divesting womens' citizenship.

MOVING TO MEXICO

Rather than face long-term or, in some cases, permanent separation from their husbands, thousands (if not hundreds of thousands) of U.S. citizens have moved out of the United States following their husbands' deportations. Courts characterize this as a choice, but it does not feel like one to those who experience it; it feels like living in exile. They lose their proximity to friends and family, as well as access to their professional career paths, and, perhaps most profoundly, they miss being home. In her book *Amor and Exile*, Nicole Salgado describes herself as living in exile because she and her husband "choose to honor our marriage in making our home together here—not with an international border between us."[15] When she moved to Mexico, she writes, "I missed my friends, my mobility, even my students. I would fantasize that I was back at the beach in San Gregorio or Half Moon Bay, inhaling the fresh, salty air. . . . That nostalgia burned brightly, like a candle amid my dark frustrations with my new residence."[16]

Leaving one's homeland to live in another country under circumstances that leave little choice presents unique challenges. Many American women who have relocated to Mexico report that their quality of life is dramatically poorer in Mexico than they were accustomed to in the United States. They struggle to acclimate to a country where they may not speak the language, and finding employment is a challenge when one's education, training, and licensing are all from a foreign country. Wages are dramatically lower in Mexico as well. Even among those who are financially secure, "there is a psychological isolation," as one woman explains.

Adapting to a new culture, particularly when forced to move, triggers both physical and emotional challenges. An American woman whose husband was deported to Mexico describes her first night in Mexico on her blog—*The Real Housewife of Ciudad Juarez*: "I cried myself to sleep that night thinking I had made the biggest mistake in the world. I cried because I felt stupid, homesick, spoiled, lost, sheltered, weak, and most of all scared shitless of what was to come." She and her husband lived in Juarez, a notoriously violent city. Within two weeks, she saw a dead body and wondered, "What will I see in the next 10 years?"[17]

The lack of choice that accompanies a move due to deportation is a theme that emerges frequently in women's narratives. "People tell me, 'That's so cool. You're moving to Cancun,'" Stephanie said, "but I'm like, no. I didn't want to move. I was happy at home." She goes on to explain that they can't imagine her lifestyle. "I'm not over there in the resorts on the beach," she says, showing me her shower, which is a water spigot dangling from a concrete wall outside the house. "I've gotten a couple of whistles," she says, "but you do what you gotta do to get clean."

For years after leaving the U.S. to live with her deported husband in central Mexico, Mary struggled to adapt to an environment where she could not find employment that utilized her professional training. She explains, "I tried teaching English, because I was a teacher back home. But that paid about two dollars an hour." Later, she recalls, "I went from having a good job with a steady income, a retirement account, and benefits to having nothing. It was stressful financially. . . . But I also felt like I lost an important part of my identity."

Another U.S. citizen whose husband was deported recalls feeling "shell-shocked" for most of the first year she lived in Mexico. "I didn't speak any Spanish," she recalls, "and every day was a struggle." She recalls being scared to leave the house. "I had heard all these things on the news about the violence and corruption in Mexico," she recounts, "so I was on high alert." She and her husband went on a bus trip from the Mexican border area further south to visit some of her husband's extended family. The bus had to stop at a routine customs checkpoint, where the passengers had to get off the bus to put their luggage through X-ray machines as part of the customs process. A woman sitting next to her warned her not to let them rob her. "I didn't know why we were being stopped," she recalls. "It was the middle of the night. I was sleeping before we stopped. My husband got off the bus to take our bags [through the customs check], but I didn't realize that's what he was doing. When the woman told me not to let them rob me, my mind started racing. I assumed that the customs officials were instead corrupt soldiers who had stopped the bus in order to rob us. I panicked so much that I fainted in the middle of the street." She now sees the experience as an indicator of how much fear and anxiety she carried with her when she first moved to Mexico. "Now, I'm not so paranoid," she says. "I do start to worry every time I read about *narco* violence rising again. We talk about moving to Canada or somewhere else, but I don't know how either of us would work there, so at least for now, we're here."

Many mixed-status couples settle in the border region so the U.S. citizen or resident spouse can cross the border to work in the United States. This ensures higher wages for the family and a much higher quality of life than would be possible based on wages in Mexico. However, crossing the border presents a major challenge in people's day-to-day lives. With waits of up to three hours on a regular basis, people often spend fifteen hours per week waiting to cross the border. One woman reported developing recurrent urinary tract infections because she could not leave the car to empty her bladder while waiting to cross. On a Facebook page for American mothers living in Tijuana, women complain regularly about their experiences in the border line. "I can't take this anymore," wrote one woman. "I'm going to have to find a job in Tijuana instead." Another writes, "I want to cry, I want to scream. I can't handle getting back in that stupid line again today."

To put it in perspective, tourists who visit Baja from San Diego and get stuck in the line waiting to return often proclaim that they won't return to Baja because the wait was so long. These women do it every day. "It is so stressful when you have to be somewhere at a certain time—work, a doctor's appointment, whatever—and you plan and plan to make it there on time. But then the line is just longer than usual. Or it's going super slow. Or you get pulled over to secondary inspection, which can add another hour to your wait. If I have to be somewhere in San Diego and I really don't want to be late, I have to leave six hours early." Another woman recalls, "The worst was when I was pregnant because I had to pee all the time. But when you're in the line alone, there's no way to get out of the car to pee. So I actually started wearing diapers. I know. Gross. But it was the only thing I could figure out."

Commuters spend time brainstorming strategies to avoid spending so many hours waiting in the border line. "I think I'm going to buy a motorcycle," one woman writes on Facebook (because motorcycles can go to the front of the line). "But I'm scared of getting hit on the freeway." Another woman posts to recommend a strategy she and her husband have developed. He gets up at three in the morning and drives the car to the border where he waits until he gets near the front of the line. At that point, she drives to a parking lot near the line, and walks to take her husband's place in the driver's seat of the car. He then walks back to the parking lot and picks up the other car.

Crossing the border with young children is even more challenging—mothers struggle to find a place to pull over to breastfeed sobbing infants or change their diapers, but finding a place to pull over in the line is nearly impossible. Toddlers cry and scream in frustration. A mother of a two-year-old reports, "When she starts crying, I just tell her, 'I understand. I want to cry too!'" There is a special line for people who can obtain a security clearance. People in this line generally wait twenty to thirty minutes to cross the border. Border Patrol describes this line as "a privilege, not a right" and reserves the right to deny people on any ground. People with criminal convictions—even minor ones like driving with a suspended license—report being denied. Women married to deportees are routinely denied based on their relationship to a deportee because they are seen as a high risk for bringing their husbands across the border.[18] Crossing the border did not used to take so long, but longer wait times go hand in hand with the increased securitization and militarization of the border.

Lawful permanent resident spouses of deportees—green card holders—face unique challenges because their residency could be revoked if it becomes apparent that they are not in fact residing in the country. A lawful permanent resident who had grown up in the United States reported that she had recently applied to become a citizen but was rejected because she had been living in Tijuana for several years due to her husband's deportation. She crosses the border Monday through Friday to work as a nurse in the U.S. "They pulled out a stack of papers," she recounts, "and they told me, 'We know you live in Mexico. You cross the border every day between 6 AM and 8 AM to go to work.' That was a blow because I've been waiting for so long for my citizenship. I lived in the U.S. my whole life—went to school there from elementary school. I work. I pay my taxes. I take care of my kids. I've never been in trouble in my life." After she found out that her application for citizenship had been denied, her husband was despondent. "I think he felt guilty," she said, "so he told me, 'That's it. I'm gonna cross.' And I was like, 'You're crazy. We'll be fine.'" She talked him off the ledge, and they continue to live in Tijuana. She still crosses the border to go to work but worries about what will happen when she needs to renew her residency. "They know I don't live in the U.S.," she says, "so they could use that against me when I renew my green card." Her income is the family's primary support, and losing her ability to work in San Diego would present a major challenge. Her husband's marginalized immigration status renders her own status vulnerable.

Deportees whose partners cross the border to work in the U.S. frequently express feelings of guilt or discomfort that their spouses shoulder all family responsibilities on the U.S. side of the border—things like taking children to doctor's appointments and buying groceries that aren't available (or that are more expensive) in Mexico. Men reported feelings of shame and embarrassment due to their financial dependence on their wives, tapping into gendered expectations and triggering feelings of emasculation.[19] "I'm so embarrassed that my wife supports us," a young man confides with tears in his eyes. "I lie about it to people and pretend like I make enough to support the family, but obviously she's the one holding us down. . . . She works on the other side [of the border]. There's no way I can compete with that."

The privileged status of women who can cross the border to work in the United States affects the dynamics of their relationships. Joanna Dreby has found in her research with Mexican migrant families in the United States that "when spouses do not share [immigration] statuses, imbalances heighten existing gender inequities in relationships."[20] For example, Dreby highlights how on the U.S. side of the border, women are more vulnerable in abusive relationships when they lack lawful status, and the partner with lawful status has "the economic edge." Because the vast majority of people the United States deports are men, women often hold this "economic edge" in postdeportation marriages. Given the deeply entrenched gendered expectation of men as providers, deportation often brings about a major change to previously established roles in relationships. This shift in traditional gendered responsibilities can be challenging for male partners, who feel inadequate, ashamed, and guilty for not being able to live up to the cultural expectation that a man should financially support his family.

Some also express fear. "I don't like to think about it, but if we get into an argument or something I'll start to panic, like, what if she just takes the kids and leaves to the other side [of the border]? They would be over there and I would be over here. What if she never let me see my kids again? I can't go over there, so there's nothing I could do." Under the Hague Convention that governs international custody disputes, a parent could fight for custody. Nonetheless, people feel like they are in a less powerful position due to their deported status.

STAYING IN THE UNITED STATES

Many couples live across international borders following one partner's deportation. People employ a variety of strategies to maintain their relationships from a distance, including phone calls, video chats, and trips to visit the deported spouse. Long-distance relationships can be challenging under any circumstance; however, when the distance is caused by deportation, the uncertainty of whether the couple will ever be able to live together in the United States adds additional stress. When her husband was deported, a U.S. citizen who calls herself "Ray's wife" described falling into a state of deep depression in a blog post:

> I wake-up and I no longer recognize my life. My husband is not next to me in bed and my bed is in this home I do not want to live in. I feel my life and my dreams slowly slipping away. I have to keep myself busy to avoid feeling the pain, desperation, and grief that is there. The reality is—"my family" and "my home" are gone and who knows how many years will be lost before we can have that back if we ever do get it back.[21]

Women who remained in the U.S. after their husband was deported experience symptoms of depression: loss of appetite, disrupted sleep patterns, and frequent episodes of crying.

Edgar—the father deported for making a verbal threat twenty years ago—had been married for sixteen years before his most recent deportation. He met his wife when they were teenagers. She was, in his words, "a good girl" who "was a very good influence in my whole life." Following Edgar's deportation, his wife stayed behind in Los Angeles. She had worked for the government for nearly twenty years. She was accustomed to a middle-class American lifestyle, and her kids were in high school. Moving to Mexico didn't feel like an option.

During the first few years of her husband's deportation, she would bring the kids to Mexico to see him once or twice a month. But the long drive and lengthy border wait took a toll on her, particularly because weekends were the only time she had to run errands, clean the house, do laundry, and take care of other things she needed to do. As a working mother without a partner in the country, her days were full. And although the kids liked seeing their father, they were teenagers with other activities they wanted to do on the weekends. When they went to Mexico, they missed out on soccer games, school events, and time with friends.

After Edgar's application for a waiver that would have allowed him to return was denied by the U.S. consulate, he attempted to return to his family unlawfully. "It was my only shot at saving my marriage," he said. "My wife is the best thing that's ever happened to me. . . . She made me a better person. But she told me that she can't live in Mexico." He was apprehended in the United States and served time in federal prison for the crime of illegal reentry. After that, he decided he would not try again. "I'm not going back," he explained, "and my wife doesn't want to live here. So I had to let her go." Their sixteen-year marriage fell apart under the stress of their physical separation. Now, instead of monthly visits, Edgar sees his kids a few times a year.

American citizen Rebekah Rodriguez-Lynn's husband was permanently barred from entering the U.S. because he had come to the country on two separate occasions without permission. When she left her husband and son behind in Mexico to return to the U.S. to finish a master's degree at Harvard, she explains, "I felt as though my limbs had been torn from my body."[22] Ultimately, her marriage fell apart under the stress of deportation.

Maintaining Contact across Borders

Couples employ a variety of coping strategies to maintain their relationships from afar. Women report relying on telephone calls and video chats to communicate with their deported spouses. "We try to get on Skype every night at the same time so we can eat dinner together and be talking," says one woman whose husband was deported a year ago. Her husband had been incarcerated before his deportation, and she drew parallels between his incarceration and his deportation. "In some ways it's better now, because I can pick up the phone and call him. In there [prison] I couldn't call him. I had to wait for his call. And then we could only talk for fifteen minutes. At least now I can call him and we can talk for however long." In other ways, she finds the relationship more difficult to maintain following his deportation. "At least when he was in there, I could go visit him more easily. I could drive out and see him on a Saturday. Now I have to save up to fly out there and it's a lot. . . . When I get there, it's better than going to prison. But I can't go that much." They hadn't seen each other in nine months.

Video chatting is frequently employed to maintain contact, although some deportees only have access to the internet by renting computers at internet cafés, which sometimes have spotty service. Several women recounted that their deported husbands were "virtually present" via video while they gave birth in the United States. "That was painful," said one woman. "He couldn't be there to hold my hand, to hold our daughter when she was first born. That's one of the most important moments in a person's life, and he couldn't be there." The couple had decided that their daughter should be born in the United States because of the availability of more advanced medical technology in the event that there was a problem during the birth, and because of concerns that their daughter could be disqualified from U.S. citizenship if born abroad.

Family members of deportees who were formerly incarcerated draw parallels between the experience of visiting their family member in the border region of Mexico and visiting in prison. "It's kind of like going out there to [the prison]," the spouse of a deportee reports. "But out here it's better because we can go out to eat instead of eating from the vending machines [laughs]. No, of course it's better. We're free to do what we want. We get to stay for longer." Just as with prison visitation, families often drive hundreds of miles to see their family member. And, as with prison visits, the process of waiting looms over the entire experience. In prison, the waiting comes first, as people routinely wait for hours to get inside.[23] With deportation, the waiting comes at the end, as people wait for hours to return to the United States. In both cases, the recipients of visits feel guilty about the waiting their family members endure. In describing the time he spends with his family when they visit from Los Angeles—a two- to three-hour drive from the border—one deportee mentions, "And the line! They start talking about that line as soon as they get here. I be checking on my phone to try to find a good time for them to go back 'cause I feel bad they have to go through that."

The lengths people go to in order to maintain their ties across international borders speak to the value they place on their relationships. Over time, the distance can take a toll, resulting in the dissolution of many marriages, or pushing the deported partner to attempt to return to the United States.

Undocumented Partners

Undocumented spouses of deportees face the even more difficult decision of whether to stay or go. If they stay in the U.S., they cannot visit their deported spouse in Mexico. If they go, they may never be able to return. With the increasingly militarized border, many undocumented immigrants within the United States decide not to leave. Whereas in the past, people without lawful status in the United States could come and go more freely, that is no longer the case. Families who are divided in this way can see each other through a fence that lines the border in Friendship Park in Tijuana. On the weekends, Border Patrol officials in the United States allow people to get near the fence that marks the border with Mexico. From there, they can speak face to face with their loved ones on the Mexican side, at least for a few hours.

HISTORICAL PREDECESSORS

The experiences of American women whose spouses have been deported are consistent with a history of discrimination against female citizens married to foreign nationals—especially foreign nationals deemed nonwhite.

For nearly a hundred years—from the 1850s through the 1930s—American women who married foreign nationals lost their citizenship.[24] The modern-day experiences of American women married to noncitizens who are excluded or deported from the United States is reminiscent of the expatriation of American women who married foreign nationals in the past.[25] By their marriage to a man from another country, women lost access to privileges otherwise guaranteed to all citizens. Although they were actually stripped of their citizenship in the past, current deportation policies have remarkably similar effects. Women's citizenship has historically been, and continues to be, underprotected.[26]

The marginalization of women's access to the rights of citizenship was embodied in the doctrine of coverture, which the United States imported from English common law. William Blackstone summarized the doctrine as follows: "By marriage, the husband and wife are one person in law; that is, the very being or legal existence of the woman is suspended during the marriage, or at least is incorporated and consolidated into that of the husband."[27] Coverture "transferred a woman's civic identity to her husband at marriage."[28] Rather than owe allegiance to the state, a married woman owed her loyalty to her husband. Any wages married women earned belonged to their husbands; they could not enter into contracts, and they could not file lawsuits because any legal transgressions against them were perceived as transgressions against their husbands.[29] Further, men gained control of their wives' property through marriage and were held responsible for crimes their wives committed because married women's civic identities were subsumed by their husbands' identities.[30] The marginalization of women as full citizens was so extreme that in a property dispute at the end of the eighteenth century, an attorney argued that a woman "is not a member; has no *political relation* to the *state* any more than an *alien*."[31] Under coverture, married women had virtually no rights apart from their husbands.

Through coverture, married women's access to the rights and responsibilities of citizenship was limited. The rights of married women whose husbands were not American were even more marginalized. In the mid-1800s, women who married men from other countries and then moved out of the United States often lost their citizenship.[32] For example, President Ulysses S. Grant's daughter married a citizen of England in 1874 and lived with him in England for a period of time.[33] She lost her citizenship, which was later restored by Congress.[34] In contrast, American men who married foreign women did not lose their citizenship.[35] Rather, under an 1855 law, their wives automatically became citizens without having to go through the naturalization process, as long as they fell within a racial category of people who were allowed to naturalize.[36] At the time, women understood that their citizenship was more vulnerable than men's. In the words of an expatriated citizen, "If for men it is even a patriotic deed to extend by marriage the influence and partnership of their country in foreign lands, why should it not be the same when it is an American girl who marries a foreigner?"[37]

The Expatriation Act of 1907 codified the loss of a woman's citizenship upon marriage to a foreigner by expressly providing that "any American woman who marries a foreigner shall take the nationality of her husband."[38] Under this law, women lost their citizenship via marriage even if they did not move out of the country. For fifteen years after the passage of the act, the "legislative command denationalized or denaturalized every woman who married an alien."[39] A woman could "resume her American citizenship" if her marriage ended.[40]

Widespread concerns about increased migration from southern and eastern Europe, which peaked in 1907, influenced the passage of the Expatriation Act.[41] Many Americans perceived immigrants from these countries as "a fearsome threat to the country's cultural and economic well-being," and women who married them were thus "discardable."[42] According to historian Candace Lewis Bredbenner, in "the nativist-tinged rhetoric of '100 percent Americanism,' a citizen woman's marriage to a foreigner became vulnerable to interpretation as a brazenly un-American act."[43]

Ethel Mackenzie challenged the law in 1915.[44] She had been active in the campaign for women's voting rights in her home state of California but was unable to vote even after the state granted the right in 1911 because she had lost her citizenship when she married a foreigner.[45] An activist with the financial means to take her case to the Supreme Court, Mackenzie could have regained her citizenship status because her husband qualified to naturalize.[46] Recognizing that this course of action "would still avail nothing to other women," she instead challenged the law in the Supreme Court.[47] Her lawyer argued her U.S. citizenship was "a right, privilege, and immunity which could not be taken away from her except as a punishment for crime or by her voluntary expatriation."[48] However, she lost.[49] The Court found the power to divest citizenship to be within Congress's plenary power, finding her decision to marry a foreigner tantamount to voluntarily relinquishing her citizenship because she did so "with notice of the consequences."[50] It reasoned that "the marriage of an American woman with a foreigner . . . may involve national complications."[51] Despite critiques from legal scholars that the law was a blatant violation of the Constitution, the Court conflated binational marriage with national security issues.[52]

Not surprisingly, women's lives were impacted profoundly when they were stripped of their citizenship. When the Nineteenth Amendment was ratified in 1920, women who had lost their citizenship could not exercise the long-awaited right to vote. According to Bredbenner, "In addition to being denied a voice at the polls, women married to aliens could be excluded or expelled from the United States, denied access to or fired from certain occupations (including female-dominated professions such as public school teaching), and exempted from many public-assistance programs" as a result of losing their citizenship.[53] For example, Lillian Larch, who had been born and raised in the United States, applied for public benefits to support her three children.[54] Since she had lost her citizenship status when she married a foreign man, the government initiated deportation proceedings against Larch and her three children on the ground that she qualified as a "public charge."[55]

The Expatriation Act was partially repealed in 1922 with the passage of the Cable Act, also referred to as the Married Women's Independent Nationality Act. The Cable Act provided that a woman married to a foreigner would no longer lose her citizenship as long as her husband was eligible to become a citizen.[56] However, women married to men who could not naturalize due to their race continued to lose their citizenship for many years after the passage of the 1922 Cable Act.[57]

Among those who lost their citizenship due to marriage, women who were prohibited from naturalizing due to their race—mainly Asian women—suffered more than their white counterparts. Because the law prohibited them from naturalizing on the basis of their race, they were blocked from recovering their citizenship after it was divested. For example, Ng Fung Sing, the daughter of Chinese parents, was born in the United States in 1898, acquiring birthright citizenship.[58] She moved to China with her parents as a child, where she eventually married a Chinese citizen.[59] Her husband died, and Sing tried to return to the United States in 1925.[60] She was denied admission and was not allowed to recover her American citizenship because she was of Chinese descent.[61] If she had been white, she would have been allowed to resume her citizenship upon her husband's death.[62] However, because she was, in the words of the court, of "yellow race," she was prohibited from returning to the country of her birth.[63]

Women who married foreigners deemed nonwhite (and not of African descent) also suffered more than women who married white foreigners. American women who married nonwhite foreigners continued to lose their citizenship for over a decade after the passage of the Cable Act since it only applied to women whose husbands otherwise qualified to naturalize. According to Professor Leti Volpp, the Cable Act of 1922 only allowed "white or black women expatriated for marrying white or black noncitizen men to be renaturalized."[64] Asian American women were most affected by the act because they were most likely to marry Asian men (particularly given that fifteen states had laws prohibiting marriages between whites and Asians).[65] Women who had married men from China, India, and Mexico all challenged the loss of their citizenship in the 1920s.[66] Congressional representative Victor Houston estimated that eighty thousand women from Hawaii alone would be unable to recover their citizenship after marrying foreign men due to the racial exclusions of the 1922 act.[67] Through a series of amendments to the Cable Act between 1930 and 1936, citizenship rights were finally restored to all women.[68]

Race continues to play a central role in the creation and enforcement of immigration law. Lines are no longer drawn between white and nonwhite to specify who qualifies for naturalization, but immigration law continues to have racially disparate impacts. Racially biased stereotypes likely contribute to a culture that allows for the underprotection of (primarily) Latina citizens' rights in this context. In a social and political context where projections about Latino population growth are perceived by some as a threat to American culture, myths surrounding Latina fertility poise Latina women as a threat: their children will contribute to the projected

Latino majority. According to anthropologist Leo R. Chavez, high fertility rates among Latinas have been discussed in national magazines as "dangerous," "pathological," "abnormal," and even a threat to national security.[69] Chavez reviewed seventy-six individual issues of ten national magazines published between 1965 and 1999 to examine how the magazines discussed Latina fertility.[70] He found many instances where the theme of high fertility rates among Mexican women was linked to Latino population growth even though Mexican women in the United States do not have dramatically more children than their Anglo counterparts.[71] A 2004 article by Harvard professor Samuel P. Huntington clearly expresses the popular misperception of the link between Latina fertility and the projected Latino majority.[72] Huntington warns that "the fertility rates of these immigrants" from Mexico present "the single most immediate and most serious challenge to America's traditional identity."[73] Myths surrounding Latina women's fertility likely contribute to the law's underprotection of Latina citizens' rights.

Although women no longer lose their citizenship upon marrying foreign nationals, citizens whose spouses are deported lose access to fundamental privileges of citizenship. As in the past, the citizenship of women whose husbands are not U.S. citizens is vulnerable, especially when the husband is not white.

MOVING AND TRANSITION

Leaving one's home entails more than just a physical move. There are logistics to figure out—what to pack, what to leave behind, whether to rent out your home or sell it (if you own it). How much will fit in the car, and how much will you have to pay to import it? Is it safe to drive with all of your earthly possessions through Mexico? What about medical care for children? Do you need to apostille (get a government validation of authenticity) your child's vaccination records in order to enroll her in school in Mexico? An online chat room for the spouses of deportees is filled with questions about moving—people who have gone through the process answer questions for those starting out. They also share how painful the process of giving up everything can be. One woman, for example, experienced a stroke during her transition phase—she attributes it to the stress of figuring out the move.

Melany describes a sharp contrast between her life in New York before her husband's deportation and her life in a rural community in central

Mexico. She left New York behind three years ago. Her view of the skyline from her home and her designer wardrobe became things of the past. Her husband had been deported when their son was only eight months old. They had gone through a lot for this child—she suffered a miscarriage in a previous pregnancy at five months' gestation. When their son was born, they were thrilled. Then, eight months after his birth, the family was abruptly separated. Her husband had taken a friend to the airport and was stopped because he hadn't yet fastened his seatbelt as he drove off. The police who apprehended him later said they arrested him because a deportation order showed up when they ran his name, and they were motivated by the $500 cash bonus ICE offered to officers who apprehended people with deportation orders.

The family now lives on less than $100 per week. They have a farm—they sell vegetables and reinvest the profits into the farm, buying food and vaccinations for animals. In the U.S., Melany describes them as "moving up and out." Now, in Mexico, they struggle financially—she feels "stuck in a continuous circle." When she first arrived, their home had no electricity and no running water. Now it does, but service can be spotty. "The longest I've been without water was three weeks," she said, "so I took a big barrel down to the river and filled it up. Then I carried it to the roof of our house and filled up the *tinaco* [a large container used to hold water]." Part of her house is missing a roof. When she first arrived, she explains, "It blew my mind more than I realized. I thought, 'People actually live like this?'" Her mother compares their lifestyle to camping. Even going to the store was a shock when she first arrived. "I had no idea I would have to go to the butcher and ask for meat, and go to the store to buy eggs in a bag. It was total culture shock," she says.

Melany's husband tried to return once. He was found "near dead" in the desert. After that, the government barred him from returning for twenty years. "We both suffer posttraumatic stress," she confides. She has a recurrent dream that she is walking through Central Park and sees her husband near an orange tree. She walks toward him, he grabs her, and she breaks into pieces. Her husband's recurrent dream recounts the trauma he experienced in the desert. Both wake up screaming with some frequency, and they feel uncomfortable if their son sleeps in another room. They meet with a psychologist on Skype to process the trauma, but it still affects them. The violence that surrounds them does not help. "I heard gunshots last night," she says, but avoids saying more on the topic for her own safety, as well as for mine.[74]

MAY

May just turned thirty-seven years old. Born in Memphis, Tennessee, to a self-described "white, upper-middle-class family with tons of privilege," she now lives in Puebla, Mexico. She moved to Mexico when her husband was deported three years ago. When she married him, she lost some of the privilege she had grown up with. "From my background," she explains, "this has been a difficult pill to swallow. I'm used to being able to spend a certain amount of energy and brain power to get the result that I want. . . . I wanted to go to the best public university in the U.S., so I worked hard, and I got in. Then I wanted to go to the [best graduate school program in my field], so I worked hard and got in." For four months, she worked twenty hours per week to assemble her husband's petition for a pardon. And she did a good job. The reviewers remarked that it was the most extensive application they had ever received. Nonetheless, they denied the petition. She found out only two weeks before we spoke. "I was holding out hope," she says. Having been subject to racial, ethnic, and socioeconomic bias since his teenage years, her husband wasn't as optimistic. Her faith is now eroding too.

"I don't think we'll ever be able to go back. . . . I'm pretty much resigned to being here forever," she says with a serious expression. And she acknowledges that living in Mexico "is not that bad." She and her husband are able to work online, so they earn much higher wages than people working in the local economy. They live comfortably and are able to travel. They took a trip to Europe last year. But she's also given up a lot.

She had secured a tenure-track teaching job in a community college. She says it was her dream job because of her passion for teaching students who have been historically underrepresented in higher education. She left that job after only a year in order to live with her husband in Mexico. In her words, "Not being able to continue my career has been one of the biggest effects" of her husband's deportation.

They spent their first year in Mexico in Morelia, the capital of Michoacán. Her husband's aunt lived there, so it seemed like a good place to start out. They left because of the violence that surrounded them. "One day we were at Home Depot," she recalls, "walking through the parking lot. All of a sudden, my husband said, 'Stay calm but walk to the car as fast as you can.' It turns out he had seen plainclothes people walking through the parking lot wielding machine guns." They also heard about people being kidnapped and held in houses within their community, and a family was gunned down at a food stand they ran only two blocks from where May lived at the time. That's when they decided to leave Michoacán for the state of Puebla.

May and her husband are mulling over whether they want to have children. She says she isn't someone who has always known she wanted kids. But, she says, she's less likely to decide to have children now that she's in Mexico than she would have been if she were in the U.S. "I have no support here, no family," she says. That's part of it. Navigating the tedious bureaucracy that characterizes most institutional interactions in Mexico—which has already been challenging for her without children—feels like a potentially insurmountable obstacle with kids. Things like picking schools and figuring out how to register for school come to mind. "It's more dangerous. I was talking with a woman from Pennsylvania who's here with her five-year-old, and she's terrified of kidnapping," she says. "They live near a town that is known for child abductions. . . . I wouldn't even think about that [in the U.S.]."

In addition to the feelings of "psychological isolation" she describes, some of the most significant aspects of May's life have been altered by her husband's deportation—her career, her decision about whether to have children, her relationship with her family members in the U.S. I summarize the approach courts have taken to analyzing claims citizens have brought based on their spouse's deportation—the reasoning that her rights as a citizen are not implicated by her husband's deportation because the law gives her the freedom to choose to marry him and continue living in the U.S. without him. And I ask, "What do you think about that?" She says, "Of course you want to live with your husband. That doesn't make sense to me."

THE LEGAL FICTION THAT DEPORTATION DOES NOT INTERFERE WITH MARRIAGE

"Why does the government even let us get married if they're just going to kick us out?" asks one deportee's wife. Spousal deportation certainly feels like an imposition on the right to marriage to those who are directly affected.

And yet, over the past half century, courts have routinely rejected arguments that the deportation of a U.S. citizen's spouse violates the citizen's right to marriage. Rather than applying the same standard used in other cases to determine whether the government has sufficient justification for infringing on the right to marriage—a high standard referred to as "strict scrutiny"—courts have not required the government to justify its intrusion into marriages when a couple faces separation due to immigration laws. Historically, noncitizens facing exclusion or removal have had very little legal recourse because the government's decisions over immigration matters have been deemed to fall under Congress's plenary power to regulate foreign affairs and international relations.[75] As such, courts are hesitant to intervene in immigration matters, and noncitizens' constitutional rights are routinely underprotected in the immigration context. Influenced by this pattern of deference, courts have concluded that "no constitutional right of a citizen spouse is violated by deportation of his or her alien spouse."[76] According to this analysis, the government does not need to justify its intrusion into the marriage, even under the lowest level of review generally referred to as rational basis review, because a justification is only required when the government has infringed upon a fundamental right.[77]

In *Silverman v. Rogers*, for example, the First Circuit Court of Appeals determined that requiring the wife of a U.S. citizen to leave the country for two years would not "destroy[] their marriage," as the plaintiff argued.[78] Rather, the court concluded that "say[ing] that the residence of one of the marriage partners may not be in the United States" is a legitimate exercise of Congress's discretion that "does not attack the validity of the marriage."[79] Similarly, in *Swartz v. Rogers*, the DC Court of Appeals rejected the argument of a citizen wife that her right to enjoy her marital status, including establishing a home and raising a family, is protected under the Due Process Clause of the Fifth Amendment and would be infringed upon by her husband's deportation.[80] The court found that deportation would not interfere with her right to marriage because even though "the physical conditions of the marriage may change . . . the marriage continues."[81] Thus, although her husband's deportation would force her to choose between "living abroad with her husband or living in this country without him," even as a citizen, she does not have an explicit "right to live in this country."[82] Therefore, "the wife has no constitutional right which is violated by the deportation of her husband."[83] The Fifth Circuit has also concluded that the deportation order of a father had "no legal effect" upon his U.S.

citizen wife and children because "it [did] not deprive them of the right to continue to live in the United States, nor [did] it deprive them of any constitutional rights."[84]

The experiences recounted in this chapter call the courts' logic into question. Deportation often fundamentally alters marriages. According to Stephanie, whose story began this chapter, "This whole thing has changed us. Me, being apart from him and now living here [in Mexico]. Him, being detained and deported. We're not the same people we used to be." Days after our interview, she decided to return to the United States. She's not sure what will happen with her marriage. She wants to work, save up some money, and return to Mexico. At the same time, the prospect seems daunting.

APPLYING THE CONSTITUTION TO SPOUSAL DEPORTATION CASES

The Supreme Court addressed a related issue in 1972 when it held in *Kleindienst v. Mandel* that the First Amendment rights of a group of American scholars and students were affected when the government denied Mandel a visa.[85] He had planned to visit the United States to deliver speeches and participate in academic events on college campuses. The Court upheld the denial of Mandel's visa because it applied a low standard of review, invoking the long line of cases that has deferred to Congress's plenary power to govern immigration. It required only that the government provide a "facially legitimate and bona fide reason" for denying the visa.[86]

The right to marriage has been protected even less than the citizens' First Amendment rights were protected in *Mandel*, where the Court at least subjected the government's actions to some review. In the marriage cases, courts have consistently ruled that the citizen spouse (or child) has no right to challenge the family member's deportation on constitutional grounds. This may be changing. The First and Ninth Circuits have recognized that a citizen's rights are implicated by the exclusion of a spouse and are therefore subject to the same level of review the Court employed in *Mandel*. In 2008, the Ninth Circuit conducted a limited review of the reason for the denial of a visa by a consular official because the decision implicated the citizen spouse's "freedom of personal choice in matters of marriage and family life," which is protected by the Due Process Clause.[87] The First Circuit similarly applied this low level of review to a visa denial that was challenged "based upon constitutional rights and interests of United States citizens," requiring the government to provide a "facially legitimate and bona fide reason" for the denial.[88]

While the recognition that the right to marriage is implicated by a spouse's deportation is a significant departure from the decisions of other circuits, these courts still applied only rational basis review, which is much less protective than the standard applied to other government infringements on marriages. Outside of the immigration realm, government actions that "significantly interfere[] with the exercise" of the right to marry are subject to "'critical examination' of the state interests advanced in support of the classification" that interfere with the right.[89] For example, *Zablocki v. Redhail* addressed a state law that required residents to "obtain[] court order[s] granting permission to marry," which would only be issued to those who were in compliance with their child support obligations and to those whose children were "not likely . . . to become public charges."[90] The Supreme Court applied strict scrutiny—its highest standard of constitutional review—to analyze the constitutionality of the statute because of marriage's "fundamental importance" to all individuals.[91] The Court reasoned, "When a statutory classification significantly interferes with the exercise of a fundamental right, it cannot be upheld unless it is supported by sufficiently important state interests and is closely tailored to effectuate only those interests."[92] Thus, in *Zablocki*, the Court found the statute to be "substantially overinclusive" and therefore not sufficiently narrowly tailored.[93] Accordingly, the Court said the statute violated the Constitution. Government intrusions into marriages are uniformly subject to strict scrutiny when the intrusion does not involve immigration law.[94]

This is a crucial distinction because government actions assessed under the lower standard of rational-basis review are often upheld, whereas those analyzed under the higher standard of strict scrutiny are often found to be unconstitutional. Under the lower standard, the government must only show that its actions are rationally related to a legitimate government interest. Given the low burden the government bears under rational basis review, it is no surprise that in both cases where courts employed this standard to consider whether visa denials violated citizens' constitutional rights, they concluded that the consular officials had facially legitimate and bona fide reasons for denying the visas.

As a result of the underprotection of binational marriages, women are currently affected in much the same way that women who were divested of their citizenship were affected in the past. When married women were stripped of their citizenship upon marriage to a foreigner in the early twentieth century, they often lost their property. Now, women whose husbands are deported often lose their homes because they can no longer afford to make mortgage payments when they lose the economic stability that having two incomes provides, or when they move to a country where wages are much lower.

As in the past, women who are constructively deported—forced to move out of the country to keep their families together—suffer emotionally because they feel ostracized from their own homeland. In 1926, congressional testimony on the problems of divesting citizenship based on marriage highlighted the emotional aspect of being rejected by one's own country.[95] Elizabeth Kite, a scholar at the Library of Congress, testified about the problems facing Mary Das, a citizen who lost her status due to her marriage to a man from India.[96] According to Kite, "She happens to live in a place where having lost her citizenship, it does not affect the holding of property. But there are other things that are very seriously menaced, particularly the humiliation and the thought of not being wanted as an American citizen."[97] These sentiments parallel those reported by women affected by spousal deportation now. According to one such woman, who now lives in Mexico with her husband, "It feels like I'm being punished . . . like my own country is telling me that I'm not wanted because of who I chose to love."

Fears of violence emerged frequently in the narratives of women whose husbands had been deported. Violence surrounding the drug trade in Mexico has reached unsurpassed heights in the past decade, and criminal organizations have branched out into other ventures as well, including kidnapping. It is not uncommon for the children of wealthy families to be escorted to school and extracurricular activities by armed body guards. The fear of what could happen permeates the lives of families that have relocated to Mexico and affects the decision of whether to leave the United States to join a deported family member.

The experiences described in this chapter highlight the extent to which many deportees' lives are deeply tied to their U.S. citizen family members, whose lives are also uprooted as a result of deportation. These connections demonstrate the harm that is caused when the law defines some family members as welcome and others as deportable. Marital relationships are just one example of the wide web of familial relationships that are affected by deportation. The next chapter focuses on the experiences of children, whose lives are similarly uprooted in the wake of a parent's deportation.

I return to the stories presented in this chapter in the conclusion and propose two legal changes in response to the problems identified here. First, I argue that courts should reconsider past decisions that have held that the deportation of a citizen's spouse does not affect her right to marriage, particularly in light of the evidence I have presented about how profoundly deportation affects people's lives and marriages. Second, I argue that people's ties to family members in the U.S. should be balanced against the government's interest in removing an individual, and that marriage to a citizen should weigh heavily against deportation.

FIVE   CHILDREN OF DEPORTEES

> I believe I have the right to live with my parents.
> I have the right to be happy.
> —Sofia Cruz, age five (to the Pope)

"Are we a nation that accepts the cruelty of ripping children from their parents' arms?" President Obama asked when he announced his Deferred Action for Parents of Americans and Lawful Permanent Residents (DAPA) Executive Action program, which was ultimately never enacted due to legal challenges.[1] The rhetoric drew attention to the program's emphasis on family unity, most likely in an effort to debunk the title of Deporter-in-Chief given to President Obama by immigrant rights advocates.

However, the answer to President Obama's rhetorical question is a resounding yes. The United States routinely "rips children from their parents' arms." The numbers speak for themselves. Due to soaring deportation rates in the past decade, the parents of over a million children in the U.S. have been deported. The Migration Policy Institute estimates that "half a million children experienced the apprehension, detention, and deportation of at least one parent in 2011 through 2013" alone.[2] Between 740,000 and 920,000 parents of American citizen children were deported between 2003 and 2013, primarily to Mexico.[3] Far from being protected from deportation, parents of U.S. citizen children constitute between one-quarter and one-fifth of all those deported from the United States in recent years.[4]

When a parent is deported, most children stay behind in the United States. But a substantial number leave the U.S. with their parent(s). There were half a million U.S. citizen children living in Mexico at the time of the most recent national census, in 2010. Given the geographic proximity of the United States and Mexico, children whose parents are deported to Mexico often move back and forth between the countries at various points in time as families struggle to cope.

The experiences of one family highlight some of the complex migratory experiences of children whose parents are deported. Gaby and Lolo are American citizens whose parents had lived in the United States for many years without lawful status. When their father, Juan, was deported to Mexico for the first time, the family followed him. Gaby and Lolo, ten and five years old respectively, moved with their parents to Juan's hometown in the state of Guanajuato. They lived in an unfinished home that looked like a construction site, with open-air windows that mosquitos flew through and no hot water. They enrolled in school, but Gaby stopped attending because she did not understand the teachers. She was (and still is) more comfortable speaking English than Spanish. The children stayed in Mexico for just under a year before their parents decided the family needed to return to California. They were not making enough money to pay for their basic needs—food, clothes, school supplies, and medical care.

Since they could enter lawfully as citizens, Gaby and Lolo were sent to live with a relative in the United States while their parents attempted to cross the border without government authorization. Border Patrol officers spotted their father, Juan, as he walked through the hills that span the border of Mexico and California, carrying their mother on his shoulders because she was too exhausted to continue walking. Since he had previously been deported, Juan was sentenced to prison for the crime of illegal reentry. The children's mother was not charged with a crime. She was returned to Tijuana, where she remained for a short time before trying again. She eventually made it across the border and was reunited with her children.

When Juan was released from prison over a year later, he tried to return to his family in the United States. He was caught again and spent another year in federal prison. Juan's incarceration affected his son Lolo greatly. His grades dropped in school, and he cried frequently for his father. At night, his mother would hear him praying over and over, "Please let my dad out. Please let my dad out." She kept a box filled with letters and drawings Juan sent his children while he was incarcerated—a tangible record of his efforts to maintain some semblance of a relationship with his children.

After Juan was released, he was deported again. This time he decided to stay in Mexico. He didn't want to risk going back to prison. Gaby—at the age of thirteen—decided to stay with her mother in Los Angeles because she wanted to continue attending school there. "I love my dad," she said during a visit with her dad in Tijuana just days after his release. She sat on his lap with her arm wrapped around his neck, her lanky body draped over her father's knees. "I just know I have more opportunities if I stay." Lolo, now eight, decided to move to Mexico in order to stay with their father. Less mature, he was not as concerned with the differences in educational opportunities. He just wanted to be with his dad.

Adjusting to life in Mexico was challenging. When Lolo first arrived, he spoke better English than Spanish and had trouble in school. His father recalls, "When he came over here, he spoke only English, you know? Over there he was doing well in school and everything. He was getting good grades, and when he got here he didn't know anything—reading or writing in Spanish. There were times he complained a lot about that." Lolo also noticed a pronounced drop in his standard of living. He went from showering regularly in hot water to bathing out of a bucket, from a refrigerator he remembers being full in the U.S. to an empty one in Mexico, from accessible medical and dental care to being unable to afford the medication he needed to treat the intestinal parasites he developed, from being able to afford new clothes and shoes when he needed them to waiting for family to send these things from the United States. He also noticed differences in the food. "Quesadillas, tacos, they're weird right here. They taste like . . . like animal. But I'm gonna learn how to eat stuff. I never seen hamburger, and the pizza is weird. . . . The first time that I eat one, ew!"

Over time, he acclimated somewhat. A year after moving to Mexico, he was more comfortable speaking Spanish, and he struggled a bit when speaking English. He made friends, and the things that had stood out to him as strange or different when he arrived had become normal to him. However, his father couldn't find work in their town, so he took a job in a city two hours away. He would come home for the weekends, but Lolo didn't see him all week. He loved his grandparents who took care of him, but it wasn't the same as being with his dad. He also missed his mom and sister, who had remained in the U.S.

During a trip to Mexico to visit her father and brother during her summer vacation, Gaby recalled their life together in the U.S. She remembered that her brother used to "play with his friends and his skateboard. Go to the skate park, with my mom and his friend would go to the beach, to the park, or to Disneyland, or with my cousins, or my grandma's house." She missed her brother's presence. "Now it's so quiet. It feels like he's gone. Well, he is gone, but like . . . if he wasn't . . . like he didn't exist." Later, she added, "I don't wanna have an empty spot in my heart, 'cause when I'm with my mom I feel like I'm missing something, and it's my dad and my brother. And if they're home, I'll be happy."

His mother cried for days when Lolo left for Mexico, but she also understood her son's desire to be with his father. Lolo had missed him so much while he was in prison for reentry. "He's happy there," she said, referring to Mexico. "He's very attached to his father." She worried, though, that his future possibilities would be limited by the choice to stay by his father's side. "If he comes back, he'll be at a disadvantage because he's not going to know English. . . . This is my fear, that he is not studying English, and that he's forgetting it."

After three years in Mexico, Lolo decided to return to Los Angeles to live with his mother and sister. He cited poverty and factors relating to a lower quality of life as the major reasons for wanting to return to the U.S. Just as he had struggled to adjust to school in Mexico when he arrived there, he had a difficult time adjusting to school in California when he returned. His English was not as good as it had once been, and he struggled with basic reading, writing, and spelling. He started getting into trouble, hanging around with gang members in his neighborhood. Driven by a desire to stop his son from going too far down the wrong path, his father abandoned his plan to stay in Mexico and returned to the United States. This time, he made it across the border.

Like Lolo and Gaby, many children whose parents are deported to Mexico go back and forth between the U.S. and Mexico during their childhoods. This makes sense given the geographic proximity of the countries and the circular migration patterns that have evolved over the years. The transitions between countries—and between schools—can interfere with children's development and academic progress. One parent reports that her third-grade son, who had been a good student in the United States, stopped talking after he transitioned to school in Mexico. "He doesn't really speak Spanish," she said, "so the change was overwhelming to him. . . . Now he doesn't really talk in English or Spanish." The trauma children experience in the context of their parent's deportation can lead to mental health problems, poor school performance, and behavioral problems. Although the links between parental deportation and delinquency or gang involvement have not been systematically studied, Lolo's trajectory hardly seems unusual. He transitioned from a traumatized child who missed his father, to an exiled citizen struggling to adapt to life in Mexico, to a rebellious teenager who struggled to adjust to life in the U.S. after having been gone for years. That is a lot for a child to manage. Regardless of which scenario children of deportees find themselves in—separated from a parent, exiled to a foreign land, or both—their development is affected by a parent's deportation.

An emerging body of social science research demonstrates that children's mental health suffers when a parent is deported, both when the children remain in the United States and when they return to the parent's country of origin. Luis Zayas, dean of social work at the University of Texas, Austin, spearheaded a major investigation documenting the mental health repercussions of parental deportation on children. According to Zayas, "The sudden, uncertain separations that come about by detention and deportation jeopardize children's fundamental attachments to the adults they rely on for love, guidance, support, and care."[5] And they experience mental health issues, "includ[ing] depression, possible conduct disorders, and having a constant sense of a diminishing and ambiguous future."[6] Children who move to Mexico due to a parent's deportation become exiles and "may lose their sense of national identity as Americans, a poignant loss that even maintaining citizenship cannot prevent."[7] They "displayed more depressive symptoms" than their counterparts who remained in the U.S.[8]

Courts have routinely dismissed children's challenges to a parent's deportation, reasoning that it "causes only an 'incidental impact' on the minor child."[9] However, a growing body of social science research exposes the myriad problems facing the families of the deported and problematizes this assumption that deporting parents results only in incidental impacts. As in the case of citizen spouses of deportees, children who leave the United States with a deported parent lose access to the rights associated with their citizenship or residency. If they stay in the U.S., separated from their deported parent(s), their right to family unity is infringed upon. After describing the problems facing children under both scenarios—separation and forced exile—this chapter turns to the law, identifying and discussing three legal mechanisms that contribute to the overall failure of the legal system to protect children whose parents face deportation.

FAMILY SEPARATION

When Gina was first deported, she reported that her sons would clamor to get on the phone with her and would beg her to come back. Five years later, she says, "They don't even want to talk to me. It's like I'm a stranger to them. They don't even know me anymore." She continues, "They only get on the phone because my mom makes them. Can you imagine how that makes my heart break?"

When children remain in the U.S. after a parent's deportation—as most do—the parent-child relationship often deteriorates over time. Many deportees described trying to stay in touch with their children soon after they left the United States. Family members would bring the children to visit, and they would try to maintain contact through phone calls or on video chats. In most cases, the visits and calls tapered off over time—especially when the father was no longer involved in a relationship with the children's mother. Deported parents described conflicts with the custodial parent or guardian over trying to see their children. "She doesn't want to bring the kids anymore," a father explains. "She says the line is too long, and it's too far. But I'm like, 'What can I do? I'm over here. I still want to see my kids.'" A sense of resignation comes up in many narratives—a sense of powerlessness over whether people will see ever see their children after they have been deported. "My ex won't even let my parents bring my son to see me anymore," one deportee explains. "I keep begging. I even had my mom try to talk to her. But she keeps saying no—she's worried that it's not safe in Mexico. I want to say that I should have rights too—I'm his father. I wouldn't bring him over here if I thought he would be in danger. No—he'll be right here with me. But if she won't let him come, there's nothing I can do about it." One mother was looking into hiring a family law attorney to require her mother—who is her children's legal guardian in the U.S.—to allow the children to visit her in Mexico. But her parental rights were terminated long ago, so she has no legal recourse.

Long-term separation of children and parents often occurs even when deported parents make efforts to reunite their families by returning to the United States. George's father has spent the last ten years in and out of prison on the basis of a single drug-related conviction, followed by several convictions for illegal reentry. The immigration and criminal enforcement systems have overlapped to produce sequential periods of short-term parental separation that have cumulatively caused George's father to be physically absent from his life between the ages of three and thirteen—virtually his entire childhood. His father went to prison when George was three years old because of a conviction for drug sales. When he was released sixteen months later, he was deported to Mexico. He immediately tried to return but was apprehended for illegal reentry and was sentenced to two years in prison. When he was released, George was seven years old. He struggled to connect to his father. They had not visited regularly because he had been housed in a prison halfway across the country from George's home, and the family did not have the funds with which to travel to visit him.

When they saw each other in Tijuana after his father's release, George tried to make small talk. He spoke mainly English, his father mainly Spanish. "Four years is a long time, huh?" he told his father, trying to make conversation. "How've you been?" George spent a few weeks during his summer vacation with his father in Mexico, becoming reacquainted before he had to return to California for school. His father tried to come back to the U.S. but was caught again at the border. This time he was sentenced to three years in federal prison. The next time he got out, George was ten. They saw each other again for a few weeks, trying to reconnect by playing basketball and going to the park. When his father tried to come back to the U.S. once again, he was apprehended and sentenced to more time in prison. Although his original criminal conviction for drug sales warranted a sixteen-month prison sentence, his subsequent three convictions for illegal reentry have cumulatively amounted to nine additional years of incarceration. For George, this means that instead of being separated for a year and a half, he has essentially grown up without his father.

When he was four years old, soon after his father was first incarcerated, George talked about his father all the time. He admired him and told stories that depicted him as a hero. That connection has eroded over the years. Now thirteen years old, he says he's not interested in seeing his father the next time he is released. "It's like if I don't even have a dad," he says.

The bonds between children separated from parents deported from the United States seem to weaken more than the bonds between children separated from parents who have migrated to the U.S. Joanna Dreby, who has studied Mexican transnational families separated due to both migration and deportation, found that fathers who leave Mexico to come to the United States maintain ties to their children in Mexico through "frequent phone calls, gifts, and remittances."[10] Being able to financially provide for the children helps to maintain the relationship. In her work on transnational Central American families, Cecilia Menjívar similarly characterizes remittances as "monetary transactions with deep emotional meaning, through which immigrants keep a sense of family."[11] However, when parents are in Mexico and children are in the United States, the economic differences between the countries do not allow for the same structure. Deportees working in Mexico cannot financially support their children in the United States; in many cases they rely on remittances from family members in the United States to supplement their earnings in Mexico. According to Dreby, "In the absence of an economic tie to their children, fathers' emotional connection also falters" in the case of deported fathers.[12]

In addition, the future prospects and expectations vary markedly between migrant fathers and deportees. Migrants typically expect to leave their children behind for a short time—a year or so—while they earn enough money to reunite the family. In contrast, deportees often have no hope of reunifying their families. Many have been barred from ever returning to the U.S. This lack of hope that the family will ever be reunited—or that the father will ever live near his children—contributes to the weakening of parent-child relationships over time when children remain in the United States. John, a thirty-nine-year-old deportee who migrated to the U.S. before he was five years old and served in the Navy during the first Gulf War, reports, "I have three sons. I'm not in touch with them now. . . . They're not really in my world. . . . Yeah, it sucks. The sentence that was given was a lifetime sentence. . . . It really scars you in a terrible way. It broke up my family." Hope of family reunification contributes to maintaining family bonds even across international borders. However, when separation seems to be permanent, it is easier for these bonds to weaken.

Mental Health Consequences

Social science research has documented mental health issues among children who remain in the United States after a parent is deported, including heightened emotional and behavioral problems that are manifested in sleep problems, depression, anxiety, and poorer grades.[13] A 2013 study compared children with parents who had either been deported or were fighting deportation with children whose parents had lawful status. It found that "children with a deported parent were more likely to demonstrate elevated levels of internalizing and externalizing problems than children without a deported parent."[14] Examples of internal problems include depression and anxiety, and external behaviors include aggression and conduct problems.[15] Another study found that children whose parents were detained or deported by immigration authorities experienced changes in their patterns of eating or sleeping (indicative of mental health issues), "cried more often, and were more afraid than the control group. More than a third were more anxious, withdrawn, clingy, angry, or aggressive."[16] Most of the children in this study experienced these symptoms cumulatively, with a majority experiencing four or more of these behaviors. Prolonged separation from a parent was associated with more behavioral changes.

References to the pain of parental separation abound in firsthand accounts from children whose parents are deported. Gaby feels like she has "an empty place in [her] heart." Julio, whose father had lived in the United States for twenty years before his deportation, tells his mother, "It hurts here inside that the police took daddy."[17] The depression some children have experienced following a parent's deportation has been so severe that it has triggered some to attempt suicide. The *New York Times* reported on an eleven-year-old girl who hanged herself eight months after her father's deportation. The doctor who tried to save her asked the immigration court to allow her father to return to help care for her siblings, explaining that she had experienced "profound grief of missing her dad, and the extra burden placed on her when the family's main support was taken away."[18]

Given the rise in interior enforcement in recent years, more parents are arrested in the presence of their children than in the past because people are targeted while they are going about their day-to-day activities. Traffic stops are the most common way that people are apprehended by immigration authorities inside the United States. Recall Gina, the mother who was deported from Colorado after missing her immigration court date in Los Angeles. She was driving with her three kids in the car when the police pulled her over. They ran her name and saw that she had an outstanding warrant. She was then detained because a deportation order had been issued when she missed her immigration court date after moving to Colorado. "My son was screaming, 'Please don't take my mommy,'" she recalls. "We all started crying." This is not unusual in modern immigration enforcement. A news report recounts the story of a young girl whose mother was detained in front of her before being deported. "I could still see my younger brother kicking and cursing at the officers," she said. "[Him] yelling, 'Don't take our mom away from us!' still haunts me."[19]

Outside of the immigration context, research has found that children who witness a mother's arrest and incarceration experience "high levels of anxiety and depression."[20] The same is true for children who witness a parent's arrest by immigration authorities. In his study on parental deportation, Dr. Zayas found that the "sudden and confusing separation" following a parent's arrest "can lead to disruption of eating and sleeping habits, to sadness, anger, guilt, and anxiety."[21] Another study found that separating children from their parents following immigration raids posed "serious risks to children's immediate safety, economic security, well-being, and longer-term development."[22]

Financial Consequences

Parental deportation also "has large negative consequences for family economic stability."[23] One study that investigated the implications of parental deportation and detention in the aftermath of immigration raids found that "households experienced steep declines in income and hardships such as housing instability and food insufficiency."[24] Specifically, three out of five households reported they sometimes or frequently experienced difficulty paying for food in the months after a parent's detention and/or deportation. These families "had almost no income" nine months following the parent's detention and/or deportation.[25] Another study found that of sixteen mothers whose families had been affected by detention or deportation, all had difficulties paying their rent, and many were forced to move.[26] In addition to losing income due to deportation, families often incur legal expenses that further undermine their financial stability. Paying immigration attorneys to fight against deportation, or to seek permission to return, costs thousands of dollars. When a family's financial security is unsettled, children often suffer.

School Performance

Children's performance in school is also negatively affected by parental separation due to deportation. Many parents I interviewed spoke of dramatic changes in their children's grades and behavior in school after their deportation. According to Frank, "My son used to get all A's when I was there. I would help him with his homework, and he was always proud to show me when he did well on a test." After his father's deportation, "that all changed. My wife says the teachers are all worried about him because he went from doing so well to doing so bad." Research confirms these anecdotal accounts. For example, one study found that children's "study and work habits began to change and children's academic performance started to suffer" in the six months following a parent's detention and/or deportation.[27] Dips in academic performance can have far-reaching consequences for children's development and their future opportunities.

Foster Care and Losing Parental Rights

Though not as common as living with another parent or with extended family members, a significant number of children whose parents are deported become wards of the state and are raised in the foster care system. This can occur even when parents would like to take their children with them to their countries of origin. Typically, children are removed from a parent's custody only upon a finding of abuse or neglect. However, this has become complicated in cases where parents are detained by immigration authorities. Behavior that could seem like neglect, such as leaving children unaccompanied, may actually be a result of the fact that a parent is detained. Immigration detention facilities and children's courts have done a poor job of communicating with one another, to the extent that many parents have missed critical court appearances involving their children because they were in immigration custody.[28] Some have permanently lost their parental rights because of missing their court appearances while detained or physically barred from entering the country.

Nina Rabin has documented structural problems that impede parents' abilities to maintain their parental rights while they are in immigration detention facilities.[29] Typically, child welfare courts require parents to participate in various programs in order to reunify with their children—parenting classes, counseling, and supervised visits, for example. However, Rabin found that parents in jail had a better chance of complying with child welfare system requirements than parents in immigration detention; parents in immigration detention were generally not able to participate in these services. A social worker Rabin interviewed explained, "If a parent is in Pima County Jail . . . [we] have relations, liaisons with the jail who make sure they participate telephonically—this doesn't happen in detention. In dependency, even assigned attorneys have a hard time ensuring they participate."[30]

The federal Adoption and Safe Families Act requires states to move toward terminating parental rights after a child has been out of the parent's care for fifteen to twenty-two months.[31] The idea is to prevent children from languishing in temporary placements for long periods of time. Depending on the state and the age of the child, a state may move to terminate parental rights in as few as six months. If parents cannot comply with the requirements of the child welfare court relatively quickly, they may permanently lose their rights to live with, make decisions about, and even see their children. Although their detention may prevent them from complying with the reunification plans, according to the Vera Institute of Justice's Anne Marie Mulcahy, "their rights are easily terminated because their failure to participate in the proceedings may be seen as a lack of interest and cooperation in getting their children out of foster care."[32] Being in detention impedes parents' abilities to comply with child welfare court orders not only because they are unable to participate in reunification services while detained, but also because many parents report being unable to communicate with the child welfare courts. When child welfare court officials are unable to locate parents held in immigration detention facilities, these parents are often deemed to have abandoned their interest in their children's cases, and their parental rights can be terminated because of that.

Parents who have been deported face the challenge of trying to communicate with courts across international borders. They too risk losing their parental rights if they cannot successfully communicate with child welfare courts to demonstrate their continued interest in parenting their children. In addition, biases against Mexico and the living conditions there can contribute to judicial decisions that children would be better off in the United States, even if that means separation from their parents.[33] In child custody cases involving one parent in Mexico and another in the United States, I have heard social workers articulate a clear preference for children staying in the United States due to the higher standard of living. This preference is so strong that it eclipses standard considerations pertaining to a child's best interest, such as the child's attachment to the parent.

In her ethnographic work examining foster care on the U.S.-Mexico border, Naomi Rodriguez observed that social workers in San Diego often found deported parents out of compliance with reunification plans because the social workers were either unaware that parents could participate in the kinds of programs required by the plans in Mexico or because they did not trust the quality of such programs there.[34] Rodriguez describes a social worker's case file she observed that indicated the social worker's intention to terminate a father's parental rights based entirely on his detention and likely deportation, concluding that the father's anticipated deportation "automatically eliminated that parent from being considered as a custodial option for their child."[35] She observed this pattern in many cases, concluding that the legal actors involved in these cases believed that "continued U.S. residency was the de facto 'best interest' option for the children . . . seemingly without investigating the viability of the array of possible custody options or the strength of the relationship between parent and child."[36] Accordingly, she concluded, "citizenship and country of residence intervened and superseded parental rights, shaping social workers' perceptions of 'good' and 'bad' parents" and foreclosing the possibility of placement with deported parents or those facing deportation.[37]

Several of the parents I interviewed spoke of feelings of powerlessness relating to losing their children to the foster care system after their deportation. Most articulated a desire to reunite with their children but had no idea where to start. Combined with the systematic bias against reunifying children with parents in Mexico, the challenges of reasserting parental rights after deportation result in the permanent separation of many children from their parents.

AMERICAN CHILDREN IN MEXICO

Over half a million U.S.-born children were living in Mexico with their parents according to Mexico's 2010 census.[38] Given that over two million people have been deported since 2010, the number is likely much higher now. Children who have grown up in the U.S. often experience the move to Mexico as a shock—they face cultural and language differences, barriers to entering schools, and often a lower standard of living.[39] Without question, there are communities in every Mexican city where residents enjoy living standards comparable to—or in some cases higher than—those of the U.S. However, most people who move to the United States from Mexico do so out of economic necessity, and many return to these underresourced communities once deported. The social safety net is much weaker in Mexico than in the United States, due in large part to Mexico's weaker economic position.

School

Children who have attended school in the United States struggle to integrate into Mexican schools. Along the border, Tijuana schools are inundated with U.S. citizen children whose parents have been deported. An estimated four thousand American citizen children attended school in Tijuana in 2013, according to the coordinator of a government program designed to help children transition from U.S. to Mexican schools. Nearly half of these four thousand children had recently transferred from U.S. schools. The transition is complicated due to language barriers—many do not speak or understand Spanish. Even for those who speak Spanish in their homes, "it's different to do all your homework in Spanish, to read in Spanish," a sixth-grade girl says, "and it's hard to make friends." There are also cultural barriers—students who come from the U.S. struggle to fit in. Children and their parents report incidents of teasing and bullying based on their children's affiliations with the United States. For example, when anti-American sentiment peaked in Mexico with the election of Donald Trump—widely understood to be anti-Mexican—children of deported parents reported increased incidents of teasing, physical aggression, and bullying in school because their children were perceived to be American. Differences in educational methods employed by U.S. and Mexican schools can also pose challenges for children who are accustomed to U.S. schools, and, given Mexico's lower socioeconomic status, there are notable differences in school infrastructure and facilities.[40] As a fifth grader who recently moved to Tijuana from California points out, "Over here they don't have the same things like over there. Like computers." Another says she misses the library at her former school in California.

Children transitioning from U.S. to Mexican schools are not unique to the border region. Research with over seven hundred students from the U.S. who were now attending schools in the interior Mexican states of Nuevo León, Zacatecas, and Puebla found that students referred to bigger buildings, libraries, and computers in U.S. schools that contrasted with their new schools in Mexico.[41] Younger children—grades one through three— were able to navigate between the schools with resilience and "without obvious anguish." Older students—who would have formed stronger bonds to the United States—had a more difficult time adjusting. The educational challenges facing these children have implications for the United States as well as for Mexico, given that most plan to return to the U.S. in the future.

Ninety-five percent of students in sixth through ninth grades reported that they would either likely (56 percent) or certainly (38 percent) return.[42]

Transitioning between countries is especially difficult for teenagers because they are more rooted in U.S. culture and the educational system. In the border region, some parents decide that it would be better for their children to continue attending school in the U.S. after they move to Mexico. Students cross the border every day to do so. Although Tijuana and San Diego are geographically close, the wait to cross the border into the U.S. can be long, as discussed in chapter 4. For some, waking their children up at 4 AM to cross the border seems worth it—especially for high school—because they feel that attending high school in the U.S. will allow their children to attend college in the country more easily.

Luis—who journeyed through Mexico from Nicaragua before reuniting with his family in Tijuana—wanted his son Junior to attend high school in San Diego. Junior had attended elementary school in Los Angeles before his father was deported in 2008 and then attended school in Mexico for two years. When it was time for high school, the family made the decision to enroll him in a school in the U.S. "I want him to go to college over there," his mom said, "so it doesn't make sense to go to high school here." His mother had to pretend they were homeless in order to enroll him in school because she didn't have a local address. The law requires that homeless children be allowed to attend school, so he was able to enroll. For four years, Junior woke up every school day at 3 AM and was in the car by 4. His mother would drive a few blocks from their house to the border, and the wait would begin. Some days it was as short as an hour; other days it was as long as four. They would leave early to be sure they would make it across in time. Junior graduated last year, an event he describes as "sad" because his father couldn't be there. "He just wanted to come home to see his dad," his mom recalls. "He didn't even want to go out to eat to celebrate." Crossing the border has become a part of his life. "I'm used to it now," he says. He is now in his second year of community college in San Diego, with plans to become a registered nurse.

In order to keep their children from spending so much time in the car, some parents look for other options in Mexico. Fourteen-year-old Arya is a U.S. citizen from California. She moved to Tijuana with her mother after her stepfather was deported. She does not speak any Spanish, and her mother did not want her to spend "too much time on the road" waiting to cross the border each day to attend school. They located an innovative program in Tijuana designed especially for people like her. The Youth Recreation and Education Center provides a communal environment where students enrolled in U.S.-based homeschooling programs share a classroom with other students. They work independently to complete their lessons with input from an onsite teacher.

Chris, who grew up in Los Angeles and was deported, founded the program in conjunction with his wife, who is a teacher in San Diego. They designed it especially for teenagers of deported parents because, he said, "It's a culture shock for them. On the other hand, for younger kids, you know, it's not that big of a deal—you know they can easily adapt to the new lifestyle." His program provides access to computers, one-on-one tutoring, and socialization for American teenagers in Tijuana. The environment allows students to leave the isolation of their homes to interact with other students during the day while also receiving educational guidance. But there are only a handful of students in the program. They miss out on more extensive social interactions that unfold on a school campus and do not have the opportunity to participate in extracurricular activities.

Some children of deported parents who move to Mexico stop attending school altogether. Carlos was fifteen years old when his mother was deported. She landed on her feet, running a modest restaurant that her boyfriend owned, but she could not cross the border. Carlos did not speak enough Spanish to function in Mexican schools and, as a teenager, he felt like he didn't fit in. At first, his mother would find people to give him rides across the border to go to school. But people would move, or the rides would fall through for other reasons. After several months, they gave up. Carlos stopped attending school and started working in the family restaurant. Now in his early twenties, his job prospects are bleak in Mexico, and he is ill prepared for a career in the U.S.

The challenges with schooling that children face when they are constructively deported from the United States due to a parent's deportation limit the opportunities available to them when they eventually choose to return to the United States, as most plan to do. Previous court cases have reasoned that the rights of citizen children are not affected by a parent's deportation because they can choose to move back to the United States—and thus invoke the rights associated with their citizenship—when they are adults. However, being forced to attend school in a different country, in a different language, with fewer resources, dramatically limits the opportunities that will be available to these children when they return.

Economic Differences

Children from the U.S. also struggle to adjust to the economic conditions in Mexico. Lolo recalls that in the United States, his family always had food in the refrigerator. They were not rich, but they were able to provide for themselves in the U.S. despite the higher cost of living because of the greater income potential. In Mexico, Lolo would open the refrigerator and find it empty. The family would scrape together their resources to buy small portions of meat, which they would supplement with large portions of tortillas and rice to stave off hunger.

Rodrigo, whose wife and children moved to Rosarito, Mexico, with him from California after his deportation, feels guilty that he cannot afford to take his children to eat at Burger King. "We're living day to day now," Rodrigo explained. "I want to give my kids a better life than this. I can't even buy them a Whopper because it's kind of expensive and I can't afford it." He works as a security guard in a Mexican shopping center occupied by American companies like Walmart and Applebee's, earning less than $100 for a seventy-two-hour work week. That breaks down to less than $1.50 per hour. In the United States, Ortega earned $600 to $700 per week doing agricultural work in California's San Joaquin valley. "We used to go every weekend to McDonald's or Burger King with the kids," he recalls, "so they were used to that. But here, it's different."

Despite their financial struggles, he and his wife have decided to stay in Mexico. The first time Rodrigo was deported, he tried going back. His wife had just given birth to his son, and he couldn't stand to be apart from them. He was caught and sentenced to federal prison for illegal reentry. He didn't meet his son until he was released two years later. This time, his wife—who had never been to Mexico before and does not speak any Spanish—moved with the couple's two children to Mexico. "My parents can't believe I moved to Mexico," she said, "but we didn't have a choice." Rodrigo adds, "It's better for me to be with my kids than to go back to prison."

Safety

The safety of American children in Mexico can be threatened as well. Consider the experiences of Juan Carlos's teenage daughter, who lived in the U.S. until she was thirteen. When she first arrived in Mexico, she did not leave the house much. She did not make friends at school because, her father explains, "She didn't fit in here." Eventually, she started dating a local boy her age. One night, they went out to the movies. On the way home, the police stopped them. They handcuffed her boyfriend, and they raped her. She was bloody and beaten when she returned home. The family rushed her to the local emergency room. When she told them who the perpetrators were, they turned her away. "They told us they wouldn't help her," her father recounts with a pained look on his face, "because they didn't want to have problems." He went to the police station to file a report, but he had little faith anything would come of it.

Concerns about drug-related violence are also very real. The U.S. State Department has issued warnings advising citizens to avoid travel to many of the states where the deported parents of U.S. citizen children are from. In effect, the U.S. government is funneling its citizen children into the very regions it recommends against visiting. In assessing the impacts of parental deportation, Luis Zayas points out that the spread of drug cartels and the related violence "would give every parent reason to fight a deportation" because "it is their children's future, maybe their very lives that are placed at risk."[43]

In light of growing awareness about the negative consequences of parental deportation, the law should be more protective of family unity and should promote the best interest of children whose parents face deportation. As Jacqueline Bhabha argues in *Child Migration and Human Rights in a Global Age*, "The right to family life is a crucial bedrock of a just migration policy."[44] Without this, American children will continue to be forced to grow up either without their parents or in a country with fewer resources and a reputation for violence—both situations that can limit the possibilities for their futures.

LIMITED PROTECTIONS AGAINST PARENTAL DEPORTATION

A case from the Ninth Circuit Court of Appeals highlights how the current legal framework fails to protect children whose parents face deportation. Andres Magaña Ortiz—a forty-three-year-old parent of three American citizen children who is married to a U.S. citizen—faced deportation after living in the U.S. for twenty-eight years. He migrated to the U.S. from Mexico when he was fifteen and built a life as a successful business owner in Hawaii. He sought relief from removal in court, and, although the judge who heard his case seemed to want to grant him relief, she felt like the law required her to deny his request. She wrote, "This Court has great sympathy for Magaña Ortiz and his family and recognizes that his removal at this time will cause sadness, economic and emotional distress, and hardship for his family, business, and community but, based on the controlling case law, this Court is constrained to find that these effects do not reach the level and force of evidence of irreparable harm."[45]

The Ninth Circuit panel that considered Magaña Ortiz's appeal similarly expressed disdain for the law governing his case. Judge Reinhardt began his concurrence as follows:

> We are compelled to deny Mr. Magaña Ortiz's request for a stay of removal because we do not have the authority to grant it. We are not, however, compelled to find the government's action in this case fair or just. The government's insistence on expelling a good man from the country in which he has lived for the past 28 years deprives his children of their right to be with their father, his wife of her right to be with her husband, and our country of a productive and responsible member of our community.

Later in the opinion, Judge Reinhardt writes,

> The government forces us to participate in ripping apart a family. Three United States citizen children will now have to choose between their father and their country. If they leave their homeland with their father, the children would be forced to move to a nation with which they have no connection. All three children were born in the United States; none has ever lived in Mexico or learned Spanish. Moving with their father would uproot their lives, interrupt their educations, and deprive them of the opportunities afforded by growing up in this country. If they remain in the United States, however, the children would not only lose a parent, but might also be deprived of their home, their opportunity for higher education, and their financial support. Subjecting vulnerable children to a choice between expulsion to a foreign land or losing the care and support of their father is not how this nation should treat its citizens.

Finally, he concludes that ordering the father's removal "is contrary to the values of this nation and its legal system. . . . Magaña Ortiz and his family are in truth not the only victims. Among the others are judges who, forced to participate in such inhumane acts, suffer a loss of dignity and humanity as well."[46]

The current legal schema allows for hundreds of thousands of American children to suffer serious emotional, physical, educational, and psychological damage by failing to allow them to bring meaningful challenges to their parents' deportation. Three major areas of the law undermine the interests of children whose parents face deportation: (1) the requirement that people establish hardship that is more extreme than the hardships that normally follow deportation; (2) the legal conclusion that parental deportation does not amount to the de facto deportation of citizen children; and (3) the elimination of judicial discretion in many cases, which effectively prohibits judges from considering whether an individual should be protected from deportation in light of the toll it would take on family members.

Exceptional and Extremely Unusual Hardship Standard

Cancellation of removal is a legal mechanism that emerged in order to allow courts to consider the effects of an individual's deportation on his or her family members. However, this relief is now available only to a small segment of the population. Many people with criminal convictions are statutorily excluded. Even those who are otherwise eligible must establish ten years of residence in the country. And the standard is very high, requiring noncitizens to establish that their deportation will cause "exceptional and extremely unusual hardship" to a family member in the U.S. This means they have to establish that the harms their family members would suffer are "substantially different from, or beyond that which would normally be expected from the deportation of an alien with close family members here."[47]

The suffering that can be expected to occur when a family is forcibly divided is thus irrelevant under the law because one must show hardship above and beyond what would normally flow from deportation. The factors that most profoundly affect children who grew up in the United States once they move to Mexico—economic loss, inadequate medical care, poorer education, lower standards of living, and speaking only English—have not been enough to establish exceptional and extremely unusual hardship in many cases.[48] The standard is so high that, according to Edith Z. Friedler, it "provides practically unattainable relief for the citizen child whose parents are subject to deportation." As one judge has argued, utilizing such a high standard "strips the phrase 'extreme hardship' of virtually all content."[49]

Legal scholar Susan Hazeldean has proposed a reinterpretation of the standard that would shift the point of comparison. She argues that rather than compare whether the consequences that would flow from a parent's deportation are "extremely unusual" in relation to other children whose parents face deportation, the standard should compare a child's experience to the experiences of a typical American child. She argues, "Since most U.S. citizens are not deprived of their constitutional right to remain in the United States or be raised by their loving, fit parents, that change in the standard of eligibility would enable many more parents facing deportation to qualify for relief and prevent harm to their children."[50] This would be a useful reform.

Rejection of De Facto Deportation Claims

The second way that the law blocks access to relief for children whose parents face deportation is that courts continue to say that deporting a parent does not amount to the constructive deportation of the child. Despite children's limited options when their parents are deported, arguments that deporting a parent amounts to the constructive deportation of a citizen child have consistently failed. According to legal scholar David Thronson, "The proposition that children's valid immigration or citizenship status alone is insufficient to overcome the removal of a parent from the United States is a firmly established starting point for courts considering the situation of citizen children whose parents face deportation."[51]

Since the 1980s, advocates have argued that deporting the parent of a citizen child amounts to the de facto deportation of the child and, as such, the child's constitutional rights should be protected in the process. However, just as with the cases discussed in chapter 4 focusing on spousal deportation, this argument has been rejected time and time again. In 1982, the Fifth Circuit concluded the deportation order of the husband and father has "no legal effect" upon an American citizen wife and children because "it does not deprive them of the right to continue to live in the United States, nor does it deprive them of any constitutional rights."[52] The Tenth Circuit rejected an argument that a parent's deportation violates a citizen child's "right to continue to have the love and affection of his parents in the United States" because, according to the court, "the deportations involved herein cause only an 'incidental impact' on the minor child, albeit a serious one."[53]

In *Acosta v. Gaffney*, the Third Circuit considered the fate of Lina Acosta, a twenty-two-month-old American citizen whose parents were ordered deported to Colombia.[54] Her attorney argued "that she will be deprived of this constitutional right of a citizen because as an infant she must remain with her parents and go with them wherever they go."[55] The court acknowledged that "it is the fundamental right of an American citizen to reside wherever he wishes, whether in the United States or abroad, and to engage in the consequent travel." However, it concluded that Lina's rights were not violated because her parents could decide to leave her behind with foster parents in the United States. Alternatively, she could decide to return to the United States when "she grows older and reaches years of discretion" such that moving with her parents to Colombia "will merely postpone but not bar, her residence in the United States if she should ultimately choose to live here."

However, this reasoning ignores the potentially insurmountable obstacles a child like Lina would face upon her return—challenges such as Lolo faced when he came back, which led him to struggle with basic reading and writing, to perform poorly in school, and to gravitate toward gang activity and delinquency. Or such as Carlos would likely face if he tried to return, having dropped out of high school at the age of fifteen when his mother was deported. As Edith Friedler notes,

> A young child who leaves this country before reaching school age will undoubtedly be at a severe disadvantage if he or she chooses to return and attempt to function as an adult member of our society. For example, where will this citizen find employment? Can we realistically expect him or her to possess basic skills which other, minimally educated United States residents acquire during their elementary school education? Such an individual may not even possess basic skills necessary to seek employment, such as filling out applications and answering questions posed by interviewers.[56]

A binational team that studied children who transitioned from U.S. to Mexican schools concluded, "US-citizen children have the right to return to the United States and may return with limited English skills, interrupted formal education, and other disadvantages."[57]

Construing the consequences of a parent's deportation as having an "incidental impact" on a child mischaracterizes the realities of children whose parents are deported. And recent social science research may provide evidence to challenge this misperception in future cases. Virtually every aspect of a child's life is affected when a parent is deported—mental health, financial stability, and educational opportunities, to name a few. Given that children are dependent on their parents for financial, emotional, and developmental support, the choice to remain in the U.S. when a parent is deported is quite limited. In light of the emerging body of research documenting the severe consequences of parental deportation on citizen children, the legal fiction that parental deportation does not amount to the constructive deportation of their children should be reconsidered.

Family Unity Claims

Under the 1996 reforms, judges cannot even consider the impact of a parent's deportation on his or her children when the parent has been convicted of an aggravated felony. Given that so many deported parents have criminal convictions—86 percent of the parents of U.S. citizen children ICE removed in 2013—eliminating judicial discretion in cases involving aggravated felonies has foreclosed the possibility of relief for many children whose parents face deportation.[58] Prohibiting judges from considering the harms caused by deportation in individual cases undermines children's fundamental human rights—rights that are protected in widely accepted international human rights instruments and that should be protected under the Constitution as well.

In *Moore v. City of East Cleveland*, the Supreme Court held that "the Constitution protects the sanctity of the family precisely because the institution of family is deeply rooted in this nation's history and tradition."[59] Like spouses, children are forced to choose between two fundamental rights when a parent is deported: (1) the right to family unity, and (2) the rights attached to their citizenship. However, children have even less of a choice between staying in the United States and moving with a parent, given their dependence on their parents to make such decisions.[60] Family unity should be constitutionally protected in immigration-related cases in the same way it is protected in other contexts.

Separating families also breaches international human rights delineated in the most widely recognized treaties on the subject. The Universal Declaration of Human Rights provides that "the family is the natural and fundamental group unity of society and is entitled to protection by society and the state." The United Nations Convention on the Rights of the Child (CRC), which has been ratified by every member state of the United Nations except the United States, requires that courts consider children's best interests prior to separating them from a parent. Specifically, the CRC requires governments to "ensure that a child shall not be separated from his or her parents against their will, except when . . . such separation is necessary for the best interests of the child." U.S. deportation policy violates this directive as there is no room for courts to consider children's best interest in cases where the parent has sustained a criminal conviction labeled an aggravated felony.

The International Covenant on Civil and Political Rights (ICCPR)—which the U.S. has ratified and is thus binding on U.S. courts—similarly prohibits arbitrary interference with family life. In order to protect this right, the United Nations Human Rights Committee charged with enforcing the ICCPR provides that in deportation cases, the government's interest in deportation must be balanced against the cost to the individual, taking into account the "length of stay in the host country, age, . . . the family's financial and emotional interdependence, and the state's interests in promoting public safety and in enforcing immigration laws." Similarly, the American Convention on Human Rights, which the U.S. signed in 1969 but has not ratified, provides that "the family is the natural and fundamental group unit of society and is entitled to protection by society and the state."[61] The convention further provides, "Every minor child has the right to the measures of protection required by his condition as a minor on the part of his family, society, and the state."

The Inter-American Commission on Human Rights considered the mandatory deportation policies the U.S. employs for people convicted of aggravated felonies in a 2010 case and concluded that the process violates the right to family unity.[62] In this case, the commission considered the deportations of two lawful permanent residents of the United States who were removed due to convictions for crimes categorized as aggravated felonies. Wayne Smith was deported based on a conviction for attempted distribution of cocaine, and Hugo Armendariz was deported due to convictions for possession of cocaine for sale, possession of drug paraphernalia, and hindering prosecution. Both were married to U.S. citizens and had citizen children. The commission concluded that the United States had violated multiple rights protected by the American Convention on

Human Rights—the rights to family unity, due process, and a fair trial. It recommended that the U.S. utilize a balancing test to weigh the state's interest in deportation against "interference with family life" on a case-by-case basis, indicating that "the reasons justifying interference with family life must be very serious indeed." Despite this international censure for violating human rights, the United States has made no steps toward bringing its law more in line with these recommendations. People convicted of aggravated felonies must be deported—absent a showing that they will be tortured upon their deportation—regardless of the consequences their deportation will cause.

The U.S. framework for deportation fundamentally conflicts with the principles outlined in most international human rights instruments. Rather than balancing citizens' interests against the government's interest, U.S. law does not even allow room for considering the consequences of parental deportation in many cases. European countries employ balancing tests like the one the Inter-American Commission recommended. Like the American Convention, the European Convention on Human Rights protects the right to family life.[63] I return to this point in the conclusion, where I propose legislative reforms modeled after the balancing test employed by the European Court of Human Rights.

How can American values and the country's immigration laws simultaneously value family unity and undermine it? Jacqueline Bhabha analyzes the "contradiction between a universal consensus on the critical importance of family unity for children and the reality of policy-induced family separation for immigration children."[64] She questions why government actions that divide families are pervasive despite this "universal consensus" that family unity and the best interests of children are not only important goals but also basic human rights. Bhabha concludes that the heart of this contradiction rests in the emphasis placed on the importance of sovereignty—in "the prerogative of the sovereign state to control its borders, to regulate the access of noncitizens to its territory, and to temper the force of human rights obligations with the exercise of exclusionary discretion."[65] The tension between a government's right to exclude and an individual's right to remain is central to the legal paradigm governing deportation. Historically, the government's right to sovereignty has reigned supreme in U.S. immigration law. However, individual rights have continually surfaced as a challenge to this government power and, in recent

Supreme Court cases, individual rights are increasingly being valued over the government's historically virtually impenetrable right to exclude.

The consequences of prioritizing the government's right to exclude over the individual's right to stay are disturbing—rampant violations of human rights, widespread mental health problems, and permanent separation of children from their parents unavoidably flow from this approach. Families are permanently divided, resulting in serious emotional and behavioral consequences that impede children's development. Hundreds of thousands of American citizen children who are living in Mexico will someday return to the United States.[66] However, their future prospects are limited by discontinuity in their schooling and by linguistic and cultural challenges that are likely to emerge because of their absence from the country. Although U.S. immigration law promotes family unity in some respects, it also "contains many provisions that keep families apart."[67] As I argue in the conclusion, justice and humanity—as well as more pragmatic public policy considerations—demand a shift in the legal paradigm toward an approach that recognizes the rights of families to stay together.

CONCLUSION RESISTANCE AND REFORMS

> I pray that soon the good men and women in Congress will ameliorate
> the plight of families like the [petitioners] and give us humane laws
> that will not cause the disintegration of such families.
> —Judge Harry Pregerson, *Memije v. Gonzales* (2007)

"We are American," one deportee in Tijuana told me, "but we can't prove it." This sentiment has been expressed by deportees from the United States who now live in El Salvador, the Dominican Republic, Cambodia, Jamaica, Guatemala, and Brazil.[1] And this is echoed by over one hundred deportees I have interviewed in Mexico. People speak of being banished from their homes and separated from their families.

As this book documents, a significant number of people who have been socialized in U.S. culture but do not have the corresponding legal status have been permanently barred from ever returning to the United States. While they were in the U.S., they did not feel less American than their citizen counterparts. As children, they started their mornings pledging allegiance to the American flag and learned about U.S. history in school. As teenagers, they liked the same music, sports teams, clothing styles, movies, and food as their friends, siblings, and neighbors who happened to be citizens. Throughout their childhoods, they celebrated uniquely American holidays like Halloween, Thanksgiving, and the Fourth of July. Their families, their property, and their entire lives were centered in the United States.

Legal scholars, sociologists, and political theorists have been exploring the meaning of citizenship in an increasingly globalized world and are theorizing new ways of thinking about citizenship and identity—theories of citizenship rooted in people's cultural associations rather than being tethered to national boundaries. Formal citizenship—the way the law defines citizenship—is merely one way of defining membership in a society. There are other ways to think about how to recognize who belongs as a full member of a country, with the accompanying rights and protections. Scholars have explored alternative approaches to understanding citizenship based on people's identities, ties to the country, political involvement, exercise of rights, and territorial presence. This chapter considers deportees' experiences in light of theoretical concepts of citizenship in order to explain the deep associations deported Americans feel with the United States despite their lack of formal citizenship. Specifically, I consider four theories of social membership based on (1) identity, (2) affiliations, (3) contract, and (4) the exercise of rights.

Under each of these theoretical constructions of citizenship or membership, deported Americans' experiences show that they are more functionally American than Mexican. First, they identify as and feel American. Others perceive them as American too. They experience stigma and rejection in Mexico because they are perceived as outsiders. Second, they have deep ties and attachments to people, places, memories, and things in the United States. In contrast, most lack these ties and connections to Mexico. Third, many have relied on the government's tacit allowance of officially unauthorized migration from Mexico and have conferred benefits on the United States during their time in the country. This relationship creates an implied contract that should recognize immigrants' membership in exchange for the benefits they have conferred on the country during their territorial presence, especially when people have lived in the country for extended periods of time. Fourth, while in the United States, deported Americans were vested with most of the same rights as citizens. In Mexico, even though they technically have the same rights as other citizens, they are unable to fully access them because of their lack of cultural familiarity and the stigma they experience. From a rights-based understanding of citizenship, they are more like citizens of the United States than of Mexico.

In the field of citizenship studies, scholars posit that identity is one way of understanding social membership. Linda Bosniak refers to this concept as "citizenship as identity," "which describes the affective ties of identification and solidarity that we maintain with groups of other people" and "is deployed to evoke the quality of belonging—the felt aspects of community membership."[2] Thinking about people's identities as an indication of citizenship or belonging taps into people's subjective understandings of their "sense of psychological membership"—"the affective elements of identification and solidarity that people maintain with others"; "the felt aspects of social membership."[3] This is the crux of what people are saying when they identify as American despite their lack of formal status. According to one deportee, "I am an American at heart and in many other aspects. It's the paperwork stating that I am an American that I regretfully lack." Another explains, "I'm American because that's where I'm from. . . . You could say I was born here [in Mexico]. I mean, I was. But I'm not *from* here."

Deported Americans regularly employed terms like "exiled" and "banished" to describe their status, thus "contesting established concepts of justice and citizenship by resisting the notion that they do not belong in the country from which they have been removed."[4] Their persistent assertions that they are American deliberately challenge their exclusion, a move that is similar to the approach taken in the Dreamers' "Unapologetic and Unafraid" campaign within the United States, which aimed to "collapse the boundary" between the categories of "American" and "undocumented" to "assert that one can be both simultaneously."[5] From this perspective, the decision to return to the United States after deportation, as so many do, can be seen as an act of resistance or civil disobedience—the deliberate violation of a law perceived as unjust by people who feel a strong sense of membership in U.S. society.[6] By returning, they physically claim the membership status they feel.

Deportees' stories also contest white hegemonic constructions of what it means to be American. Their narratives of belonging depict both positive and negative aspects of life in the United States. Memories of competing in a school spelling bee competition and being elected homecoming king are accompanied by memories of police harassment and abusive working conditions their parents experienced. People recall poverty, violence, and juvenile halls alongside outings to Disneyland and trick-or-treating at Halloween.

Their memories are tied to the communities typically inhabited by recent immigrants from Mexico and Central America, which do not represent the stereotypical image of the United States but are integral parts of the country nonetheless. By identifying as American, they demand membership in a society that systematically marginalizes people like them. Despite powerful forces of exclusion, their ties to their communities, to social institutions like churches and schools, and to property, careers, friends, and family make the United States home.

In the words of one deportee,

> If you ask me, "What are you?" I'm gonna say I'm American. That's where I grew up. That's what I know. I mean, I'm Mexican American. Don't get me wrong. A lot of white people hate us over there. But that's where I'm from. If you ask me, "Are you Mexican?" I'm gonna say no. I could sing you "The Star-Spangled Banner," but I don't even know what the Mexican anthem is. I don't know how to get a job here, how to enroll my boy in school. . . . I don't even know how to catch the bus. I'm American just like my brothers and sisters over there [who are citizens]. But they kicked me out. My papers say I'm Mexican but there's a lot more to it than what my birth certificate says.

Identifying as being American does not necessarily imply assimilation into mainstream U.S. culture. Rather, it can be employed to embrace the multifaceted nature of U.S. society. One deportee who lived in the U.S. from the age of four months until he was thirty-three years old explains, "I'm a citizen of the United States all in but for documentation. . . . I went to school there—preschool, kindergarden, elementary, high school, and university while in prison. It's my first language. The culture—it's my culture. If there is one culture in the United States. So I identify with the U.S. I identify myself as an American even though I was born in Mexico." While recognizing the complexity of U.S. society—the divisions, the racism, the tendency toward exclusion, the term "American" still represents who they are. According to one deportee, "When I say I'm American, I'm not trying to say I'm white. No. I'm Chicano. I'm brown and I'm proud. But that don't make me less American."

Deported Americans contest their social construction as others and their exclusion from the territorial boundaries of the United States. Although they recognize that they faced barriers to full inclusion when they resided within the United States, they challenge the legitimacy of exclusionary legal definitions of citizenship and membership, drawing instead on their life experiences to assert that they are functionally American. Sociologist Leisy Abrego has found that members of the 1.5 generation of immigrants within the United States—immigrants who came to the U.S. as children—are more likely than immigrants who migrated as adults to challenge policies of exclusion.[7] She attributes this to their socialization in U.S. schools and their adherence to American values. They were taught to stand up for their rights and that the U.S. is a country of immigrants. In this context, the defiant assertion of Americanness even after forcible removal can be seen as a form of resistance and an indication of their roots in U.S. culture. As Susan Coutin found in her study of Salvadoran migrants who had come to the U.S. as children and had been deported, "From a place of extreme marginalization, deportees nonetheless claim membership in ways that challenge both removal and social exclusion."[8]

Deportation reinforces, rather than undermines, people's identification with the United States. Being separated from the country solidifies the feeling that the United States is where they belong. This is consistent with social psychologist Nira Yuval-Davis's observation that "the emotional components of people's constructions of themselves and their identities become more central the more threatened and less secure they feel."[9] Whereas a study of immigrants within the United States who had migrated under the age of five found that 40 percent reported their ethnic identity by their country of origin, all of the people I interviewed who migrated before they turned five identified as American or Mexican American after they had been deported. This confirms Yuval-Davis's point—people seem to feel a stronger sense of identification with the American aspects of their identities postdeportation. Indeed, several people noted that they identified with their Mexican heritage while in the United States, referencing things like hanging the Mexican flag in their homes or getting tattoos relating to their Mexican heritage. Within Mexico, however, they report being perceived as *gabachos* (Americans) or *pochos* (a derogatory term for Mexican Americans) who do not fit into Mexican cultural norms. Many surround themselves with social networks composed of other Americans, most often other deportees or Americans who have retired in Mexico. In many respects, their worldviews are more similar to those of American expatriates than to those of other Mexican citizens, with the critical distinction that they did not leave their homeland by choice.

Philosopher Leo Zaibert employs the concept of "homeland" as a way to understand the implications of deportation for noncitizens who identify the U.S. as their home. He prioritizes the "sense of cultural identity and community that pervades all members of the nation" in defining one's homeland and recognizes that "sometimes a country can be someone's homeland, even if that someone is not a citizen of that country."[10] Political philosopher Joseph Carens argues that these feelings of belonging—of connections "through one's sense of emotional attachment, identification, and loyalty" point to a "psychological dimension of membership" that can give rise to claims of citizenship, albeit not claims currently recognized by the law.[11] The "conventional view" of citizenship imagines "a tight fit between the legal and psychological dimensions of citizenship"—that people will feel this psychological connection to the country where they have formal or legal citizenship.[12] However, in the case of deported Americans, there is a disconnect between these legal and psychological dimensions of citizenship.

The depth of the psychological identification with the United States demonstrated by deported Americans is tied to their socialization in the country. Childhood years are formative years—we develop our selves, our identities, our ways of seeing the world. All of the people I interviewed grew up attending U.S. schools, which, Roberto G. Gonzalez notes in his study of undocumented youth in the United States, provide immigrant children "the important opportunity to integrate into a country's legal and cultural framework, albeit temporarily," promoting the development of their "identities as American children."[13] Schools played such a central role in the lives of the people I interviewed that most of them specifically named the schools they attended; some even mentioned the names of specific teachers who had made an impression. Many brought up pledging allegiance to the American flag each morning in elementary school—a memory that stands out as a tangible claim to an American political affiliation.

Deported Americans generally felt like they belonged in the United States, at least when they were children. As discussed in chapter 2, many recounted stories of the moments that they realized that they were either undocumented or deportable. Those without any lawful status in the United States generally became aware of their immigration status when they started to get interested in applying for jobs or college, or obtaining a driver's license. For people who had lawful status, the deportation process itself changed their status from legal or illegal. Many reported feelings of shock and surprise when they learned that they could be deported; they had felt so much a part of U.S. society that they had not realized that deportation was a possibility. Once people have felt so integrated into a society, applying a different label does not change their psychological feelings of culture, identity, and belonging. Rather, the identification with U.S. society stays with people even after they have been forcibly removed.

This psychological identification is perhaps most evident among deportees who previously served in the U.S. military but later were deported due to criminal convictions. Most would have qualified to become citizens due to their military service if they had filled out the correct paperwork. But, having failed to do so, hundreds of U.S. veterans now find themselves deported. The U.S. government says it does not track how many American veterans have been deported, but a substantial number of noncitizens serve in the military. In 2009, for example, 14,508 noncitizens were enlisted.[14] Hector Barajas, a veteran of the U.S. Army who launched a grassroots organization to serve the needs of this population in Mexico, estimates there are thousands of deported vets scattered around the world, including veterans of the wars in Korea, Vietnam, Iraq, and Afghanistan.

In an interview at the Deported Veterans Support House—a shelter Barajas founded—a veteran of the U.S. Marine Corps sums up the bizarre paradox of being a deported veteran: "I risked my life for this country. I thought I was American." Barajas jumps in, adding, "We fought side by side with our brothers. We wore the uniform. We were proud of our country." Later he asks, "Can you imagine how it feels to go through all that and then be kicked out like we're nothing?" This group of veterans copes by surrounding themselves with others who identify as American despite their deportation—the sense of camaraderie and support people pull from these associations is another example of their American identities.

To sociologist Nira Yuval-Davis, belonging is, at its core, "about emotional attachment, about feeling 'at home.'"[15] If citizenship is viewed through the lens of identity, the social membership of deportees who were socialized in the United States is hard to deny.

SOCIAL MEMBERSHIP BASED ON AFFILIATIONS

In addition to stating that they see themselves as American, many deportees invoke their membership in U.S. society by describing the people, places, institutions, and cultural references that tie them to the country. In doing so, they recount their deep connections to the United States. According to one man,

> Yeah, I see myself as American because I grew up there. I listen to rap or oldies, not *banda* or *rock en español*. I watch Monday night football, not soccer. . . . I wear fitted [baseball] hats. My pants are probably baggier than most people here. I miss the places where I grew up—Pecan Park, Popeye's Chicken . . . Taco Bell . . . and the biggest thing—my family.

He ties his claim to membership to specific places and to family, in addition to his internal sense of identity. As the previous chapters have discussed, many deportees are part of American families, and separation from family members is one of the most difficult aspects of being deported. The desire to reunite with family members in the U.S. drives many to attempt to return. The inextricable connections between deported Americans and loved ones in the United States demonstrate their integration into U.S. society.

Claims to membership based on the strength of people's ties to the country are consistent with a long history of preferential treatment of noncitizens who have resided in the United States for longer periods of time and who have stronger affilations with the country. In *Americans in Waiting*, Hiroshi Motomura—a preeminent immigration law scholar—describes "immigration as affiliation" as one of three prominent themes undergirding U.S. immigration law.[16] Immigration as affiliation "is the view that the treatment of lawful immigrants and other noncitizens should depend on the ties that they have formed in this country" and that "the longer they are here, and the more they become enmeshed in the fabric of American life, the more these lawful immigrants and citizens should be treated equally."[17] Motomura traces the origin of this affiliation-based reasoning to the emergence of "the first deportation statutes," which, for example, made a noncitizen eligible for deportation on the basis of engaging in prostitution, but only within three years of entering the country.[18] Once people had been in the country for more than three years, it was considered less appropriate to deport them even if they engaged in misconduct.

Motomura's book describes numerous historical examples where affiliation-based claims shaped and informed U.S. immigration law. For example, advocates mounted arguments for leniency in deportation cases in the 1930s by citing the "human cost of deportation in terms of broken families and economic hardship," contributing to the emergence of cancellation of removal as a formal mechanism for relief from deportation.[19] In a line of cases beginning in 1971, courts limited the differential treatment of citizens and noncitizens in non-immigration-related matters and "stressed that these lawful immigrants had meaningful ties in the United States," citing the fact that they pay taxes, may serve in the military, may have lived in a state for years, and contribute to the economy.[20]

In addition to exploring this historical evolution, Motomura also discusses how affiliation-based claims to membership play out in current immigration laws. Noncitizens with more extensive ties to U.S. society—or those who have spent more time in the country—are generally more protected from deportation than their counterparts with weaker ties, or those who have spent less time in the U.S. For example, the view of immigration as affiliation is evident in "safe harbors" that "make it harder to deport noncitizens who are more settled here."[21] Thus, noncitizens who have resided in the U.S. longer than five years are not subject to deportation on the basis of a single "crime of moral turpitude." People who have been in the country longer are shielded from this ground of deportation. Further, relief from deportation—where it is still available under the law—"depends heavily on the noncitizen's ties in the United States, especially the hardships that the noncitizen's deportation will cause for close relatives who are citizens or lawful immigrants."[22] The importance of an individual's affiliation with U.S. culture and society is codified into federal criminal law in a provision allowing judges to impose lower sentences for people who unlawfully entered the country but are "culturally assimilated." The strength of immigrants' affiliations with American society is legally significant, and there is precedent for providing greater protections to those who are more tied to U.S. society.

Deported Americans' claims to membership in the United States are consistent with legal scholar Cristina Rodríguez's recognition that "membership can turn on the extent of one's earned connection to American society and may not be merely a function of legal status."[23] For example, in *U.S. v. Verdugo-Urquidez* the Court found that noncitizens are protected by the Fourth Amendment when they are part of "a class of persons who are part of a national community or who have otherwise developed sufficient connection with this country to be considered part of the community."[24] In *Mathews v. Diaz*, the Supreme Court upheld a federal law that limited noncitizens' eligibility for Medicare to lawful permanent residents who had lived in the United States for five years.[25] The Court's reasoning in the case reinforces the idea that "it is unquestionably reasonable for Congress to make an alien's eligibility depend on both the character and duration of his residence."[26] In *Landon v. Plasencia*, where the Court expanded procedural due process protections to lawful permanent residents seeking to reenter the U.S., the Supreme Court reasoned that "once an alien gains admission to our country and begins to develop the ties that go with permanent residence his constitutional status changes accordingly."[27] The Court characterized Plasencia's interest as "without question, a weighty one" that implicated her "right 'to stay and live and work in this land of freedom,'" and "to rejoin her immediate family."[28] This weighty interest noncitizens have in continuing to live in the United States expands over time as people's lives become more inextricably linked to the country.

Deportees' accounts of their connections to people, places, and cultural practices from the United States invoke the same kind of affiliation-based reasoning. When he was deported, Hector (the founder of the Deported Veterans Support House) left behind his family—all U.S. citizens—including his three-year-old daughter, his parents, and his wife. He decided to live near the border in Mexico so he could receive visits from his daughter. He talked about her all the time and aspired to someday to reunite with her in the United States. His apartment was decorated with drawings she'd sent him. Hector worked to keep the relationship strong by communicating with her on Skype every night, but, as he explained, "It's not the same. I want to be able to hug her, to touch her. And for her to respect me—she's at that age where she's trying to push the limits, and with me not being there, it's hard to do anything about it." He continued, "It's hard. Until you've lived it, you don't know the desperation, the anxiety, the crying yourself to sleep at night." The pain of his deportation centered around this separation from his daughter, a sign of the depth of his affiliation with the United States through direct family ties.

A parent-child relationship is the kind of relationship that U.S. immigration law generally treats as important. Children can obtain citizenship through their parents even when they are not born in the United States because of the law's recognition of the importance of family unity; as adults, children can sponsor their parents to become citizens. However, the law did not protect Hector's relationship with his daughter because he was convicted of a crime. The singular moment when he committed the crime effectively erased his right to family unity, as well as his daughter's. To Hector, and to others whom I interviewed, ties to their families, their memories, and their culture tether them so tightly to the United States that they continue to argue for their inclusion based on these affiliations, in opposition to laws that define their connections as irrelevant. In the words of Hector, "I'm never going to give up trying to go home. I'll get there one day. When I die, they'll take me back in a casket. Give my family a flag and everything. I have a right to be buried in a military cemetery. . . . But I'm trying to go back before then." Remarkably, in 2018, Hector achieved this goal. He was pardoned by the governor of California, where his crime had occurred, and was subsequently allowed to return to the United States as a citizen.

Affiliation-based arguments go to the heart of the problems families experience due to deportation. When all of people's attachments are to the United States, and virtually none are to Mexico, it is incongruous that their citizenship would be tied to the country they experience as foreign.

IMMIGRATION AS CONTRACT

In addition to membership claims based on affiliation, noncitizens residing in the United States arguably have claims to membership in U.S. society under theories rooted in contract law. Just as Hiroshi Motomura's *Americans in Waiting* traces the history of affiliation-based claims in the development of U.S. immigration law, it also traces the influence of contracts-based claims in the field. Broadly, Motomura characterizes "immigration as contract" as "a set of concepts of fairness and justice that are associated with contracts and sometimes with property rights. These ideas are often phrased in terms of promises, invitations, expectations, notice, and reliance."[29] The idea is not that actual, enforceable contracts govern immigration law; this is certainly not the case. Nonetheless, key theoretical concepts of contract law have influenced immigration law, and immigration as contract is a useful framework to apply in considering the rights and obligations of both migrants and governments.

Contracts are usually created through overt agreements between people; these are called express contracts. In the context of immigration law, the closest thing to an express contract arises when the government offers people lawful admission by authorizing a visa or green card. In exchange for allowing the individual to come to the United States, the government expects that the individual will leave at the expiration of a visa, pay taxes, and otherwise comply with the country's laws. Through this lens, deportation may be seen as a legitimate response when people fail to hold up their end of the bargain by remaining in the country after a visa expires or by engaging in criminal acts. This is the most pervasive rationale for deporting lawful permanent residents on the basis of criminal convictions—they violated the terms of their agreement when they were convicted of a crime.

However, this argument does not hold up in the case of people who came to the U.S. as children because it is illogical to think that children can enter into any such agreement when they come to the United States. Children are not even allowed to enter into contracts given their immaturity. But there is also a broader problem with this justification for deportation, rooted in the doctrine of unconscionability. When one party has more bargaining power than the other party, an otherwise legitimate contract may be unenforceable against the party with less power. Courts specifically consider whether the disadvantaged party has "an absence of meaningful choice" in the agreement. This is an apt concept in the case of migration from Mexico, which is propelled by two primal forces: (1) poverty in Mexico and (2) the desire to reunite with family members in the United States. Deporting people for failing to live up to their end of the bargain undermines fundamental notions of justice when the only reason people agreed to the bargain in the first place was to escape dire economic conditions or to reunite with their families. The problem of unconscionability applies to people who came as children and adults, most of whom feel like they left Mexico out of necessity.

Even in cases where the bargaining power between the government and a migrant does not lead to unconscionability, the more time one spends in the country, the less legitimate it becomes to deport people for failing to keep up their end of the bargain. Political philosopher Joseph Carens explains, "As irregular migrants become more and more settled, their membership in society grows in moral importance, and the fact that they settled without authorization becomes correspondingly less relevant."[30] According to Carens, "Over time, the circumstances of entry grow less important. Eventually, they become altogether irrelevant. That was recognized in Europe in the 1970s, when people who had originally been admitted as 'guest workers,' with the explicit expectation that they would leave after a limited period, nevertheless were granted resident status."[31] For people who have been in the country for long periods of time, as in the case of deported Americans, affiliation-based claims to membership trump arguments for exclusion based on broken promises or even unauthorized entry because, over time, the strength of people's social ties far outweighs the harm caused by the broken promise.

In the case of people who entered the United States without specific government authorization, express agreements, promises, or expectations are not overtly articulated between migrants and the government. However, an implied contract may exist even when an express agreement has not been reached. Implied contracts arise in two situations. First, when facts suggest that two parties had an agreement that created an obligation, an implied contract may be assumed. Second, when one party provides a service or benefit to another, the party who received the benefit has a duty to compensate the party who provided the service to avoid being unjustly enriched. This obligation arises even in the absence of an agreement.

In some ways, the United States has entered into an implied contract with migrants who entered from Mexico without official permission because its lax enforcement at the border for many years demonstrated an unstated, tacit agreement that effectively invited migrants to come to the United States to work. Millions have done so, working for low wages that have allowed U.S. companies and consumers to profit. According to Professor Motomura, "A national policy of acquiescence means that unauthorized migrants come to the United States as part of a tacit arrangement that is mutually beneficial. In spite of the letter of the law, this arrangement amounts to an invitation extended by the combination of willing employers, limited enforcement, and legal mechanisms that allow unauthorized migrants to stay as a matter of government discretion."[32]

The United States has historically allowed migration from Mexico in order to fulfill its economic needs, by relaxing enforcement at the border as needed and by creating temporary work programs specifically for Mexicans. In the nineteenth and early twentieth centuries, the U.S. did not regulate its border with Mexico, which was relatively porous. Mexicans who lived near the border at that time report that they were able to come and go as they pleased; there was an unstated agreement that Mexican laborers could go for work, and the U.S. would look the other way because many of its industries depended on inexpensive Mexican labor. The U.S.-Mexico border continued to be porous for much of the twentieth century. For example, during the Bracero Program in the 1940s—a guest worker program that offered temporary lawful status to 200,000 people from Mexico annually—as many as four undocumented Mexican migrants came to the U.S. for every documented participant in the program.[33] And they found work. Many employers preferred hiring undocumented workers because they worked for lower wages, and the regulations of the Bracero Program designed to protect workers' rights did not apply.[34] Although border enforcement practices have changed and no longer communicate that migrants from Mexico are welcome, the centuries-long history of welcoming unauthorized workers from Mexico created deeply entrenched migration patterns that link families between the two countries. More than half of the population of Mexico has at least one close friend or family member who lives in the United States.[35] This is a predictable result of the U.S. government actively recruiting migrants to come to the U.S., both lawfully through authorized, temporary work programs and outside the legal process, by allowing migrants to come to work in the U.S. even without official authorization over hundreds of years.

Migrants who came to the U.S. years ago have relied on the government's tacit acceptance of their presence and have put down roots. Most people who have entered the United States without permission "came at employer invitation and government acquiescence in spite of the letter of immigration law."[36] In contract law, the exchange of benefits and a reliance on them can give rise to obligations. At what point has the United States received such benefits from the unauthorized immigrant population that it incurs an obligation to allow people to continue to live in the country?

According to the Institute on Taxation and Economic Policy, the U.S. government itself receives $12 billion in taxes from unauthorized immigrants each year, which would seem to amount to the kind of "unjust enrichment" contract doctrine seeks to prevent. U.S. consumers have reaped the benefits of migrants' low-wage labor by paying less for products and services than the market would otherwise require. Particularly in the case of people who have relied on the government's silent acceptance of their presence over years, the government arguably has an obligation to recognize that people have become members of U.S. society because, in the words of Joseph Carens, "social membership does not depend upon official permission. . . . People who live and work and raise their families in a society become members, whatever their legal status."[37]

CITIZENSHIP AS THE EXERCISE OF RIGHTS

Theorists also conceive of "citizenship as entitlement to, and enjoyment of, rights."[38] Under this view of citizenship, people who are entitled to rights in a given society are treated as members by virtue of having rights and "are usually presumed thereby to enjoy citizenship."[39] Within the United States, lawful immigrants are generally entitled to the same rights as citizens, with some exceptions such as the right to vote and, of course, the risk that they can be deported. Undocumented immigrants are also entitled to many rights within the United States, although the overarching specter of deportability impedes practical access to many of these rights. Prior to their deportation, the people I interviewed fell into both of these categories—some were lawful permanent residents whereas others were undocumented.

Many were accustomed to legal protections within the United States, as evidenced by the surprise they articulated at the lack of protections they experienced in their deportation proceedings. Chapter 1 describes the reactions of several deportees to being deported without appearing in court. Gina kept trying to get into court to explain her situation to a judge, and Luis perceived his deportation process as unjust because he was not allowed to see a judge. Their reactions demonstrate the extent to which they had become accustomed to their rights being protected in the United States. Jose specifically contrasted the protections afforded to noncitizens under criminal and immigration law: "I feel like if they're going to take people to court before making them pay a fine or putting them in jail for a few days, they should at least take me to court before they tell me I can never come back. They just took me into an office and gave me a paper that said I'm barred for life."

The perception that deportation is unjust because it is a double punishment or that it violates the constitutional prohibition against double jeopardy emerged in many interviews. "I did my time," explains one young man, "and now I'm serving my second sentence, but this one is for life." Since he was deported for an aggravated felony, lawful return is nearly impossible. Invoking claims to protection from double jeopardy demonstrates a level of familiarity with the American justice system that is indicative of membership in U.S. society.

In addition to being accustomed to legal protections within the United States, deported Americans have a difficult time obtaining legal protections within Mexico, which points to their lack of belonging there. Most are unable to articulate what rights they might be entitled to in Mexico because the legal system is foreign to them. In addition, the stigma associated with being deported subjects them to violations of their rights. They express fear of being targeted by police because of their deported status and their recognizable American appearance. Some shared stories of specific police harassment based on tattoos or deported status. "They snatched me up one day when I was just standing here outside my house," Mike explained, "I think because of all my tattoos. They put a paper bag over my head so I couldn't see and drove me somewhere. I don't know where. Over here, you don't have rights. It's not like over there." The outsider position deported Americans occupy in Mexican society prevents them from accessing the rights that typically accompany citizenship.

The deep ties to the United States articulated by deportees who migrated as children demonstrate their functional status as Americans. In contrast, the social isolation and stigmatization they experience in Mexico based on the perception that they are Americans threatens their integration into Mexican society and keeps them from becoming full citizens there. They are caught in between, not recognized as citizens by the country they identify with but also rejected in the country where they are entitled to formal citizenship.

People's strong connections to the U.S. should have legal relevance. Previous court decisions have distinguished deportation, which applies to noncitizens, from denationalization, which applies to citizens. But these cases have not considered the unique experiences of people who came to the United States as children and are essentially American. Similarly, cases that have dismissed constitutional challenges to deportation based on a claim that the practice violates the right to marriage or family unity of a U.S. citizen family member have been based on the assumption that the impact of a family member's deportation is incidental. Chapters 4 and 5 explored how the consequences of deportation on the spouses and children of deportees are life altering, as opposed to incidental. Research documenting the profound implications of deportation should inform future court decisions. I turn now to describe two distinct areas where the law would be improved by incorporating the reality of people's postdeportation experiences into courts' legal analysis.

REFORM THROUGH THE COURTS

Many of the laws governing deportation proceedings would have to change dramatically if courts were to apply the same constitutional protections that apply to every other area of the law. Although it would not cure all of the problems caused by deportation, incorporating constitutional norms into immigration proceedings would at least make the human toll of deportation legally relevant, whereas now—in many cases—it is not.

The Supreme Court has been moving away from its historically strict adherence to the plenary power doctrine, albeit slowly. It seems that two centuries of immigration exceptionalism may be yielding, and that courts are more willing to impose constitutional limits on the government's power in immigration cases. Stephen Legomsky predicts that rather than being completely overruled, the plenary power will gradually fade away "by steady erosion."[40] In a *New York Times* opinion piece during the 2016 presidential race, Peter Spiro described the plenary power doctrine as the judicial equivalent of a "blank check" giving Congress virtually unrestricted power to regulate immigration law.[41] He argued that despite national outcry over Donald Trump's proposal to bar Muslim immigrants from the United States, it would likely not be overturned by the judiciary because of the plenary power doctrine. According to Spiro, this profound disconnect between the values of the American public and the archaic plenary power doctrine pointed to the need for the Supreme Court to "bring its reading of the Constitution in line with the public's own, more progressive constitutional norms." When President Trump's administration attempted to enact a version of this travel ban, federal courts did as Spiro had hoped and found it to be unconstitutional. And, although the Supreme Court ultimately upheld a a modified version, it placed severe limits on the travel ban while it considered the initial case, a move that indicates a greater willingness to limit the government's actions in the immigration realm than in the past. Also, in 2017, the Supreme Court found that gender discrimination in an immigration law violated the Equal Protection Clause of the Fourteenth Amendment, incorporating standard constitutional limits into the immigration realm.[42] Courts are indeed chipping away at the plenary power doctrine.

Building on Legomsky's prediction that plenary power will fade away, I propose two potential constitutional challenges that would further erode the doctrine. Coupled with qualitative information about the experiences of deportees and their family members, recent developments in the Supreme Court's jurisprudence open the door to new possibilities for applying constitutional limits in deportation cases. Here, I consider two legal challenges that would respond to different problems facing deportees. First, based on the American identities of people who grew up in the United States, I argue that courts should treat their deportation in the same way that they treat the denationalization of citizens because the effects are virtually identical. This argument focuses on the rights and experiences of deportees themselves. Second, I argue that courts should recognize the profound consequences of deportation on U.S. citizen family members of deportees and should protect the fundamental rights to marriage and family unity in deportation cases in the same way these rights are protected in all other areas of the law.

Deportation and Denationalization

United States law treats denationalization—stripping people of their citizenship—completely differently from deportation. Whereas divestment of citizenship is considered cruel and unusual punishment, deportation has not been seen in the same way by courts. However, in many respects, people with strong ties to the United States experience their deportation as a citizen would experience denationalization.[43] Thus, based on the American identities of some deportees, deportation should similarly be rejected as cruel and unusual, at least for this population. As political philosopher Joseph Carens posits, "Human beings who have been raised in a society become members of that society: not recognizing their social membership is cruel and unjust."[44]

In *Trop v. Dulles*, the Supreme Court held that stripping an individual of his citizenship for deserting the military amounted to cruel and unusual punishment and was thus barred by the Constitution.[45] A plurality of the Court found the practice amounted to punishment even though it was not technically defined in penal law.[46] In its reasoning, the Court distinguished deportation from divestment of citizenship because the authority to deport is derived from "the sovereign power to exclude" foreigners from the country.[47] But the Court's distinction between denationalization and deportation—its finding that denationalization is punitive while deportation is not—does not hold up when viewed from the perspective of deported Americans. Critical race scholar Mari Matsuda calls scholars to "look[] to the bottom" by "studying the actual experience" of "groups who have suffered through history" and have "experienced discrimination."[48] Through the eyes of deported Americans, denationalization looks remarkably similar to deportation. The justification to allow one but to forbid the other is logically indefensible when viewed through this lens.

In *Trop*, the Court recognized that banishment is "a fate universally decried by civilized people."[49] This is just as true for deported noncitizens who identify as Americans. Leo Zaibert argues, "There exists no principled, reasonable way to distinguish the cruelty that denationalization brings to its citizens from the cruelty that deportation brings to some noncitizens."[50] The most important losses a denationalized person faces relate not to citizenship status but to connections to family, community, and culture. These are the losses that make deportation so cruel for those who identify as American.

Margaret Jo Randall, a U.S. citizen who was denationalized after becoming a citizen of Mexico, fought for nine years to regain her U.S. citizenship between 1984 and 1993. She persisted in her efforts to regain her citizenship not because she was concerned about being stateless. Rather, her cultural and emotional ties to the United States motivated her. According to Randall, "What I was asking for . . . was the opportunity to live in the country that I feel in my heart is my country, and that is the country I was born in; it's the country I grew up in; it's the country where my parents resided, which was [where] my children were citizens, the country that culturally and emotionally pulled me."[51] Randall's words sound remarkably similar to those of the deportees I have interviewed—they want to be accepted back into the country where they grew up, where their families are, and that they identify with. Her sentiments invoke claims to membership based on psychological identity and affiliation, which are both key aspects of deported Americans' claims to membership.

The *Trop* Court distinguished between deportation and denationalization by taking the government's perspective and focusing on the source of the government's authority for each sanction. However, a sanction's effect on people's lives is more instructive in assessing its legitimacy than the source of the government's authority. The cruel nature of denationalization lies in forcing people from their homes, and isolating them from their culture and families. Judge Learned Hand highlighted the harms of deporting people who had grown up in the United States in a 1926 dissent:

> Whether the relator came here in arms or at the age of ten, he is as much our product as though his mother had borne him on American soil. He knows no other language, no other people, no other habits, than ours; he will be as much a stranger in [his country of origin] as any one born of ancestors who immigrated in the seventeenth century. However heinous his crime, deportation is to him exile, a dreadful punishment, abandoned by the common consent of all civilized people.[52]

People who grew up in the United States perceive their deportation as exile or banishment, thus tying their experiences directly to the experience of a citizen ejected from his or her country. Deportees frequently described themselves as being banished, kicked out, thrown away, and exiled from the United States. When speaking of the U.S., people often referred to it as home, "back home," and the place where they are from.

In *Trop*, the Supreme Court was not only concerned about a denationalized citizen experiencing "banishment, a fate universally decried by civilized people." It was also concerned about the consequences of a citizen becoming stateless. According to the Court, denationalization "strips the citizen of his status in the national and international political community" to the extent that "the expatriate has lost the right to have rights."[53] In contrast, the deportees I interviewed did not become stateless after they were deported. They are citizens of Mexico and are entitled to the rights that accompany citizenship there. But even though they are not technically stateless, deportees experience stigmatization and rejection that impedes their ability to exercise rights within Mexican society, making their experience more similar to that of stateless citizens.

Susan Coutin theorizes a "space of non-existence" for people living in the United States without lawful status.[54] They are physically present, but legally they do not exist. Deported Americans occupy a similar space of nonexistence in Mexico. Their paradox is the opposite—they have lawful status in Mexico, but they do not feel like they physically or culturally belong there. They feel "invisible" or like they "don't exist," in the words of some deportees, because they have been physically removed from the world where they felt like they belonged. They have been isolated from everything that gave their lives meaning.

On arrival, the struggles with proving one's existence are very concrete, as described in chapter 2. Establishing one's identity in Mexico is challenging, as many deportees arrive without identification and have been absent from the country for many years. People struggle to obtain copies of their birth certificates—many recounted having to travel to the towns where they were born to physically retrieve copies. Applying for an identification requires presenting utility bills in your name. But to open a utility account in one's name requires government-issued identification. One deportee recounts, "Oh man. I struggled with getting myself set up here. I wanted to work, but to work I needed an ID. To get an ID I needed my birth certificate. To get a birth certificate I needed an ID. There were so many circles like that, like I couldn't get one thing I needed without another thing I didn't have." After people work through the bureaucratic challenges of establishing their lawful identities within Mexico, however, they continue to inhabit this space of nonexistence because the stigma and isolation they experience persists long after their arrival.

As chapter 3 discusses, the social isolation deportees feel is profound, even among those who have integrated successfully into communities in Mexico. Deportees who have established careers, become homeowners, and are raising families in Mexico report struggling with feelings of rejection, losing their identities, and feeling like they don't belong. Jose explains, "I know I'm blessed. I have my house, my car, my kids, my job. I'm doing better than a lot of my friends at home. But I still don't belong. No matter what I do, people don't like me just because of who I am. They see me as American. When I try to say I'm from here, they laugh. . . . Even if I weren't deported, they wouldn't like me because I'm American—a pocho. But if they find out I'm deported, they hate me for that too. For being a loser."

Deportation is experienced as a social death—the loss of people's very sense of self.[55] Scholarship addressing social death explores "how human value is made unintelligible through racialized, sexualized, spatialized, and state-sanctioned violence."[56] Populations who experience social death occupy such marginalized positions in society that they are denied "the right to have rights," according to the literature.[57] Although they are formal citizens of Mexico, deportees who identify as American do not become full members of Mexican society due to the stigma that accompanies their deported status and the perception that they are different by virtue of their American upbringing.

This loss of the right to have rights is the same concern the Supreme Court identified regarding statelessness in *Trop*, highlighting the similarities between deportation and denationalization for this population. Even though they are not rendered stateless, deported Americans experience "the total destruction of the individual's status in organized society" that the Court was concerned about in *Trop*. They lose their careers, their homes, their social status, their families, and their pride.

Cases that have upheld the constitutionality of deportation despite legal challenges that it violates the Eighth Amendment's prohibition against cruel and unusual punishment—the provision the Supreme Court rested its decision on in *Trop*—hinge on the fact that deportation is a civil rather than criminal sanction. However, that distinction is fading away given the enmeshing of immigration and criminal law in the past two decades. In the 2010 case of *Padilla v. Kentucky*, the Supreme Court held that criminal defense attorneys are ineffective when they do not properly advise their clients about the immigration consequences of criminal plea bargains because deportation is "an integral part—indeed, sometimes the most important part—of the penalty" for a crime.[58]

Although the Court maintained that deportation "is not, in a strict sense, a criminal sanction," its reasoning suggests otherwise. The Court emphasized that "deportation is a particularly severe 'penalty'" that is "intimately related to the criminal process" and is "enmeshed" with criminal convictions. This recognition of deportation as a severe penalty flowing from criminal convictions highlights the punitive nature of deportation under current law and undermines historical arguments that distinguished deportation from punishment. Over one hundred years ago, Justice Brewer recognized the cruel nature of deportation, writing that "every one knows that to be forcibly taken away from home and family and friends and business and property, and sent across the ocean to a distant land, is punishment, and that oftentimes most severe and cruel."[59] The practice is especially cruel for people who came to the United States as children who are functionally— though not formally—American, and to the families they leave behind. In many cases, deportation is just as cruel as denationalization.

Right to Marriage and Family Unity in Deportation Cases

In all areas other than immigration law, government infringements on marriages or family unity are allowed only when the government can prove the infringement is necessary to further a compelling interest, and when the infringement is narrowly tailored to further this interest. As chapter 4 discusses, this is the highest standard of constitutional review, meant to protect the rights to marriage and family unity. The same standard should apply when families are threatened with separation due to deportation.

Marriage is quite clearly recognized as a fundamental right worthy of constitutional protection. The Supreme Court recognized the importance of marriage as early as 1888, in *Maynard v. Hill*, when it found that marriage "creat[es] the most important relation in life."[60] In 1967, the Court concluded in *Loving v. Virginia* that "the freedom to marry has long been recognized as one of the vital personal rights essential to the orderly pursuit of happiness by free men."[61] The choice of whom to marry is, according to the

Loving opinion, one of the "'basic civil rights of man,' fundamental to our very existence and survival."[62] Most recently, in 2015, the Court reiterated the importance of marriage and its status as a fundamental right when it extended the right to marriage to same-sex couples in *Obergefell v. Hodges*.[63]

Obergefell both reinforced and expanded the constitutionally protected right to marriage. Justice Kennedy's majority opinion in *Obergefell* begins by emphasizing "the transcendent importance of marriage," stating that marriage has historically "promised nobility and dignity to all persons."[64] The opinion notes that marriage "allows two people to find a life that could not be found alone" and "is essential to our most profound hopes and aspirations."[65] According to *Obergefell*, marriage is "the foundation of government" that operates as an essential "bond of society."[66]

Living with one's spouse is such a central aspect of marriage that the right to marriage should also protect the right of a married couple to live together. Marriage simply cannot fulfill many of its "transcendent" or functional purposes when spouses are prevented from living together. In *Obergefell*, the Court discussed companionship and the "intimate association" of spouses as important aspects of marriage.[67] The benefits of companionship are necessarily limited when people reside across international borders from one another. Companionship and intimacy are such important aspects of marriage that a law that infringes upon the right to live together as a married couple should be understood to infringe upon the marriage itself. The Supreme Court has recognized the right to "establish a home and bring up children" as central to marriage.[68] This recognition is premised on the unstated assumption that the married couple would live together in the home they establish.

Although physical proximity is not a prerequisite to marriage, living together is an important aspect of a union. In fact, cohabitation is one of its defining characteristics. It is generally expected that once two people are married, they will live together. Upon the dissolution of a marriage, it is similarly expected that the couple will no longer live together. The centrality of cohabitation to marriage is evident in the doctrine of common law marriage, whereby couples who live together can be recognized as married at least in part because of their cohabitation. Conversely, marriages were historically understood to end when it was "improper or impossible for the parties to live together."[69]

In the field of immigration law, cohabitation is a required element of establishing a valid marriage. According to the Immigration and Nationality

Act, a spouse of a citizen must have been "living in marital union with the citizen spouse" for the three years before filing an application to adjust status from lawful permanent resident to citizen.[70] The United States Citizenship and Immigration Services (USCIS) policy manual, which governs the conduct of immigration adjudicators conducting these interviews, provides that "USCIS considers an applicant to 'live in marital union' with his or her citizen spouse if the applicant and the citizen actually reside together."[71] If a couple cannot prove cohabitation, the application may be denied.[72]

When noncitizens apply to become lawful permanent residents based upon marriage to a citizen, they must attend an interview with an immigration officer.[73] Interview questions frequently focus on establishing whether a marriage is bona fide, as opposed to a sham marriage entered into solely for an immigration benefit. According to USCIS's manual, "You will often have to question both the petitioner and the beneficiary to determine whether the marriage is bona fide."[74] "No cohabitation" is an "indication that a marriage may have been contracted solely for immigration benefits." The Board of Immigration Appeals defines a "sham marriage," which renders an applicant ineligible for immigration benefits through his or her spouse, as a marriage "the parties entered into with no intent, or 'good faith,' to live together." Further, immigration law prioritizes marital cohabitation to the extent that it has codified shorter waiting periods for immigrant spouses to gain entry to the United States, so that they can live with their American spouse, than for other family members.

The requirements for petitioning for relief under the Violence Against Women Act (VAWA) reinforce the importance of living with one's spouse to marriage.[75] In addition to establishing a good faith marriage to a U.S. citizen or lawful permanent resident, a victim of domestic violence petitioning for immigration relief under VAWA must also establish that she lived with her spouse at some point.[76] Cohabitation is such an important indication of the validity of the marriage that it is codified as a requirement separate and apart from the marriage being entered into in good faith.

To be sure, people who cannot physically reside together may still cultivate meaningful marriages. For example, many prisoners serving lengthy sentences maintain strong bonds with their spouses despite the separation.[77] The Supreme Court recognized that the right to marriage persists during one's incarceration in *Turner v. Safley*, holding that prisoners maintain the right to get married during their incarceration.[78] Reasoning that "the religious and personal aspects of the marriage commitment . . . are unaffected by the fact of confinement," the Court found that despite physical incarceration of one spouse, several key aspects of marriage persist.[79] These aspects include marriage as an "expression[] of emotional support and public commitment."[80] From a functional perspective, "marital status often is a precondition to the receipt of government benefits" and to "other, less tangible benefits."[81] Accordingly, in *Turner*, the Court held that a prisoner maintains the right to enter into a marriage despite being incarcerated.

Yet the fact that prisoners' marriages are recognized and valued does not undermine the centrality of cohabitation to the institution of marriage. Prisoners are subject to a wide range of severe restrictions on their liberty. Recognizing that they maintain a right to marriage despite these liberty restrictions does not mean that marriage is unaffected by the distance between spouses. Rather, some relationships survive a spouse's imprisonment despite the distance. While it is certainly true that a couple may maintain some important aspects of marriage although they are geographically separated, living with one's spouse remains a crucial aspect of marriage. Deportation policies that undermine a couple's ability to live together undeniably interfere with fundamental aspects of marriage, including companionship and intimacy. The erosion of both marriages and relationships between parents and children documented in chapters 4 and 5 demonstrate the profound toll of family separation across borders. Even when people try to maintain their relationships at first, the obstacles associated with living in different countries can result in the permanent dissolution of families.

A married couple's right to live together at home was key in the most important marriage rights case of the twentieth century—*Loving v. Virginia*.[82] *Loving* specifically held that "restricting the freedom to marry solely because of racial classifications violates the central meaning of the Equal Protection Clause" and the Due Process Clause because the "racial classifications embodied in these statutes" infringed upon the "fundamental freedom" to marry and thus were "subversive of the principle of equality at the heart of the Fourteenth Amendment."[83] But the *Loving* case was also about married people's choice to live together in their home state.

Mildred and Richard Loving, an interracial couple, got married in the District of Columbia.[84] When they returned to their home in Virginia, where state law prohibited interracial marriages, they were prosecuted.[85] Instead of serving jail time, the Lovings were banished from Virginia and were prohibited from living together in their home.[86] The Lovings moved to Washington, DC, where they were allowed to live together as a married couple, but they missed their families and wanted to return home to Virginia—where they felt at home. Richard Loving clearly articulated this concern in comments to his lawyer, whom he asked to tell the Supreme Court Justices, "I love my wife, and it is unfair that I can't live with her in Virginia."[87] In holding that the Virginia statute infringed upon the Lovings' right to marriage, the Court implied that the option to live with one's spouse in a different state did not cure the state's infringement on their right to marriage.

When the Supreme Court concluded that Virginia's law impermissibly interfered with the right to marriage on substantive due process grounds, the Court did not engage in the reasoning that is now common in deportation-based challenges predicated on the right to marriage. The Court could have reasoned that the Lovings' right to marriage was not infringed upon by the Virginia statute because they were free to live together as a married couple in Washington, DC. But in *Loving*, the alternative of living somewhere else as a married couple did not render the interference with their marriage null. Rather, the Court vindicated their right to live as a married couple in the state they chose.[88]

The Supreme Court has also recognized family unity—living with one's family members—as a fundamental right entitled to due process protections. In *Moore v. City of East Cleveland*, the Court protected a grandmother's right to share a home with her grandsons.[89] The Court applied strict scrutiny to a statute that would have prohibited this living arrangement, explaining that "when the government intrudes on the choices concerning family living arrangements, this Court must examine carefully the importance of the governmental interests advanced and the extent to which they are served by the challenged regulation."[90] In reaching its conclusion, the Court found the Due Process Clause protects "freedom of personal choice in the matters of marriage and family life."[91] As in *Loving*, the Court did not reason that the grandmother could preserve her right to live with her grandsons by moving from her home to another location where this living arrangement would be allowed. Rather, the Court protected the grandmother's right to live in her home with her grandsons.

In the same way that the Lovings' right to marriage was impermissibly infringed upon when they were forced to live away from their home to preserve their marriage, the rights of U.S. citizens who are forced to leave the country to live with a deported family member are similarly infringed upon. The Supreme Court has not explicitly recognized the right to live at home with one's spouse as a fundamental component of the right to marriage, but more than half of the justices on the Supreme Court signaled their support for acknowledging a citizen's right to live in the United States with her husband in the 2015 case of *Kerry v. Din*.[92] Although the case focused specifically on the doctrine of consular nonreviewability, it has broader relevance to the question of whether an American citizen's right to marriage is implicated when a noncitizen spouse is prevented from entering, or is forcibly removed from, the United States. Din, a U.S. citizen, argued that her right to marriage implied the right to live with her husband in the United States, and the denial of his visa interfered with that right such that the government must provide a "facially legitimate and *bona fide* reason" for its decision.[93]

Din's claim challenged the long-standing rule that consular decisions are not subject to judicial review. Although her claim ultimately failed, only three justices concluded unequivocally that her rights were not implicated by her husband's exclusion.[94] The four dissenting justices reached the opposite conclusion, stating that Din, as a citizen, has a constitutionally protected liberty interest in "her freedom to live together with her husband in the United States."[95] Justice Breyer's dissent recognized that "the institution of marriage . . . encompasses the right of spouses to live together and raise a family" in the United States.[96] The two concurring members of the Court—Justices Kennedy and Alito—concluded that they need not determine whether Din had a right to bring the claim.[97] They assumed her liberty interests were implicated by the visa denial and concluded the information the government supplied regarding the reason for the denial was sufficient. While Justice Kennedy was careful to specify that the case "should not be interpreted as deciding whether a citizen has a protected liberty interest in the visa application of her alien spouse," the concurrence's assumption that the U.S. citizen's marital rights were implicated by the denial of her husband's visa is significant.[98]

Outside of the immigration context, protecting people's liberty interest to decide whom to marry has animated Supreme Court decisions protecting the right to marriage.[99] In *Loving*, the Court explained, "the Fourteenth Amendment requires that the freedom of choice to marry not be restricted by invidious racial discriminations."[100] The Court echoed the importance of choice in selecting one's spouse in *Obergefell*: "Like choices concerning contraception, family relationships, procreation, and childrearing, all of which are protected by the Constitution, decisions concerning marriage are among the most intimate that an individual can make."[101] This freedom to choose whom one marries is fundamentally limited, however, when the decision to marry someone who is not a U.S. citizen results in the loss of a citizen's right to live in her country as a married person.

In the 1990s, Hiroshi Motomura argued that constitutional protections of family unity should apply in immigration cases but concluded at the time that "courts are likely to rule that *Moore* and similar precedents are trumped by the plenary power doctrine, which generally precludes constitutional judicial review in immigration cases."[102] Now, over twenty years later, he argues that the climate is changing. The expansion of marital rights exemplified by *Obergefell* coupled with the plurality's willingness to either conclude or assume that a citizen's rights are implicated by her husband's exclusion from the country in *Din* point toward the possibility of the Supreme Court reconsidering the longtime exclusion of family unity cases from constitutional constraints.

The Supreme Court recognizes that "freedom of personal choice in the matters of marriage and family life is, of course, one of the liberties protected by the Due Process Clause."[103] The right to live with one's family members is constitutionally protected, and family unity is widely recognized as a cornerstone of U.S. immigration law.[104] Combined with the right of citizens to live in their homeland, the fundamental rights to marriage and family unity should include the right to live with one's spouse, parent, or other significant family member in the United States.[105] As Justice Breyer articulated in his 2015 dissent in *Kerry v. Din*, "The institution of marriage . . . encompasses the right of spouses to live together and to raise a family" in the United States.[106] The same could be said for the right to family unity.

Extending constitutional protection to cases where the family member of a U.S. citizen faces deportation would not prevent all deportations affecting the lives of U.S. citizens, but it would subject the government's decision to heightened review and would create a mechanism for assessing whether deportation is appropriate in light of the harm it would cause. By focusing on spousal and parental relationships here, I do not mean to exclude other important familial bonds. Siblings, grandparents, grandchildren, aunts, uncles, and cousins also experience loss when a family member is deported. Many of the arguments I make regarding spousal and parental relationships could be extended to apply to other family relationships given that the Supreme Court has recognized that the right to family unity includes extended family members.

The legal challenges I have just described would incorporate constitutional protections into deportation cases where the potential deportee is functionally American, or where the family members of an individual facing deportation would suffer due to the individual's removal. If the Supreme Court were to apply constitutional norms in these cases, perhaps it would eventually be willing to subject all immigration cases to the same constitutional limitations that apply in other areas of the law. This would, in turn, have the potential to imbue deportation cases with a greater sense of proportionality and could transform the field of immigration law.

LEGISLATIVE REFORMS

Legislative reforms could also respond to some of the more troubling aspects of the deportation regime, many of which stem from the 1996 legislative reforms. I suggest two: (1) returning to individualized determinations where judges balance the government's need to deport against the harm it will cause, even in aggravated felony cases; and (2) creating a lawful path to return to the United States based on demonstrated rehabilitation.

Returning to a Balancing Test

The United States used to employ a balancing test that vested immigration judges with the power to decide whether an individual should be deported, even in cases involving crimes. The government's interest in deporting the individual was weighed against the harm the deportation would cause. Factors like the length of time the individual had been in the country, whether he or she came as a child and was socialized in the United States, and the strength of the individual's ties to the United States were considered. This is the kind of process international human rights bodies uniformly recommend in order to guard against human rights abuses in the deportation process. When the Inter-American Commission on Human Rights found that U.S. deportation policy directed toward people with aggravated felony convictions violates international human rights law, it recommended using such a test, as discussed in chapter 5. Similarly, European and Canadian courts engage in this kind of balancing test in deportation cases.

The European Court of Human Rights requires member states to consider whether "the 'impact of the challenged policy or procedure on private or family life is proportionate to the legitimate aim pursued.'"[107] Although it does not uniformly protect family unity and has "often deferred to immigration-control exigencies and sidestepped children's strong claim to family life," children's rights are at least considered in relation to the government's interest in deporting or restricting entry for a parent.[108] The European Convention on Human Rights clearly provides that "everyone has the right to respect for his private and family life," and it gives some specific guidance regarding enforcement of this right. It provides

> there shall be no interference by a public authority with the exercise of this right except such as is in accordance with the law and is necessary in a democractic society in the interests of national security, public safety or the economic well-being of the country, for the prevention of disorder or crime, for the protection of health or morals, or for the protection of the rights and freedoms of others.[109]

In this context, Ines Hasselberg has found that deportation appeals she documented in the United Kingdom often "focused much of their attention on the relationships, feelings, ambitions and regrets of the appellant and their family."[110]

In weighing the interest in deportation against the effects on the individual (and related people), the European Court of Human Rights directs decicion makers to consider a wide range of factors that touch on the harms my research with deportees has uncovered. For example, the length of time an individual has resided in the country and the "social, cultural, and family ties" with both the country seeking to deport the individual and the receiving country are considered. These factors would allow judges to weigh the deep connections deported Americans have developed to the United States and the lack of connections most have to Mexico. The effects of the deportation on family members are also considered, as is the length of time that has passed since a criminal conviction occurred. This last provision would respond to the injustice demonstrated in the narratives of many whose deportations are based on transgressions that occurred decades earlier and are no longer indicative of who they are. Under its case law, the European Court of Human Rights considers the following factors in balancing the government's need to deport against the harm of deportation on a case-by-case basis:

- the nature and seriousness of the offence;
- the length of the applicant's stay in the country from which they are to be expelled;
- the time elapsed since the offence was committed and the applicant's conduct during that period;
- the nationalities of the various people involved;
- the applicant's family situation, such as the length of the marriage and other factors expressing the effectiveness of a couple's family life;
- whether the spouse knew about the offence at the time they entered into a family relationship;
- whether there are children of the marriage, and if so, their age;
- the seriousness of the difficulties which the spouse is likely to encounter in the country to which the applicant is to be expelled;
- the best interests and well-being of the children, in particular the seriousness of the difficulties which any children of the applicant are likely to encounter in the country to which the applicant is to be expelled;
- the solidity of the social, cultural, and family ties with the host country and with the country of destination.[111]

Under this framework, deportation is deemed necessary only when the government's interests outweigh those of the individual facing deportation and of the individual's family. Jacqueline Bhabha has studied European courts' approaches to children's rights in the context of parental deportation and concludes that they have generally developed a "robust" system for protecting "the right to respect for the family life of deportable aliens."[112] At the same time, she notes that parents who have been law abiding generally receive favorable outcomes whereas those who have broken the law do not.[113] She also critiques the court for prioritizing the perspective of parents over the experiences children will face if a parent is deported. The European Court of Justice—which enforces the laws of the European Union—has been more protective of children's rights to family unity. The Court of Justice has ruled against parental deportation in order to protect "the child's right of residence" in his or her country of citizenship.[114] This approach protects the fundamental rights of children to reside in their countries, and protects parents from deportation in order to protect their children's rights.

A balancing test modeled on the approach of the European Court of Human Rights would allow courts to protect against many of the harms the narratives in this book have highlighted.[115] The European Court uses an inclusive definition of family and protects "private life" as well as family life. It applies the protections on family unity beyond spouses and children to include "wider family relations—like grandparents, grandchildren, aunts, uncles, nephews, nieces, adult siblings, and adult children—also form[ing] part of family life."[116] This approach protects the rights of people in nontraditional family structures or whose strongest connections are to siblings, grandparents, nonmarital partners, or even friends.[117]

With any standard that is implemented on a case-by-case basis, there is a risk of inequality arising out of different judicial perspectives. While providing this discretion would be much preferable to the current system, it may also result in unequal treatment of similarly situated people. Some courts would undoubtedly weigh an individual's unlawful presence more heavily, and others might be unduly influenced by the pervasive characterization of immigrants who have committed crimes as dangerous. The moral panic that has emerged surrounding "criminal aliens" may cloud the judgment of well-meaning judicial officers because the rhetoric of dangerousness is so pervasive.

Incorporating a rebuttable presumption that the harm likely to result from deportation outweighs the government interest in cases where a noncitizen is married to, or is the parent of, a U.S. citizen would add an additional layer of protection for these family relationships. Joseph Carens argues that in cases where a noncitizen who is married to a citizen faces deportation, "his ties to the United States, his interest in living there, and his spouse's interest in living there all assume a new importance and greatly outweigh any interest the state had in deporting him in order to enforce its immigration laws."[118] A rebuttable presumption that the noncitizen should be able to stay in the country would recognize the importance of the relationships while also giving the government the opportunity to rebut this presumption with evidence that would either show that the relationship was not worthy of protection, as in the case of a marriage entered into for the purpose of obtaining immigration benefits or relationships characterized by abuse, or in cases where the government's interest in deportation is so compelling that it overpowers the presumption. Although it would not be absolute, the presumption would create a structural protection against the unfounded yet influential fears of immigrants—and specifically of "criminal aliens"—that, as Leo Chavez describes, are "pervasive when not explicitly mentioned."[119]

The crux of the 1996 reforms was that people with (somewhat) serious criminal convictions should be automatically expelled from the country. The law characterizes this population as unworthy of protection. However, as the experiences of deported Americans reveal, the human cost of excluding people with criminal convictions from protection against deportation is enormous. Passing legislation aimed at extending protections to so-called "criminal aliens" would be a political challenge, to say the least. It would require a radical transformation in public discourse from one that demonizes noncitizens who have been convicted of crimes to one that recognizes their humanity.

The stories described in previous chapters exemplify how, once the circumstances surrounding a crime or conviction are better understood, people seem less like "criminals," with all of the negative connotations the term implies, and more like ordinary people who have made mistakes. For example, Luis—who journeyed to Mexico from Nicaragua—was convicted of a serious crime. He discharged a firearm at an undercover police officer and was sentenced to twelve years in prison for assault. He explains, "I thought I was being attacked." An undercover officer "came up to [him] from behind." The incident was caught on camera, which, according to Luis, "showed that he never identified himself" as a police officer. Instead of going to trial and risking the possibility of a life sentence if he were convicted, Luis pled no contest to lesser charges. Now he has been out of prison for over ten years and has not been in any trouble with the law during that time. He launched a successful tattoo business and spends most of his free time with his wife and children. He says in some ways he feels like he is serving a life sentence. "I can do good for the rest of my life," he recounts, "but they ain't ever gonna let me go back."

The demonization of immigrants as criminals fuels support for mass deportation efforts. For example, when President George Bush signed the Immigration Act of 1990, which expanded the list of serious crimes that qualified as aggravated felonies, he wrote that the reform fit within his "Administration's war on drugs and violent crime." Specifically, he framed people newly eligible for deportation as aggravated felons as threats who "jeopardize the safety and well-being of every American resident."[120] However, more recent Supreme Court cases addressing aggravated felonies highlight the disconnect between the rhetoric and reality. Most of the cases the Court has considered involve longtime lawful permanent residents facing permanent deportation for relatively minor offenses—things like participating in insurance fraud, possessing a sock to hold a pipe, or lighting a small fire (a crime that resulted in a sentence of one day in jail).[121] The conduct underlying convictions for aggravated felonies is much more benign than the images evoked by the labels "aggravated felony" or "criminal alien," or by the public rhetoric framing immigrants as "murderers and rapists," which, in reality, account for less than 2 percent of the "criminal alien" population the U.S. reports it has deported. The success of any legislative proposal to reincorporate a balancing test for people convicted of serious crimes would depend on legislators'—and the public's—willingness to see past dehumanizing labels and to recognize those with criminal convictions as multidimensional people who are more similar to people without convictions than public discourse implies.

Creating a Path to Return Home

Most of the deportees I interviewed can never lawfully return to the U.S., and there should be a legal mechanism that would allow them to eventually come home, even if they have been convicted of aggravated felonies or have made false claims to citizenship (both of which result in permanent deportation). Among other things, the 1996 reforms eliminated the possibility of seeking a waiver to return to the country for most lawful permanent residents with aggravated felony convictions; this is out of step with international practices. Most countries cap the length of an individual's deportation order at ten years; after that, people can apply to return. The U.K. bars people for between three and ten years.[122] In cases punishable by less than ten years in prison, Canada deems foreigners wishing to visit rehabilitated ten years after their sentence has been completed, such that the criminal conviction no longer has any bearing on whether they should be allowed entry. In cases punishable by ten years' imprisonment or more, people may be considered for admission five years after completion of the criminal sentence if they demonstrate rehabilitation.

The permanent nature of so many deportation orders from the United States is counterproductive. Family relationships are more likely to deteriorate in the face of permanent separation, and those who are deported for the rest of their lives often lose hope, descending into depression or addiction. Without any hope of lawful return, many also resort to any means necessary to return to their families, crossing the border without government authorization in dangerous situations. If they make it to the U.S., they are forced to live in the shadows and are blocked from participating in the mainstream economy. Creating opportunities for people who have already been deported to qualify to return, even if they have been convicted of an aggravated felony, would give people hope and motivation to engage in prosocial activities during the period of their deportation. It may also reduce the number of people who reenter without permission. When the aggravated felony category was originally created in the Anti–Drug Abuse Act of 1988, people deported for aggravated felonies were eligible to seek readmission after they had been out of the country for ten years. Reinstating this option as a realistic and attainable possibility would be both normatively and functionally preferable to the current schema that bars people for the rest of their lives.

This reform would also recognize the resilience of many deportees and the success stories this book has documented. Despite the potentially insurmountable obstacles deportation creates—language barriers, homelessness, family separation, poverty, and profound identity crises, to name a few—many deportees have achieved success. They have launched small businesses, returned to school, and have created meaningful lives. However, even though their lives demonstrate rehabilitation, they are barred from ever returning on the basis of convictions that occurred decades ago. Deportees equate their deportation orders to life sentences because of their permanence. Creating a realistic path to return home would reward people's success, deter unlawful reentry, and would incentivize others to follow this path.

Laws are socially constructed, and legal definitions of citizenship are not set in stone. Citizenship theory looks beyond definitions of formal citizenship to consider other ways of recognizing social membership based on people's lived experiences, through their identities, affiliations, contractual agreements, and the exercise of rights. The strong sense of membership deported Americans experience in each of these realms should influence the law governing the deportation of this population. Courts could recognize the social membership of noncitizens who spent their formative years in the United States by treating their deportation as denationalization and thus barring the practice for people who are functional Americans. Courts could also protect the marital rights of citizen family members of deportees by subjecting deportation decisions to the highest level of constitutional review in order to assess whether it is really necessary to deport the spouse, parent, child, or sibling of a U.S. citizen or permanent resident. In addition, legislative changes could reduce many of the harmful consequences of deportation, although legislation that includes people with criminal convictions seems unlikely in the near future given the widespread moral panic surrounding "criminal aliens" and fears of the Latino threat more broadly.

EPILOGUE

From a moral perspective, the more someone has become integrated into a society, the more troubling their deportation becomes. The experiences recounted throughout this book highlight many ways in which deportation is particularly cruel for people who grew up in the United States. Deported Americans are more likely to experience mental health issues (including thoughts of suicide), to turn to substance abuse to numb their pain, and to risk their lives and freedom trying to return to the United States than are other deportees. They compare the experience of deportation to death, and many say they would rather be in prison in the United States than be free in Mexico.

Scholars who have studied the consequences of deportation firsthand compare deporting long-term residents to "violent dismemberment," calling it "destructive and inhumane" and "tragic."[1] In her ethnography of deportees in Mexico, Deborah Boehm is struck by the inhumanity of deportation, writing, "Each day, human lives are deemed 'precarious,' categorized as less than, marked, and made abject, dehumanized beyond recognition by the public." Her observations cause her to ask, "Who counts as human? Whose lives count as lives? And finally, what makes for a grievable life?"[2] When people come face to face with the consequences of U.S. deportation policy, the moral and ethical implications of the practice are deeply troubling. The United States is systematically and forcibly removing millions of Latino men from the boundaries of the country despite strong evidence of their attachments and claims to membership in American society.

Separating families or forcing citizens to move abroad offends people's sense of intuitive justice. U.S. citizen children or spouses of deportees are pushed to move to areas the State Department warns citizens to avoid because they are unsafe. Citizens married to deportees frequently report being met with shock when they explain to other Americans that their spouses do not automatically become citizens by virtue of their marriage. "But you're married," people often say after hearing about their families' separation or exile, assuming that marriage would take care of any immigration law obstacles.

Based on the ethical problems that surround deporting long-term residents, Joseph Carens argues that people earn a right to stay somewhere once they have lived there long enough. He draws upon the depth of the connections that develop over time to demonstrate the moral problems with uprooting long-term residents from the place they consider home:

> In fifteen years connections grow: to spouses and partners, sons and daughters, friends and neighbors and fellow-workers, people we love and people we hate. Experiences accumulated: birthdays and braces, tones of voice and senses of humor, public parks and corner stores, the shape of the streets and the way the sun shines through the leaves, the smell of flowers and the sounds of local accents, the look of the stars and the taste of the air—all that gives life its purpose and texture. We sink deep roots over fifteen years, and these roots matter even if we were not authorized to plant ourselves in the first place.[3]

While radical, Carens's idea that people who have resided in the country for many years should be exempt from deportation is not unheard of. In 1953, President Harry Truman's Commission on Immigration and Naturalization recommended that lawful permanent residents who had been in the country for twenty years should become nondeportable.[4] France used to grant lawful residency to people who could prove they had been residing there for at least ten years.

This book only scratches the surface in describing the harms people experience when they are deported. By focusing on the unique experiences of deportees who came to the U.S. as children, I do not mean to suggest that the experiences of migrants who came as adults are any less important. Many immigrants come to the United States out of desperation, faced with extreme poverty, violence, or insecurity in their countries of origin. And many have strong claims that they should be allowed to stay in the United

States for a variety of reasons that have nothing to do with their identification with or attachments to U.S. culture or society. This book focuses on merely one segment of the deportation problem, and the solutions I propose are far from the kind of comprehensive immigration reform that is truly needed to respond to the plurality of immigrant experiences.

The question of whether deportation is a legitimate social practice depends on the lens through which it is viewed. "Seen through the lens of the state, deportation could be a 'just' measure, understood as a duty of surveillance that protects deserving citizens from dangerous border crossers and potential terrorists."[5] Through the lens of history, its legitimacy is suspect—it has been used as a tool for social cleansing and exclusion of marginalized populations. From the perspectives of people most affected by it, deportation looks inhumane. People compare the experience of deportation to losing their limbs, to being raped, and to death. Although deportation is allowed under the law, that does not mean that the practice itself is legitimate. Deportees' experiences challenge us to think about whether deportation should be viewed as a legitimate exercise of state control.

Society's tolerance of punitive practices changes over time. Punishments like public executions or torture that have been widely accepted in the past are now understood to be morally reprehensible. Perhaps one hundred years from now, future generations will see the practice of deportation as we now see the practice of public execution—as inhumane, uncivilized, and wrong. Until then, it is imperative to consider what alternative mechanisms could be employed to accomplish the same goals espoused by current deportation policy—at least the legitimate ones—while causing far less harm.

NOTES

INTRODUCTION

Note: Unless otherwise indicated, quotes from deportees throughout the book are from interviews I conducted. Pseudonyms are used to protect privacy.

1. Tim Rogers, "Obama Has Deported More Immigrants Than Any Other President," *Splinter*, January 7, 2016, https://splinternews.com/sure-looks-like-voters-really-care-about-healthcare-an-1826523310.

2. United States Department of Homeland Security, *2016 Yearbook of Immigration Statistics* (Washington, DC: U.S. Department of Homeland Security, 2017), 108–14. From FY 2009 through FY 2016, an additional 1.39 million people were returned to Mexico, meaning the U.S. government likely apprehended them at the border, detained them, and returned them to Mexico without initiating formal removal proceedings (105).

3. I use the term "American" throughout the book to refer to people from the United States for lack of a better term, although I recognize that it can also refer to people from other countries in North, Central, and South America.

4. Kevin Johnson refers to this contradiction as the "huddled masses myth." Kevin R. Johnson, *The Huddled Masses Myth* (Philadelphia: Temple University Press, 2004); Daniel Kanstroom, *Deportation Nation: Outsiders in American History* (Cambridge, MA: Harvard University Press, 2010).

5. Rubén G. Rumbaut, "Ages, Life Stories, and Generational Cohorts: Decomposing the Immigration First and Second Generations in the United States," *International Migration Review* 38 (2004): 1167.

6. Roberto G. Gonzales, *Lives in Limbo: Undocumented and Coming of Age in America* (Oakland: University of California Press, 2015), 6.

7. Kate Linthicum, "Dreamers Are Building New Lives—Back in Mexico," *Los Angeles Times*, November 4, 2014, http://www.latimes.com/world/la-fg-c1-mexico-dreamers-20141104-story.html#page=1.

8. White House, Office of the Press Secretary, "Remarks by the President on Immigration," June 15, 2012, https://obamawhitehouse.archives.gov/the-press-office/2012/06/15/remarks-president-immigration.

9. Prior to the 2010 congressional vote on the DREAM Act, the White House assured the public that "all criminal grounds of inadmissibility and removability that apply to other aliens seeking lawful permanent resident status would apply and bar criminal aliens from gaining conditional or unconditional Lawful Permanent Resident status under the DREAM Act." Luis Miranda, "Get the Facts on the DREAM Act," *White House Blog*, December 1, 2010, https://obamawhitehouse.archives.gov/blog/2010/12/01/get-facts-dream-act.

10. "Diaspora," *Merriam-Webster* (online dictionary), http://www.merriam-webster.com.

11. Daniel Kanstroom, *Aftermath: Deportation Law and the New American Diaspora* (New York: Oxford University Press, 2012), xi.

12. Linthicum, "Dreamers Are Building New Lives."

13. Susan Bibler Coutin, "Exiled by Law: Deportation and the Inviability of Life," in *The Deportation Regime: Sovereignty, Space, and the Freedom of Movement*, ed. Nathalie Peutz and Nicholas de Genova (Durham, NC: Duke University Press, 2010), 361.

14. David C. Brotherton and Luis Barrios, *Banished to the Homeland: Dominican Deportees and Their Stories of Exile* (New York: Columbia University Press, 2011), 197.

15. Angela M. Robertson, Remedios Lozada, Lawrence A. Palinkas, José Luis Burgos, Carlos Magis-Rodriguez, Gudelia Rangel, and Victoria D. Ojeda, "Deportation Experiences of Women Who Inject Drugs in Tijuana, Mexico," *Qualitative Health Research* 22 (2012): 499.

16. Cristina M. Rodríguez, "Immigration, Civil Rights and the Evolution of the People," *Daedalus* 142 (2013): 228.

17. Rodriguez, "Immigration," 228.

18. Tanya Golash-Boza studied the effects of deportation from the U.S. in the Dominican Republic, Guatemala, and Brazil. She found that "deportation nearly always involves an emotional cost. This cost, however, varies tremendously depending on the circumstances of the deportation and the strength of the deportees' ties to the United States and to their countries of birth." Tanya Maria Golash-Boza, *Deported: Immigrant Policing, Disposable Labor, and Global Capitalism* (New York: New York University Press, 2015), 218.

19. I recorded many of the interviews. However, in many cases I chose not to record the interview because I felt the interviewee would be less likely to speak frankly if I were recording. If recording was not possible, I took detailed notes during the interview, jotting down direct quotes when something stood out in the conversation. After each interview, I filled in details immediately following the interview. When direct quotes are included in the book, they are derived from either recordings or the direct language I transcribed during the interview. Where I did not record or write down direct language from an interview subject, I paraphrase the information provided based on my notes. Each interview generally lasted an hour or two, although the length varied.

20. Out of respect for their privacy, I have changed many people's names and those of their family members, except when their true names have already been widely used

in the media. In some cases, I have changed other minor details in order to protect people's identities. My understanding of people's stories has been enhanced by reviewing court records and speaking with their family members. For the sake of clarity, I frequently omit the names of people I only reference once in the book, reserving names for the key characters whose stories I return to.

21. Mark Hugo Lopez and Susan Minushkin, *Hispanics See Their Situation in U.S. Deteriorating, Oppose Key Immigration Enforcement Measures* (Washington, DC: Pew Research Center, 2008).

22. Ines Hasselberg, *Enduring Uncertainty: Deportation, Punishment and Everyday Life* (New York: Berghahn, 2016).

23. Deborah Boehm, *Returned: Going and Coming in an Age of Deportation* (Oakland: University of California Press, 2016), 4.

24. United States Customs and Border Protection, "U.S. Border Patrol Fiscal Year Budget Statistics," December 12, 2017, https://www.cbp.gov/document/stats/us-border -patrol-fiscal-year-budget-statistics-fy-1990-fy-2017; United States Department of Homeland Security, *Budget in Brief*, FY 2005–14, https://www.dhs.gov/publication/dhs-budget.

25. Craig Whitlock, "U.S. Surveillance Drones Largely Ineffective along Border, Report Says," *Washington Post*, January 6, 2015, https://www.washingtonpost.com/world /national-security/us-surveillance-drones-largely-ineffective-along-border-report-says /2015/01/06/5243abea-95bc-11e4-aabd-d0b93ff613d5_story.html.

26. Kanstroom, *Deportation Nation*, 18.

ONE. IN THE SHADOW OF DUE PROCESS

1. These exceptions are discussed in more detail in this chapter. They are reinstatement of removal, expedited removal, administrative removal for aggravated felony convictions, removal in absentia, and stipulated removal.

2. Immigration and Nationality Act § 241(a)(5).

3. One history of citizenship studies argues that citizenship was "a limited and discriminatory institution" for at least a century after the American Revolution. Peter Riesenberg and Henry S. Matteo, *Denationalization v. "the Right to Have Rights": The Standard of Intent in Citizenship Loss* (Lanham, MD: University Press of America, 1997), 2. The claim that immigration law is actively employed to keep people out may sound jarring. After all, the United States is a nation of immigrants. However, as this chapter explores, U.S. immigration law has always privileged some groups, welcoming wealthier, whiter migrants, while excluding others. See Ediberto Roman, *Citizenship and Its Exclusions: A Classical, Constitutional, and Critical Race Critique* (New York: New York University Press, 2010), 12 ("Western societies have uniformly accepted the aspects of citizenship discourse that have championed equality and inclusion; but at the same time, these same societies have repeatedly denied disfavored groups full social, civil, and political citizenship rights").

4. Dred Scott v. Sandford, 60 U.S. 393 (1856).

5. Mae M. Ngai, *Impossible Subjects: Illegal Aliens and the Making of Modern America* (Princeton, NJ: Princeton University Press, 2004), 7; Natalia Molina, *How Race Is Made*

in America: Immigration, Citizenship, and the Historical Power of Racial Scripts (Berkeley: University of California Press, 2014), 2.

6. See United States v. Thind, 261 U.S. 204 (1923) (concluding people from India were not white), and Ozawa v. United States, 260 U.S. 178 (1922) (barring Japanese people from naturalizing because they were not white).

7. According to Daniel Kanstroom, *Fong Yue Ting* has "been cited by the Supreme Court more than eighty times." Daniel Kanstroom, *Deportation Nation: Outsiders in American History* (Cambridge, MA: Harvard University Press, 2010), 17; Gabriel J. Chin, "Segregation's Last Stronghold: Race Discrimination and the Constitutional Law of Immigration," UCLA *Law Review* 46 (1998): 6 ("*Plessy, Lockwood, Davis*, and other disgraceful cases of that era are not just dead but dishonored, usually discussed if at all as evidence of a lamentable history of bigotry in American law. The cases that created the plenary power doctrine, by contrast, not only continue to be cited but, in the words of one distinguished authority, 'said nearly everything the modern lawyer needs to know about the source and extent of Congress's power to regulate immigration'") quoting T. Alexander Aleinikoff, "Federal Regulation of Aliens and the Constitution," *American Journal of International Law* 83 (1989): 862; Kevin R. Johnson, *The Huddled Masses Myth* (Philadelphia: Temple University Press, 2004), 14 (discussing the racist origins of the plenary power doctrine and the fact that it remains the law of the land).

8. Chae Chan Ping v. United States, 130 U.S. 581, 606 (1889).

9. *Chae Chan Ping*, 130 U.S. at 609; Hiroshi Motomura, *Americans in Waiting: The Lost Story of Immigration and Citizenship in the United States* (New York: Oxford University Press, 2006), 29 (arguing the case was "premised on Anglo-Saxon racial superiority").

10. Fong Yue Ting v. United States, 149 U.S. 698, 706 (1893).

11. *Fong Yue Ting*, 149 U.S. at 706.

12. *Fong Yue Ting*, 149 U.S. at 733 (Brewer, J., dissenting) and 149 U.S. at 738.

13. *Chae Chan Ping*, 130 U.S. at 606.

14. David Scott FitzGerald and David Cook-Martin, *Culling the Masses: The Democratic Origins of Racist Immigration Policy in the Americas* (Cambridge, MA: Harvard University Press, 2014), 1.

15. Yick Wo v. Hopkins, 118 U.S. 356 (1886).

16. In 1903, the Supreme Court held that noncitizens facing deportation from the interior of the United States were entitled to procedural due process protections, such as the right to appear in court prior to being deported. Yamataya v. Fisher, 189 U.S. 86 (1903). In 1982, the Court expanded procedural due process protections to lawful permanent residents facing exclusion from reentering the country after a brief absence. Landon v. Plasencia, 459 U.S. 21 (1982); Hiroshi Motomura, "The Curious Evolution of Immigration Law: Procedural Surrogates for Substantive Constitutional Rights," *Columbia Law Review* 92 (1992): 1652 (arguing that although courts were historically "unwilling[] to give the procedural due process requirement any real content," they have been moving toward imbuing immigration law with greater substantive protections through the guise of procedural due process).

17. *Yamataya v. Fisher*, 189 U.S.

18. Motomura, "The Curious Evolution," 1646.

19. Fiallo v. Bell, 430 U.S. 787 (1977).

20. Daniel Kanstroom and M. Brinton Lykes, "Migration, Detention, and Deportation: Dilemmas and Responses," in *Deportations Delirium: Interdisciplinary Responses*, ed. Daniel Kanstroom and M. Brinton Lykes (New York: New York University Press, 2015), 12.

21. Kanstroom and Lykes, "Migration, Detention, and Deportation," 11.

22. The term Manifest Destiny was coined by John L. O'Sullivan in 1845, who described it as "the right of our manifest destiny to over spread and to possess the whole of the continent which Providence has given us for the development of the great experiment of liberty and federaltive [sic] development of self government entrusted to us. It is right such as that of the tree to the space of air and the earth suitable for the full expansion of its principle and destiny of growth." Alan Brinkley, *American History: A Survey*, vol. 1, 9th ed. (New York: McGraw-Hill, 1995), 352.

23. Gilbert G. Gonzalez, *Culture of Empire: American Writers, Mexico, and Mexican Immigrants, 1880–1930* (Austin: University of Texas Press, 2004), 9.

24. Gloria E. Anzaldúa, *Borderlands/La Frontera: The New Mestiza*, 2nd ed. (San Francisco: Aunt Lute, 1999), 29.

25. John Morton Blum, William S. McFeely, Edmund S. Morgan, Arthur M. Schlesinger, and Kenneth M. Stampp, *The National Experience: A History of the United States to 1877*, 8th ed. (Belmont, CA: Wadsworth, 1993).

26. Leticia Saucedo, "Mexicans, Immigrants, Cultural Narratives, and National Origin," *Arizona State Law Journal* 44 (2012): 307–8.

27. See, e.g., *In re* Rodriguez, 81 F. 337 (1897).

28. Ken Gonzalez Day, *Lynching in the West: 1850–1935* (Durham, NC: Duke University Press, 2006).

29. Laura E. Gomez argues that Mexicans were treated as "off-white" during this time period because they were legally defined as white under naturalization laws, but they were socially treated as nonwhite. Laura Gomez, *Manifest Destinies: The Making of the Mexican American Race* (New York: New York University Press, 2008), 84–85. Natalia Molina refers to the period between 1924 and 1965 as "an immigration regime that remade racial categories that still think the way we think about race, and specifically about Mexicans," whom, she argues, "are still not deemed fully American and are largely equated with illegality." Molina, *How Race Is Made in America*, 16.

30. Ngai, *Impossible Subjects*, 75.

31. Stephen W. Bender, *Run for the Border: Vice and Virtue in U.S.-Mexico Border Crossings* (New York: New York University Press, 2012), 125.

32. Roman, *Citizenship and Its Exclusions*, xi.

33. Leo R. Chavez, *The Latino Threat: Constructing Immigrants, Citizens, and the Nation*, 2nd ed. (Palo Alto, CA: Stanford University Press, 2013).

34. Chavez, *The Latino Threat*, 4.

35. The depiction of Mexicans as diseased has also played an important role in the history of excluding and deporting Mexicans from the United States. Molina, *How Race Is Made in America*, 94.

36. Ana Gonzalez-Barrera, "More Mexicans Leaving Than Coming to the U.S.," Pew Research Center, November 19, 2015, http://www.pewhispanic.org/2015/11/19/more -mexicans-leaving-than-coming-to-the-u-s/.

37. Peter Brimelow's 1995 best seller *Alien Nation* clearly articulates this fear that the "white majority" will be overridden by Latino immigrants, particularly from Mexico. He argues that "the American nation has always had a specific ethnic core. And that core has been white." Brimelow presents a multiracial, multiethnic society, and specifically a growing population of people of Mexican origin, as threatening to the very foundation of American culture. Peter Brimelow, *Alien Nation: Common Sense about America's Immigration Disaster* (New York: Harper Perennial, 1996), 10. Invasion rhetoric has been employed in political campaigns as well. In 1994, California governor Pete Wilson's reelection campaign featured commercials showing migrants from Mexico flooding across the border into the United States coupled with the words "they keep coming." FitzGerald and Cook-Martin, *Culling the Masses*, 134.

38. Samuel Huntington, "The Special Case of Mexican Immigration: Why Mexico Is a Problem," *American Enterprise* (December 2000): 20, 22. Similarly, in 2009, Pat Buchanan questioned "whether we're going to survive as a country" because of a projected growth in the Hispanic population in the United States. Chavez, *The Latino Threat*, 1.

39. Ann Coulter, ¡*Adios, America! The Left's Plan to Turn Our Country into a Third World Hellhole* (Washington, DC: Regnery, 2015).

40. Ron Nixon, "Border Wall Could Cost 3 Times Estimates, Senate Democrats' Report Says," *New York Times*, April 18, 2017.

41. United States v. Ortiz, 422 U.S. 891, 904 (1975); City of Indianapolis v. Edmond, 531 U.S. 32, 38 (2000).

42. Ngai, *Impossible Subjects*, 154–55.

43. Judith Warner studied the use of this terminology in public discourse and found that "the term 'immigrant' has positive connotations in relation to the development and operation of democracy and U.S. history while 'illegal aliens' are vilified." Judith Ann Warner, "The Social Construction of the Criminal Alien in Immigration Law, Enforcement Practice and Enumeration: Consequences for Immigrant Stereotyping," *Journal of Social and Ecological Boundaries* 1, no. 2 (2005–6): 56.

44. D. Carolina Nuñez, "War of the Words: Aliens, Immigrants, Citizens, and the Language of Exclusion," *Brigham Young University Law Review* 2013 (2014): 1517, 1520.

45. Alfredo Mirandé, *Gringo Justice* (Notre Dame, IN: University of Notre Dame Press, 1987), 17.

46. Kelly Lytle Hernandez, *Migra! A History of the U.S. Border Patrol* (Berkeley: University of California Press, 2010), 205–6.

47. Hernandez, *Migra!*, 206.

48. Hernandez, *Migra!*, 206.

49. Hernandez, *Migra!*, 209.

50. Graham C. Ousey and Charis E. Kubrin, "Immigration and Crime: Assessing a Contentious Issue," *Annual Review of Criminology* 1 (June 27, 2017), https://doi.org/10 .1146/annurev-criminol-032317-092026; Bianca E. Bersani, "An Examination of First

and Second Generation Immigrant Offending Trajectories," *Justice Quarterly* 31 (February 16, 2012), http://dx.doi.org/10.1080/07418825.2012.659200; Robert J. Sampson, "Rethinking Crime and Immigration," *Contexts* 7 (2008): 28–33.

51. Department of Homeland Security, *Immigration Enforcement Actions: 2015* (Washington, DC: U.S. Department of Homeland Security, Office of Immigration Statistics, 2017), table 8, https://www.dhs.gov/sites/default/files/publications/Enforcement _Actions_2015.pdf.

52. False claims to citizenship and alien smuggling are less common but are also included in the category of immigration crimes.

53. U.S. Sentencing Commission, "Figure A: Offenders in Each Primary Offense Category, Fiscal Year 2015," http://www.ussc.gov/sites/default/files/pdf/research-and -publications/annual-reports-and-sourcebooks/2015/FigureA.pdf; U.S. Sentencing Commission, "Table 3: Change in Guideline Offenders in Each Primary Offense Category, Fiscal Year 2014–2015," http://www.ussc.gov/sites/default/files/pdf/research-and -publications/annual-reports-and-sourcebooks/2015/Table03.pdf; Michael Light, Mark Hugo Lopez, and Ana Gonzalez-Barrera, "The Rise of Federal Immigration Crimes," Pew Research Center, March 18, 2014, http://www.pewhispanic.org/2014/03/18/the -rise-of-federal-immigration-crimes/.

54. Ingrid V. Eagly, "Prosecuting Immigration," *Northwestern University Law Review* 104, no. 4 (2010): 1281.

55. U.S. Sentencing Commission, "Table 4: Race of Offenders in Each Offense Category, Fiscal Year 2015," http://www.ussc.gov/sites/default/files/pdf/research-and -publications/annual-reports-and-sourcebooks/2015/Table04.pdf.

56. Judith Ann Warner found that the mechanisms the government uses to track deportation skew the statistics by including people with criminal convictions from many years prior to their deportation and by including people whose convictions are based on immigration offenses. She warns that "Office of Immigration statistics which imply a rapidly increasing immigrant crime wave will promote stereotyping on a very dubious basis in a nation already suffering a xenophobic reaction to the new immigration and the threat of terrorism." Warner, "The Social Construction of the Criminal Alien," 71.

57. Guillermo Cantor, Mark Noferi, and Daniel E. Martinez, *Enforcement Overdrive: A Comprehensive Assessment of ICE's Criminal Alien Program* (Washington, DC: American Immigration Council, 2015), 14–15, http://immigrationpolicy.org/special-reports /enforcement-overdrive-comprehensive-assessment-criminal-alien-program.

58. Cantor, Noferi, and Martinez, *Enforcement Overdrive*, 14–15.

59. Cantor, Noferi, and Martinez, *Enforcement Overdrive*, appendix 1 (1.5 percent of the people deported through the Criminal Alien Program had most serious convictions of sexual assault, and 0.5 percent of homicide).

60. *In re Lawrence*, 190 P.3d 535 (2008).

61. Nancy Mullane, *Life after Murder: Five Men in Search of Redemption* (New York: Public Affairs, 2012).

62. Michelle Alexander, *The New Jim Crow: Mass Incarceration in the Age of Colorblindness* (New York: New Press, 2010).

63. Mona Lynch, "Backpacking the Border: The Intersection of Drug and Immigration Prosecutions in a High-Volume US Court," *British Journal of Criminology* 57, no. 1 (2015): 112–31, https://doi.org/10.1093/bjc/azv105.

64. Cantor, Noferi, and Martinez, *Enforcement Overdrive*. Similar racial profiling occurred in Secure Communities, where 93 percent of the people identified through the program were Latino. Launched in 2008, Secure Communities was a federal program that required local police to run fingerprints of those arrested through federal databases to identify immigration issues. If a potential immigration problem was found, the local agency would keep the person in custody until he or she could be transferred to ICE custody, frequently holding people for days longer than they otherwise would have been detained in order to facilitate this transfer. Aarti Kohli, Peter Markowitz, and Lisa Chavez, *Secure Communities by the Numbers: An Analysis of Demographics and Due Process* (Berkeley, CA: Warren Institute, 2011), 5–6.

65. Narina Nuñez, Minday J. Dahl, Connie M. Tang, and Brittney L. Jensen, "Trial Venue Decisions in Juvenile Cases: Mitigating and Extralegal Factors Matter," *Legal and Criminological Psychology* 12 (2007): 21, 37.

66. Juliet Stumpf, "Doing Time: Crimmigration Law and the Perils of Haste," UCLA *Law Review* 58, no. 1705 (2011): 26.

67. Heike Drotbohm and Ines Hasselberg, "Deportation, Anxiety, Justice: New Ethnographic Perspectives," *Journal of Ethnic and Migration Studies* 41, no. 4 (2014): 551–62.

68. Ingrid V. Eagly, "Criminal Justice for Noncitizens: An Analysis of Local Enforcement," *New York University Law Review* 99 (2013): 1126, 1128.

69. Nathalie Peutz and Nicholas De Genova, *The Deportation Regime: Sovereignty, Space, and the Freedom of Movement* (Durham, NC: Duke University Press, 2010), 10.

70. Daniel Kanstroom frames contemporary U.S. deportation policy as a social cleansing apparatus aimed at removing "those with undesirable qualities, especially criminal behavior." Daniel Kanstroom, "Deportation, Social Control, and Punishment: Some Thoughts about Why Hard Laws Make Bad Cases," *Harvard Law Review* 11 (2000): 1892. Similarly, anthropologist Susan Bibler Coutin argues that American law "constitute[s] certain noncitizens as expendable others," whom it then deports. Susan Bibler Coutin, "Exiled by Law: Deportation and the Inviability of Life," in *The Deportation Regime: Sovereignty, Space, and the Freedom of Movement*, ed. Nathalie Peutz and Nicholas de Genova (Durham, NC: Duke University Press, 2010), 357.

71. Barack Obama, Second Presidential Debate, October 16, 2012; "Remarks by the President in Address to the Nation on Immigration," The White House, November 20, 2014, https://obamawhitehouse.archives.gov/the-press-office/2014/11/20/remarks -president-address-nation-immigration; Graham Lanktree, "Trump Says Immigrant Gang Members 'Slice and Dice' Young, Beautiful Girls," *Newsweek*, July 26, 2017, http:// www.newsweek.com/trump-says-immigrant-gang-members-slice-and-dice-young -beautiful-girls-642046.

72. Lucas Guttentag, "Immigration Legislation and Due Process: The Forgotten Issue," *International Migration Review* 19 (1996): 33–34.

73. Anil Kalhan, "Revisiting the 1996 Experiment in Comprehensive Immigration Severity in the Age of Trump," *Drexel Law Review* 9 (2017): 263.

74. Kalhan, "Revisiting the 1996 Experiment," 263.

75. Anti–Drug Abuse Act of 1988, Pub. L. No. 100–690, § 7342, 102 Stat. 4181, 4469–70.

76. César Cuahtémoc García Hernández, "Creating Crimmigration," *Brigham Young University Law Review* 2013 (2014): 1469–70.

77. American Immigration Council, "Aggravated Felonies: An Overview," December 16, 2016, https://www.americanimmigrationcouncil.org/research/aggravated-felonies-overview ("Today, the definition of 'aggravated felony' covers more than thirty types of offenses, including simple battery, theft, filing a false tax return, and failing to appear in court").

78. Three hundred thousand people were deported from the United States for aggravated felony convictions between fiscal years 1992 and 2006. In recent years, somewhere in the neighborhood of forty thousand people per year with aggravated felony convictions have been deported annually. Transactional Records Access Clearinghouse (TRAC), "New Data on the Processing of Aggravated Felons," January 5, 2007, http://trac.syr.edu/immigration/reports/175/; TRAC, "How Often Is the Aggravated Felony Statute Used?," 2006, http://trac.syr.edu/immigration/reports/158/.

79. TRAC, "How Often Is the Aggravated Felony Statute Used?"

80. TRAC, "How Often Is the Aggravated Felony Statute Used?"

81. Department of Homeland Security, *Immigration Enforcement Actions: 2013* (Washington, DC: U.S. Department of Homeland Security, Office of Immigration Studies, 2014), table 7, https://www.dhs.gov/sites/default/files/publications/Enforcement _Actions_2013.pdf.

82. Marc R. Rosenblum and Doris Meissner, *The Deportation Dilemma: Reconciling Tough and Humane Enforcement* (Washington, DC: Migration Policy Institute, 2014), 3–4, http://www.migrationpolicy.org/research/deportation-dilemma-reconciling-tough -humane-enforcement.

83. Department of Homeland Security, *Immigration Enforcement Actions: 2015*, table 6.

84. Executive Office for Immigration Review, FY 2016 Statistics Yearbook, 1.

85. Department of Homeland Security, *Immigration Enforcement Actions: 2013*, 6; Department of Homeland Security, *Immigration Enforcement Actions: 2015*.

86. Immigration and Nationality Act § 238.

87. Immigration and Nationality Act § 238(b).

88. Jeremy Slack, Daniel E. Martínez, and Scott Whiteford, eds., *In the Shadow of the Wall* (Tucson: University of Arizona Press, 2013), 121.

89. Slack, Martínez, and Whiteford, *In the Shadow of the Wall*.

90. Department of Homeland Security, *Immigration Enforcement Actions: 2015*, table 6; TRAC, "ICE Bypassing Immigration Courts? Deportations Rise as Deportation Orders Fall," August 13, 2012, http://trac.syr.edu/immigration/reports/291/.

91. Daniel Kanstroom, *Aftermath: Deportation Law and the New American Diaspora* (New York: Oxford University Press, 2012), 66.

92. Trina Realmuto, "Practice Advisories: Reinstatement of Removal," Legal Action Center, April 29, 2013, http://www.legalactioncenter.org/sites/default/files /reinstatement_of_removal_4-29-13_fin.pdf ("Every circuit has held that the court of appeals has jurisdiction over petitions for review of reinstatement orders").

93. Immigration and Nationalization Act § 240(e)(1).

94. For example, one study "found that asylum seekers in expedited removal proceedings were at risk of being returned to countries where they may face persecution." Denise Noonan Slavin and Dana Leigh Marks, "Who Should Preside Over Immigration Cases," in *Deportations Delirium: Interdisciplinary Responses*, ed. Daniel Kanstroom and M. Brinton Lykes, 89–112 (New York: New York University Press, 2015), 104.

95. Maritza I. Reyes, "Constitutionalizing Immigration Law: The Vital Role of Judicial Discretion in the Removal of Lawful Permanent Residents," *Temple Law Review* 84 (2012): 646 (citing Theagene v. Gonzales, 411 F.3d 1107, 1113 (9th Cir 2005)).

96. See Bill Ong Hing, *Deporting Our Souls: Values, Morality, and Immigration Policy* (New York: Cambridge University Press, 2006).

97. Hing, *Deporting Our Souls*, 60.

98. Hing, *Deporting Our Souls*, 60.

99. Paredes-Urrestarazu v. INS, 36 F.3d 801 (9th Cir. 1994).

100. Diaz-Resendez v. INS, 960 F.2d 493 (5th Cir. 1992).

101. Hing, *Deporting Our Souls*, 63.

102. Mellouli v. Lynch, 135 S. Ct. 1980 (2015).

103. Padilla v. Kentucky, 130 S. Ct. 1473 (2010).

104. Paul Grussendorf, "Immigration Judges Need Discretion," *SF Gate*, April 11, 2013, https://www.sfgate.com/opinion/openforum/article/Immigration-judges-need -discretion-4428406.php.

105. Dana Leigh Marks, "Let Immigration Judges Be Judges," *The Hill*, May 9, 2013, http://thehill.com/blogs/congress-blog/judicial/298875-let-immigration-judges-be -judges.

106. Judge Zsa Zsa DePaolo was speaking at a public event that I attended.

107. James P. Vandello, "Perspective of an Immigration Judge," *Denver University Law Review* 80, no. 4 (2003): 780.

108. Nancy Morawetz, "Understanding the Impact of the 1996 Deportation Laws and the Limited Scope of Proposed Reforms," *Harvard Law Review* 113 (2000): 1950.

109. Randy Capps, Heather Koball, Andrea Campetella, Krista Perreira, Sarah Hooker, and Juan Manuel Pedroza, *Implications of Immigration Enforcement Activities for the Well-Being of Children in Immigrant Families: A Review of the Literature* (Washington, DC: Urban Institute and Migration Policy Institute, 2015), 5.

110. Report No. 81/10, Case 12.562, Wayne Smith, Hugo Armendariz et al. (July 12, 2010).

111. Presidential Statement of Signing of the AEDPA, 32 Weekly Comp. Pres. Doc. 720 (April 24, 1996).

112. Court documents. It is worth noting that this framework is based on traditional notions of family. People whose lives do not correspond to these norms—gay couples, people without children, or people who embrace more nontraditional lifestyles— would likely face even greater challenges convincing a judge to exercise discretion to allow them to stay. I return to this issue in the conclusion, where I discuss an approach employed by the European Court of Human Rights that uses expansive definitions of family and also considers an individual's right to private life.

113. Immigration and Nationality Act (INA) of 1952 § 242(a)(2)(C), 8 U.S.C. § 1252(a)(2)(C) (2012). There are some very narrow exceptions. For example, an individual may be eligible for protection under the Convention against Torture.

114. See 8 U.S.C. § 1182(a)(9)(A)(ii) (2012) (stating that a noncitizen who has been convicted of an "aggravated felony" and has been previously ordered removed is inadmissible "at any time"). For people who did not enter as lawful permanent residents, INA 212(h) provides an avenue to apply for a waiver from this lifetime bar. However, it is extremely difficult for people with aggravated felonies to qualify for this waiver.

115. Ingrid V. Eagly and Steven Shafer, "A National Study of Access to Counsel in Immigration Court," *University of Pennsylvania Law Review* 164, no. 1 (2015): 1–91.

116. Jayashri Srikantiah and Lisa Weissman-Ward, *Access to Justice for Immigrant Families and Communities: Study of Legal Representation of Detained Immigrants in Northern California* (Northern California Collaborative for Immigrant Justice, 2014), https://www.lccr.com/wp-content/uploads/NCCIJ-Access-to-Justice-Report-Oct.-2014.pdf, 18.

117. Eagly and Shafer, "A National Study," 9.

118. See, e.g., Aguilera-Enriquez v. INS, 516 F.2d 565 (1975).

119. *Aguilera-Enriquez*, 516 F.2d at 574 (J. DeMascio, dissenting).

120. Quality control is also a critical issue in immigration cases. Even those who can hire attorneys often receive deficient representation. Immigration judges in New York courts reported in 2011, for example, that the representation by immigration attorneys in cases they presided over "does not meet a basic level of adequacy" in almost half of the cases that appear before them. New York Immigrant Representation Study Report, "Accessing Justice: The Availability and Adequacy of Counsel in Removal Proceedings," *Cardozo Law Review* 333 (2011): 357.

121. Department of Homeland Security, *2015 Yearbook of Immigration Statistics* (Washington, DC: U.S. Department of Homeland Security, 2016), table 39.

122. The United States expels people from its boundaries through two legal mechanisms: removal and return. People who are removed are ordered to leave the country, by either an immigration judge or an immigration official. The fact that they were removed subjects them to administrative and criminal penalties if they seek to return. In contrast, people who are returned are generally apprehended at the border and are sent back without an order of removal. While more people were removed under President Obama's administration, fewer people were returned.

123. Kanstroom and Lykes, "Migration, Detention, and Deportation," 4–5.

124. In 2015, Mexicans constituted 242,456 out of a total of 333,341 people deported from the United States. Department of Homeland Security, *2015 Yearbook of Immigration Statistics*, table 41.

125. Records from ICE confirm that a sizeable number of people deported from the interior have long-term ties to the country—17 percent of those apprehended in the interior of the country between 2003 and 2013 had lived in the United States for over ten years. Marc R. Rosenblum and Kristen McCabe, *Deportation and Discretion: Reviewing the Record and Options for Change* (Washington, DC: Migration Policy Institute, 2014), 24, https://www.migrationpolicy.org/research/deportation-and-discretion-reviewing-record-and-options-change.

126. Marjorie S. Zatz and Nancy Rodriguez, *Dreams and Nightmares: Immigration Policy, Youth, and Families* (Oakland: University of California Press, 2015).

127. James Lee and Bryan Baker, *Estimates of the Lawful Permanent Resident Population in the United States: January 2014* (Washington, DC: U.S. Department of Homeland Security, 2017), 3, https://www.dhs.gov/sites/default/files/publications/LPR%20Population%20Estimates%20January%202014.pdf.

128. Tonatiuh Guillén López, "Entre la convergencia y la exclusión: La deportación de mexicanos desde Estados Unidos de América" [Between convergence and exclusion: The deportation of Mexicans from the United States], *Realidad, Datos y Espacio Revista Internacional de Estadistica y Geografia* 3, no. 3 (2012): 164, 174, http://www.inegi.org.mx/RDE/RDE_07/Doctos/RDE_07_opt.pdf. People deported to Mexico in recent years have generally spent more time in the United States than people who were deported in the past. Only 3 percent of people surveyed upon their removal to Tijuana in 2004 had lived in the U.S. for three years or more, but this number jumped to 38 percent in 2011. López, "Entre la convergencia y la exclusión."

129. Slack, Martínez, and Whiteford, *In the Shadow of the Wall*, 11.

130. For example, the Supreme Court has previously held that mandatory civil detention does not violate the Constitution in the immigration realm even though the Constitution would bar the practice in other contexts. Demore v. Kim, 538 U.S. 510, 522 (2003). But see Zadvydas v. Davis, 533 U.S. 678 (2001) (applying some substantive due process limits in the immigration realm by holding that the plenary power doctrine does not allow the government to indefinitely detain immigrants subject to deportation).

131. Fong Yue Ting v. United States, 149 U.S. 698, 756 (1893) (Field, J., dissenting).

132. Office of the High Commissioner of Human Rights, *Recommended Principles and Guidelines on Human Rights at International Borders* (Geneva: UNHR, 2014), http://www.ohchr.org/Documents/Issues/Migration/OHCHR_Recommended_Principles_Guidelines.pdf.

133. United States Commission on Civil Rights, *With Liberty and Justice for All: The State of Civil Rights at Immigration Detention Facilities* (2015), 123, http://www.usccr.gov/pubs/Statutory_Enforcement_Report2015.pdf.

134. There are signs that this may be changing. For example, in 2001 the Supreme Court ruled that indefinitely detaining immigrants violates the Constitution (Zadvydas v. Davis, 533 U.S. 678), and in 2017 the Supreme Court held an immigration law to violate the Equal Protection Clause of the Constitution because it discriminated on the basis of gender (Sessions v. Morales-Santana, 137 S. Ct. 1678 (2017)). Kevin Johnson analyzed a series of Supreme Court decisions on immigration-related issues in 2017 and concluded that "the court appears to be moving toward applying ordinary constitutional norms to immigration law." Kevin Johnson, "No Decision in Two Immigration-Enforcement Cases," *SCOTUSblog*, June 26, 2017, http://www.scotusblog.com/2017/06/no-decision-two-immigration-enforcement-cases/.

135. Jennifer Chacón argues that the 1996 immigration reforms "normalized a national discourse that positions all immigrants, and particularly those perceived as 'illegal Mexican immigrants,' as a crime and security problem that needs solving, rather

than an integral part of the national community." Jennifer M. Chacón, "The 1996 Immigration Laws Come of Age," *Drexel Law Review* 9 (2017): 299–300.

TWO. RETURN TO A FOREIGN LAND

1. In longitudinal research with undocumented young people in Los Angeles, Roberto G. Gonzales found that undocumented immigrants who came to the U.S. as children often did not realize they were undocumented until their teenage years. Roberto G. Gonzalez, *Lives in Limbo: Undocumented and Coming of Age in America* (Oakland: University of California Press, 2015). He describes adolescence as a traumatic time for his undocumented respondents when "the condition of illegality, which is temporarily suspended during childhood and early adolescence, becomes a significant part of everyday life in adulthood" as they come "into closer contact with legal exclusions" such as bars to applying for college and financial aid, getting jobs, and obtaining driver's licenses.

2. He made this statement in English. Using the term "rare" in this context sounds more natural in Spanish, where the phrase "No soy raro" would literally translate to "I'm not weird."

3. Academics point out the "othering" of referring to people as aliens. According to Gerald Neuman, the term "calls attention to their 'otherness' and even associates them with nonhuman invaders from outer space." Gerald L. Neuman, "Aliens as Outlaws, Government Services, Proposition 187, and the Structure of Equal Protection Doctrine," UCLA *Law Review* 42 (1994), 1428; Kevin R. Johnson, "Aliens and the U.S. Immigration Laws: The Social and Legal Construction of Nonpersons," *University of Miami Inter-American Law Review* 28 (1996): 272 ("The word alien immediately brings forth rich imagery. One thinks of space invaders seen on television and in movies").

4. The Migrant Border Crossing Study found that 23 percent of the deportees they surveyed reported verbal abuse during the deportation process. Daniel E. Martínez, Jeremy Slack, and Josiah Heyman, *Bordering on Criminal: The Routine Abuse of Migrants in the Removal System* (Washington, DC: American Immigration Council, 2013), 2, https://www.americanimmigrationcouncil.org/research/bordering-criminal-routine
-abuse-migrants-removal-system.

5. Martínez, Slack, and Heyman, *Bordering on Criminal*, 6.

6. Jeremy Slack, Daniel E. Martínez, and Scott Whiteford, *In the Shadow of the Wall* (Tuscon: University of Arizona Press, 2013), 119.

7. Martínez, Slack, and Heyman, *Bordering on Criminal*, 5.

8. Martínez, Slack, and Heyman, *Bordering on Criminal*, 5.

9. Deborah Boehm, *Returned: Going and Coming in an Age of Deportation* (Oakland: University of California Press, 2016), 27.

10. Boehm, *Returned*, 28.

11. Cecilia Menjívar, "Liminal Legality: Salvadoran and Guatemalan Immigrants' Lives in the United States," *American Journal of Sociology* 111, no. 4 (2006): 999–1037.

12. Michael Sangiacomo and Alfredo Corchado, "Man Who Was Kidnapped after Deportation Is Freed Following Payments, 5 Days of Beatings," *Dallas News*, August 1,

2017, https://www.dallasnews.com/news/immigration/2017/08/01/man-kidnapped
-deportation-freed-following-payments-5-days-beatings.

13. Stephen Bochner, "Culture Shock Due to Contact with Unfamiliar Cultures," *Online Readings in Psychology and Culture* 4 (2003), http://dx.doi.org/10.9707/2307-0919.1073.

14. *Merriam-Webster* (online dictionary), http://www.merriam-webster.com.

15. In a study in Sonora, sociologist Paola Molina found that the five deportees she interviewed who had entered the United States as children "were experiencing culture shock at finding themselves in Mexico." Paola Molina, *Re-immigration after Deportation: Family, Gender, and the Decision to Make a Second Attempt to Enter the U.S.* (El Paso: LFB Scholarly, 2013), 120. Similarly, Katie Dingeman-Cerda and Rubén Rumbaut documented "reverse culture shock" among deportees to El Salvador who had migrated to the United States as children. Katie Dingeman-Cerda and Rubén Rumbaut, "Alienation in Salvadoran Society," in *Deportations Delirium: Interdisciplinary Responses*, ed. Daniel Kanstroom and M. Brinton Lykes, 227–50 (New York: New York University Press, 2015), 235.

16. These themes emerged in most of my interviews. A study of deported women in Tijuana similarly found that once deported, "women lacking social networks in Tijuana described feelings of fear, isolation, and disorientation with the neighborhoods or street culture of Tijuana and other border cities into which they were released." Angela M. Robertson, Remedios Lozada, Lawrence A. Palinkas, José Luis Burgos, Carlos Magis-Rodriguez, Gudelia Rangel, and Victoria D. Ojeda, "Deportation Experiences of Women Who Inject Drugs in Tijuana, Mexico," *Qualitative Health Research* 22, no. 4 (2012): 499–510.

17. A CURP is like a Social Security number and is required for most government transactions in Mexico.

18. Diana Carolina Peláez and Maria Dolores París, "Mujeres deportadas en Tijuana: Separación familiar y sentimientos de exilio" [Deported women in Tijuana: Family separation and feelings of exile], Seminario Internacional Sobre Migracion de Retorno [International workshop on return migration] (Tijuana: El Colegio de la Frontera Norte, 2013), https://www.colef.mx/emif/resultados/articulos/2013%20-%20Mujeres%20deportadas%20en%20Tijuana%20separacion%20familiar%20y%20sentimientos%20de%20exilio.pdf.

19. Peláez and París, "Mujeres deportadas."

20. Laura Velasco and Marie Laure Coubes, *Reporte sobre dimensión, caracterización y areas de atención a mexicanos deportados desde Estados Unidos* [Report on the dimension, characterization and areas of attention of Mexicans deported from the United States] (Tijuana: El Colegio de la Frontera Norte, 2013), 12, https://www.colef.mx/estudiosdeelcolef/reporte-sobre-dimension-caracterizacion-y-areas-de-atencion-mexicanos-deportados-desde-estados-unidos/?lang=en.

21. Velasco and Coubes, *Reporte sobre mexicanos deportados*, 16.

22. Velasco and Coubes, *Reporte sobre mexicanos deportados*, 21–22.

23. In 2017, largely in response to concerns over the fate of DACA recipients, Mexico passed legislation aimed at making it easier for Mexican nationals who were educated in the United States to enter higher education in Mexico.

24. My findings are consistent with sociologist Paola Molina's study, which included interviews with seventy recently deported individuals in Nogales, Sonora, Mexico. She found that "for the permanent U.S. settlers who had crossed as minors, returning to Mexico was like moving to a foreign country." Molina, *Re-immigration after Deportation*, 7.

THREE. LIFE AFTER DEPORTATION

1. Ng Fung Ho v. White, 259 U.S. 276, 284–85 (1922).

2. Jeremy Slack, Daniel E. Martínez, and Scott Whiteford, eds., *In the Shadow of the Wall* (Tuscon: University of Arizona Press, 2013), 120.

3. Heike Drotbohm and Ines Hasselberg, "Deportation, Anxiety, Justice: New Ethnographic Perspectives," *Journal of Ethnic and Migration Studies* 41, no. 4 (2014): 551–62 ("Deportation . . . is not a singular event. It is a process that begins long before, and carries on long after, the removal from one country to another takes place").

4. According to Dr. Ietza Bojorquez, one of the authors of the study cited in note 5, deportees in Mexico experience mental health problems at much higher rates than the general Mexican population.

5. Ietza Bojorquez, Rosa M. Aguilera, Jacobo Ramírez, Diego Cerecero, and Silvia Mejía, "Common Mental Disorders at the Time of Deportation: A Survey at the Mexico-United States Border," *Journal of Immigrant and Minority Health* 17, no. 6 (2015), doi:10.1007/s10903-014-0083-y.

6. Bojorquez et al., "Common Mental Disorders."

7. American Psychological Association, "Trauma," accessed August 8, 2016, http://www.apa.org/topics/trauma/.

8. Tonatiuh Guillén López, "Entre la convergencia y la exclusión: La deportación de mexicanos desde Estados Unidos de América" [Between convergence and exclusion: The deportation of Mexicans from the United States], *Realidad, Datos y Espacio Revista Internacional de Estadistica y Geografia* 3, no. 3 (2012), http://www.inegi.org.mx/RDE/RDE_07/Doctos/RDE_07_opt.pdf.

9. David C. Brotherton and Luis Barrios, *Banished to the Homeland: Dominican Deportees and Their Stories of Exile* (New York: Columbia University Press, 2011), 195. Susan Bibler Coutin's ethnographic work on deportees in El Salvador similarly uncovered suicidal ideation. Susan Bibler Coutin, *Exiled Home: Salvadoran Transnational Youth in the Aftermath of Violence* (Durham, NC: Duke University Press, 2016).

10. Rachel S. Taylor, *Sent "Home" with Nothing: The Deportation of Jamaicans with Mental Disabilities* (Washington, DC: Georgetown Law Human Rights Institute, 2011).

11. Julianne Hing, Seth Freed Wessler, and Jorge Rivas, "Torn Apart by Deportation," *Colorlines*, October 22, 2009, https://www.colorlines.com/articles/torn-apart-deportation.

12. Rory Carroll, "Stuck in Tijuana Waiting for a Miracle," *Guardian*, April 11, 2014, http://www.theguardian.com/world/2014/apr/11/undocumented-migrants-stuck-tijuana-mexico-us.

13. Laura Velasco and Sandra Albicker, *Estimación y caracterización de la población residente en "El Bordo" del Canal del Rio Tijuana* [Estimates and characteristics of the

resident population in "El Bordo" of the Tijuana River Channel] (Tijuana: El Colegio de la Frontera Norte, 2013), 6.

14. Marie-Laure Coubes, Eduardo González Fagoaga, Silvia Mejía Arango, René Nevarez Sanchez, and Laura Velasco Ortiz, "Estudio sobre los usuarios del Desayunador Salesiano Padre Chava: Reporte ejecutivo" [Study of the users of the Salesian Father Chava Breakfast Room: Executive report] (Tijuana: El Colegio de la Frontera Norte, 2015), 12, http://www.colef.mx/wp-content/uploads/2015/03/Reporte-ejecutivo -estudio-desayunador.pdf.

15. Of those under the age of sixty, 62 percent reported these symptoms. Coubes et al., "Estudio sobre los usarios," 19.

16. Miguel Pinedo, Jose Luis Burgos, and Victoria D. Ojeda, "A Critical Review of Social and Structural Conditions That Influence HIV Risk among Mexican Deportees," *Microbes and Infection/Institut Pasteur* 16, no. 5 (2014): 379–90.

17. Victoria D. Ojeda, Angela M. Robertson, Sarah P. Hiller, Remedios Lozada, Wayne Cornelius, Lawrence A. Palinkas, Carlos Magis-Rodriguez, and Steffanie A. Strathdee, "A Qualitative View of Drug Use Behaviors of Mexican Male Injection Drug Users from the United States," *Journal of Urban Health* 88, no. 1 (2011): 111, doi:10.1007/s11524-010-9508-7.

18. Ojeda et al., "A Qualitative View of Drug Use Behaviors," 111.

19. Ojeda et al., "A Qualitative View of Drug Use Behaviors," 112.

20. Angela M. Robertson, Remedios Lozada, Lawrence A. Palinkas, José Luis Burgos, Carlos Magis-Rodriguez, Gudelia Rangel, and Victoria D. Ojeda, "Deportation Experiences of Women Who Inject Drugs in Tijuana, Mexico," *Qualitative Health Research* 22, no. 4 (2012): 499.

21. Robertson et al., "Deportation Experiences of Women." Nine of twelve women "described feeling lonely and sad following their most recent deportation, often because they were separated from children and other family members in the United States and elsewhere in Mexico" (505).

22. Angela M. Robertson, M. Gudelia Rangel, Remedios Lozada, Alicia Vera, and Victoria D. Ojeda, "Male Injection Drug Users Try New Drugs Following Deportation to Tijuana, Mexico," *Drug and Alcohol Dependence* 120, no. 1–3 (2012), doi:10.1016/j.drugalcdep.2011.07.012.

23. Robertson et al., "Deportation Experiences of Women."

24. Kimberly Brouwer, Remedios Lozada, Wayne A. Cornelius, M. Firestone Cruz, Carlos Magis-Rodriguez, María Luisa Zúñiga, and Steffanie A Strathdee, "Deportation along the U.S.-Mexico Border: Its Relation to Drug Use Patterns and Accessing Care," *Journal of Immigrant and Minority Health* 11, no. 1 (2009), doi:10.1007/s10903-008-9119-5.

25. Bojorquez et al., "Common Mental Health Disorders," 1732.

26. Bojorquez et al., "Common Mental Health Disorders," 1732.

27. Ojeda et al., "A Qualitative View of Drug Use Behaviors," 111.

28. Norberto Santana Jr., "Criminal Deportations Fuel Border Crime Wave," *Orange County Register*, August 21, 2013, http://www.ocregister.com/articles/tijuana-189703 -border-deportees.html.

29. Santana, "Criminal Deportations Fuel Border Crime Wave."

30. Katherine Beckett and Steve Herbert, *Banished: The New Social Control in Urban America* (New York: Oxford University Press, 2010), 17.

31. Department of Justice, "Department of Justice and the Department of Homeland Security Announce Safeguards for Unrepresented Immigration Detainees with Serious Mental Disorders or Conditions," April 22, 2013, http://www.justice.gov/eoir/press /2013/SafeguardsUnrepresentedImmigrationDetainees.html.

32. Hilario Ochoa Movis, "Recibe unos 400 migrantes el Hospital de Salud Mental," *El Mexicano*, November 19, 2012, http://www.el-mexicano.com.mx/informacion /noticias/1/3/estatal/2012/11/19/630452/recibe-unos-400-migrantes-el-hospital-de-salud -mental.aspx.

33. Bojorquez et al., "Common Mental Health Disorders," 1732.

34. Leonardo Rivas Rivas, "Returnees' Identity Construction at a BA TESOL Program," *Profile Issues in Teachers' Professional Development* 15, no. 2 (2013): 185–97.

35. Seth Freed Wessler, "Call Centers: Returning to Mexico but Sounding 'American,'" *Al Jazeera America*, March 16, 2014, http://america.aljazeera.com/features/2014/3 /mexico-s-call-centers.html.

36. Call Center Service International, "Contact Center and IT Development Success in Mexico," accessed December 5, 2017, http://www.bajacallcenters.com.

37. Andy Uhler, "For Returnees to Mexico, English Is a Lucrative Skill," *Marketplace*, March 10, 2015, http://www.marketplace.org/2015/03/10/world/returnees-mexico -english-lucrative-skill.

38. Uhler, "For Returnees to Mexico, English Is a Lucrative Skill."

39. Jill Anderson, "From U.S. Immigration Detention Center to Transnational Call Center," *Voices of Mexico* 95 (2012): http://www.revistascisan.unam.mx/Voices/pdfs /9517.pdf.

40. Anderson, "From U.S. Immigration Detention Center," 87.

41. Anderson, "From U.S. Immigration Detention Center," 87–88.

42. Elliot Spagat and Omar Millan, "Deported Mexicans Find New Life at Call Centers," *Washington Times*, August 22, 2014, https://www.washingtontimes.com/news /2014/aug/22/deported-mexicans-find-new-life-at-call-centers/.

43. Spagat and Millan, "Deported Mexicans Find New Life."

44. Judy Woodruff, "Young Returnees Start Over in Mexico after Growing Up in the U.S.," *PBS Newshour*, January 6, 2016, http://www.pbs.org/newshour/bb/young -deportees-start-over-in-mexico-after-growing-up-in-the-u-s/.

45. Wessler, "Call Centers."

46. Spagat and Millan, "Deported Mexicans Find New Life."

47. Wessler, "Call Centers."

48. Anderson, "From U.S. Immigration Detention Center," 89.

49. Tanya Maria Golash-Boza, *Deported: Immigrant Policing, Disposable Labor, and Global Capitalism* (New York: New York University Press, 2015), 498–99.

50. Golash-Boza, *Deported*, 502.

51. Golash-Boza, *Deported*, 501–2.

52. Jose Enrique Arrioja, "Tourism Seen Jumping to No. 3 Mexico Cash Source by 2018," *Bloomberg*, June 25, 2013, http://www.bloomberg.com/news/articles/2013-06-25 /tourism-seen-jumping-to-mexico-s-3rd-biggest-cash-source-by-2018.

53. Eunice O. Albarrán, "De deportados a empresarios: 30 mil paisanos logran abrir su negocio aquí," *La Razón*, March 27, 2017, https://www.razon.com.mx/de-deportados -a-empresarios-30-mil-paisanos-logran-abrir-su-negocio-aqui/.

54. Jacqueline Hagan, Ruben Hernandez-Leon, and Jean-Luc Demonsant, *Skills of the Unskilled: Work and Mobility among Mexican Migrants* (Oakland: University of California Press, 2015).

55. In the study, 51 percent of the people surveyed reported transferring some kind of skills from the U.S. to Mexico, including 11 percent language skills, 2 percent formal education, 39 percent on-the-job technical skills, and 11 percent social skills. Hagan, Hernandez-Leon, and Demonsant, *Skills of the Unskilled*, table 5.2.

56. Hagan, Hernandez-Leon, and Demonsant, *Skills of the Unskilled*.

57. Katie Dingeman-Cerda and Rubén G. Rumpaut, "Alienation in Salvadoran Society," in *Deportations Delirium: Interdisciplinary Responses*, ed. Daniel Kanstroom and M. Brinton Lykes, 228–31 (New York: New York University Press, 2015).

58. Ines Hasselberg, *Enduring Uncertainty: Deportation, Punishment and Everyday Life* (New York: Berghahn, 2016), 6.

59. Hasselberg, *Enduring Uncertainty*, 7.

60. Rivas, "Returnees' Identity Construction," 191.

61. The study does not specify whether the participants were deported or returned voluntarily, but they did spend their formative years in the United States and now live in Mexico.

62. Douglas S. Massey and Kristin E. Espinosa, "What's Driving Mexico-US Migration? A Theoretical, Empirical, and Policy Analysis," *American Journal of Sociology* 102, no. 4 (1997): 939–99; Jodi Berger Cardoso, Erin Randle Hamilton, Nestor Rodriguez, Karl Eschbach, and Jacqueline Hagan, "Deporting Fathers: Involuntary Transnational Families and Intent to Remigrate among Salvadoran Deportees," *International Migration Review* 50 (2016), doi:10.1111/imre.12106.

63. Other estimates are lower, placing the number of deportees who intend to remigrate to the U.S. closer to one-third. Jacqueline Hagan, Karl Eschbach, and Nestor Rodriguez, "U.S. Deportation Policy, Family Separation, and Circular Migration," *International Migration Review* 42, no. 1 (2008), https://doi.org/10.1111/j.1747-7379.2007 .00114.x. The Migrant Crossing Border Study, with a sample of 1,100 deportees in Mexico, found that 55 percent intended to return. Slack, Martínez, and Whiteford, *In the Shadow of the Wall*, 114.

64. Slack, Martínez, and Whiteford, *In the Shadow of the Wall*, 114. Similarly, Paola Molina interviewed seventy recent deportees in Nogales, Mexico, and found that of the twenty respondents who intended to cross again, fourteen were "permanent U.S. settlers" for whom "crossing again meant returning home to their families and lives." Paola Molina, *Re-immigration after Deportation: Family, Gender, and the Decision to Make a Second Attempt to Enter the U.S.* (El Paso: LFB Scholarly, 2013), 86.

65. Slack, Martínez, and Whiteford, *In the Shadow of the Wall*, 116.

66. Grace Meng, "Turning Migrants into Criminals: The Harmful Impact of US Border Prosecutions," Human Rights Watch, 2013, 57, https://www.hrw.org/report/2013/05/22/turning-migrants-criminals/harmful-impact-us-border-prosecutions#page.

67. François Crépeau, "Report of the Special Rapporteur on the Rights of Migrants," United Nations General Assembly, Human Rights Council, April 2, 2012, https://www.ohchr.org/Documents/HRBodies/HRCouncil/RegularSession/Session20/A-HRC-20-24_en.pdf.

68. In 2015, the federal government filed 21,598 charges for immigration crimes, while 11,621 were filed for drug offenses, including drug dealing, drug possession, and organized crime–related drug crimes.

69. Transactional Records Access Clearinghouse (TRAC), "Despite Rise in Felony Charges, Most Immigration Convictions Remain Misdemeanors," June 26, 2014, http://trac.syr.edu/immigratin/reports/356/.

70. TRAC, "Most Immigration Convictions Remain Misdemeanors."

71. Federal Bureau of Prisons, "Statistics, Offenses," August 29, 2016, https://www.bop.gov/about/statistics/statistics_inmate_offenses.jsp; Meng, "Turning Migrants into Criminals," 3.

72. Meng, "Turning Migrants into Criminals," 133.

73. Meng, "Turning Migrants into Criminals," 135. Angela Viramontes, an assistant federal defender in Riverside, California, said she had heard a judge tell her colleague, "If I apply it in this case, I'd have to apply it to all cases."

74. Meng, "Turning Migrants into Criminals," 133.

75. Maria Jimenez, *Migrant Deaths at the U.S.-Mexico Border* (San Diego: ACLU and Mexico's National Commission of Human Rights, 2009), https://www.aclu.org/files/pdfs/immigrants/humanitariancrisisreport.pdf.

76. Hasselberg, *Enduring Uncertainty*, 99.

77. Woodruff, "Young Returnees Start Over in Mexico." Maggie had grown up in the United States and voluntarily returned to Mexico at the age of eighteen. Although she was not deported, her experience of returning to Mexico is similar to those of deported Americans after spending her formative years in the United States.

78. Woodruff, "Young Returnees Start Over in Mexico."

FOUR. DEPORTED BY MARRIAGE

1. In a 2009 report analyzing deportations between 1997 and 2007, Human Rights Watch estimated that "at least one million spouses and children have faced separation from their family members due to these deportations." Human Rights Watch, *Forced Apart (By the Numbers): Non-citizens Deported Mostly for Nonviolent Offenses* (2009), 3–4, https://www.hrw.org/report/2009/04/15/forced-apart-numbers/non-citizens-deported-mostly-nonviolent-offenses.

2. Daniel Kanstroom, *Aftermath: Deportation Law and the New American Diaspora* (New York: Oxford University Press, 2012), 135.

3. In marriages characterized by abuse, the deportation of an abusive spouse may have positive effects because it creates distance between the abuser and the abused. At

the same time, sociologist Joanna Dreby found in her research with migrant families in the United States that the deportation of an abusive spouse may not be experienced as a positive development even by the abused spouse because of the financial implications that accompany deportation. Dreby describes the experience of Gladys, whose husband was deported following an arrest. "The relationship had been abusive, but Gladys did not experience relief with his arrest. Rather, she felt it turned her life upside down. Before he was deported, she had been a stay-at-home mother." Even while the couple was separated, her husband had continued to support the family financially before his deportation. After his deportation, Gladys's work schedule greatly limited the time she could spend with her children. Joanna Dreby, *Everyday Illegal: When Policies Undermine Immigrant Families* (Oakland: University of California Press, 2015).

4. Linda Kelly, "Preserving the Fundamental Right to Family Unity: Championing Notions of Social Contract and Community Ties in the Battle of Plenary Power," *Villanova Law Review* 41 (1996): 776–77 (concluding that courts "do not give any serious consideration to the U.S. citizen's fundamental right to marry and to marital privacy" in immigration law cases).

5. Kerry v. Din, 135 S. Ct. 2128, 2138 (2015) (plurality opinion).

6. See, e.g., Swartz v. Rogers, 254 F.2d 338, 339 (D.C. Cir. 1958) (concluding that although "the physical conditions of the marriage may change [if she stayed in the United States without her husband] . . . the marriage continues").

7. See, e.g., Mostofi v. Naplitano, 841 F. Supp. 2d 208 (D.D.C. 2012) (rejecting claim that visa denial violates spouse's constitutional right to "freedom of personal choice in marriage and family life because they have 'done nothing more than say that the residence of one of the marriage partners may not be in the United States'").

8. Obergefell v. Hodges, 135 S. Ct. 2584, 2594–96 (2015).

9. *Kerry*, 135 S. Ct. at 2140 (Kennedy, J., concurring).

10. *Kerry*, 135 S. Ct. at 2139 ("But rather than deciding, as the plurality does, whether Din has a protected liberty interest, my view is that, even assuming she does, the notice she received regarding her husband's visa denial satisfied due process").

11. *Kerry*, 135 S. Ct. at 2142 (Breyer, J., dissenting).

12. David B. Thronson, "Unhappy Families: The Failings of Immigration Law for Families That Are Not All Alike," in *Deportations Delirium: Interdisciplinary Responses*, ed. Daniel Kanstroom and M. Brinton Lykes, 33–56 (New York: New York University Press, 2015).

13. Cervantes v. Immigration & Naturalization Serv., 510 F.2d 89, 91–92 (10th Cir. 1975) (framing a parent's deportation as having an "incidental impact" on a child's life).

14. Over 90 percent of people deported from the United States are Latino men, and most marriages are between heterosexual couples. Department of Homeland Security, *2014 Yearbook of Immigration Statistics* (Washington, DC: Department of Homeland Security, 2016), 103–6, https://www.dhs.gov/sites/default/files/publications/DHS%20 2014%20Yearbook.pdf; Tanya Golash-Boza and Pierrette Hondagneau-Sotelo, "Latino Immigrant Men and the Deportation Crisis: A Gendered Removal Program," *Latino Studies* 11 (2012): 271 (discussing the targeted deportation of Latino men).

15. Nathaniel Hoffman and Nicole Salgado, *Amor and Exile: True Stories of Love across America's Borders* (Boise, ID: Cordillera West, 2014), 74.

16. Hoffman and Salgado, *Amor and Exile*, 34.

17. "Moving to Mexico" and "Only in Mexico," *The Real Housewife of Ciudad Juárez*, August 18 and 19, 2010, http://therealhousewifeofciudadjuarez.blogspot.com/2010/.

18. Jean Guerrero, "American Wives of Deported Mexicans Say They're Excluded from SENTRI," KPBS, August 10, 2016, http://www.kpbs.org/news/2016/aug/10/us-citizen-wives-deported-mexicans-excluded-sentri/.

19. Ines Hasselberg, *Enduring Uncertainty: Deportation, Punishment and Everyday Life* (New York: Berghahn, 2016), 98 (documenting similar feelings of emasculation based on financial dependence articulated by male respondents); Tanya Maria Golash-Boza, *Deported: Immigrant Policing, Disposable Labor, and Global Capitalism* (New York: New York University Press, 2015), 226 ("For deportees like Victor and O'Ryan [in Jamaica], a gendered shame surrounding their inability to provide for themselves and to cope emotionally with their new situations complicated financial and emotional stresses").

20. Dreby, *Everyday Illegal*, 175.

21. "Updates—Nov. 4," *Raysdeportation* (blog), November 4, 2011, http://raysdeportation.blogspot.com/2011_11_01_archive.html.

22. Rebekah Rodriguez-Lynn, "How America's Immigration Laws Tore My Family Apart for Good," *Huffington Post*, April 28, 2015, http://www.huffingtonpost.com/rebekah-rodriguezlynn/immigration-family-tore-apart_b_7129574.html. Deportation and the separation it brings about is often described by those experiencing it as feeling like losing part of one's body. "6 Years Down . . . ," *A Guide to Belonging Everywhere* (blog), September 1, 2015, https://happycosmopolite.wordpress.com/2015/09/01/6-years-down/: "Our sentences (because it does feel like some horrid punishment) will be up September 2019, and it's sort of incredible to think that I have made it this long with an amputation as severe and heart breaking as being denied my family and a part of my home."

23. Megan Comfort, *Doing Time Together: Love and Family in the Shadow of the Prison* (Chicago: University of Chicago Press, 2007).

24. Linda K. Kerber, *No Constitutional Right to Be Ladies: Women and the Obligations of Citizenship* (New York: Hill and Wang, 1998); Nancy F. Cott, "Marriage and Women's Citizenship in the United States, 1830–1934," *American Historical Review* 103 (1998): 1444.

25. Expatriation Act of 1907, ch. 2534, 34 Stat. 1228, 1228–29 (1907), *repealed by* Nationality Act of 1940, ch. 876, 54 Stat. 1137 (1940).

26. Historian Nancy F. Cott suggests that "there is something peculiar—more tenuous or vulnerable—about women's (or perhaps married women's) citizenship in the United States." Cott, "Marriage and Women's Citizenship," 1441.

27. William Blackstone, *Commentaries on the Laws of England*, vol. 1 (1765), 441.

28. Kerber, *No Constitutional Right to Be Ladies*, 11–12.

29. Candice Lewis Bredbenner, *A Nationality of Her Own: Women, Marriage, and the Law of Citizenship* (Berkeley: University of California Press, 1998), 18–19.

30. Bredbenner, *A Nationality of Her Own*, 18–19.

31. Kerber, *No Constitutional Right to Be Ladies*, 25.

32. Kerber, *No Constitutional Right to Be Ladies*, 40–41.

33. Kerber, *No Constitutional Right to Be Ladies*, 40–41.

34. Kerber, *No Constitutional Right to Be Ladies*, 40–41.

35. Kerber, *No Constitutional Right to Be Ladies*, 37.

36. This requirement only applied to "any woman who might lawfully be naturalized under the existing laws," thus excluding Asian women and others due to race. Kerber, *No Constitutional Right to Be Ladies*, 37.

37. Bredbenner, *A Nationality of Her Own*, 105 (quoting Letter of Linda E. Hardesty de Reyes-Guerra to NWP Headquarters, May 1922).

38. Expatriation Act of 1907, ch. 2534, 34 Stat. 1228, 1228–29 (1907), *repealed by* Nationality Act of 1940, ch. 876, 54 Stat. 1137 (1940).

39. Bredbenner, *A Nationality of Her Own*, 47.

40. Expatriation Act of 1907 ch. 2534, 34 Stat. at 1229.

41. Bredbenner, *A Nationality of Her Own*, 5–6.

42. Bredbenner, *A Nationality of Her Own*, 5–6.

43. Bredbenner, *A Nationality of Her Own*, 6.

44. Mackenzie v. Hare, 239 U.S. 299, 299 (1915).

45. Bredbenner, *A Nationality of Her Own*, 65.

46. Bredbenner, *A Nationality of Her Own*, 65.

47. Bredbenner, *A Nationality of Her Own*, 65 (quoting "Becomes Citizen for Wife's Vote," *Women's Journal and Suffrage News* 44, no. 401 (1913)).

48. *Mackenzie*, 239 U.S. at 308.

49. *Mackenzie*, 239 U.S. at 300 (equating a woman's marrying a foreigner to voluntarily renouncing her citizenship).

50. *Mackenzie*, 239 U.S. at 311–12.

51. *Mackenzie*, 239 U.S. at 312.

52. Bredbenner, *A Nationality of Her Own*, 6.

53. Bredbenner, *A Nationality of Her Own*, 68.

54. Bredbenner, *A Nationality of Her Own*, 1.

55. Bredbenner, *A Nationality of Her Own*, 173.

56. Meg Hacker, "When Saying 'I Do' Meant Giving Up Your U.S. Citizenship," *Genealogy Notes* (2014): 56, 58, http://www.archives.gov/publications/prologue/2014/spring/citizenship.pdf.

57. Kerber, *No Constitutional Right to Be Ladies*, 42–43.

58. Leti Volpp, "Divesting Citizenship: On Asian American History and the Loss of Citizenship through Marriage," *UCLA Law Review* 53 (2005): 407 (citing *Ex parte* Ng Fung Sing, 6 F.2d 670, 670 (D.D.C. 1925)).

59. Volpp, "Divesting Citizenship," 407.

60. Volpp, "Divesting Citizenship," 407.

61. Volpp, "Divesting Citizenship," 407.

62. *In re* Fitzroy, 4 F.2d 541, 542 (D. Mass. 1925) (holding that upon "termination of the marriage and her continuation or resumption of domicile [in the United States], her original citizenship revive[d]").

63. Volpp, "Divesting Citizenship," 407–8.

64. Volpp, "Divesting Citizenship," 433.

65. Volpp, "Divesting Citizenship," 433–35.

66. Volpp, "Divesting Citizenship," 435–36, 438.

67. Volpp, "Divesting Citizenship," 441–42.

68. Cott, "Marriage and Women's Citizenship," 1469; Volpp, "Divesting Citizenship," 444–46.

69. Leo R. Chavez, "A Glass Half Empty: Latina Reproduction and Public Discourse," *Human Organization* 63 (2004): 174.

70. Chavez, "A Glass Half Empty," 175.

71. Chavez, "A Glass Half Empty," 175–76, 178.

72. Samuel P. Huntington, "The Hispanic Challenge," *Foreign Policy*, March–April 2004, 32.

73. Huntington, "The Hispanic Challenge," 32.

74. Violence against journalists who write about organized crime in Mexico is pervasive.

75. See Daniel Kanstroom, *Deportation Nation: Outsiders in American History* (Cambridge, MA: Harvard University Press, 2010), 70–75 (tracing the history of the plenary power doctrine); Stephen H. Legomsky, "Ten More Years of Plenary Power: Immigration, Congress, and the Courts," *Hastings Constitutional Law Quarterly* 22 (1994–95): 926.

76. Burrafato v. U.S. Dep't of State, 523 F.2d 554, 555 (2d Cir. 1975).

77. *Burrafato*, 523 F.2d at 556–57 (concluding that when an American citizen challenged the exclusion of her husband from the country, "no constitutional rights of American citizens over which a federal court would have jurisdiction [were] 'implicated' here," and thus declining to require the government to present a "facially legitimate and bona fide" reason for the denial of a visa).

78. Silverman v. Rogers, 437 F.2d 102, 103, 107 (1st Cir. 1970), *cert. denied*, 402 U.S. 983 (1971).

79. *Silverman*, 437 F.2d at 102.

80. Swartz v. Rogers, 254 F.2d 338, 339 (D.C. Cir. 1958).

81. *Swartz*, 254 F.2d at 339.

82. *Swartz*, 254 F.2d at 339.

83. *Swartz*, 254 F.2d at 339; Mostofi v. Naplitano, 841 F. Supp. 2d 208, 213 (D.D.C. 2012) (rejecting claim that visa denial violates spouses' constitutional "right to freedom of personal choice in marriage and family life because they have 'done nothing more than say that the residence of one of the marriage partners may not be in the United States'" (quoting *Silverman*, 437 F.2d at 107)); Udugampola v. Jacobs, 795 F. Supp. 2d 96, 101 (D.D.C. 2011) (concluding that a visa applicant's wife and daughter "cannot demonstrate that the defendant's denial of the visa implicated a constitutionally protected interest" and, thus, their claim was not entitled to judicial review); Bangura v. Hansen, 434 F.3d 487, 496 (6th Cir. 2006) ("A denial of an immediate relative visa does not infringe upon their right to marry" because "the Constitution does not recognize the right of a citizen spouse to have his or her alien spouse remain in the country" (quoting Almario v. Attorney Gen., 872 F.2d 147, 151 (6th Cir. 1989)) (alteration in original)).

84. Garcia v. Boldin, 691 F.2d 1172, 1183 (5th Cir. 1982).

85. Kleindienst v. Mandel, 408 U.S. 753 (1972).

86. *Mandel*, 408 U.S. at 769.

87. Bustamante v. Mukasey, 531 F.3d 1059, 1062 (9th Cir. 2008).

88. Adams v. Baker, 909 F.2d 643, 647 (1st Cir. 1990) ("Thus, if the Department of State's determination that Adams was ineligible to receive a visa . . . was based on a 'facially legitimate and bona fide reason,' we will be constrained to uphold Adams' exclusion").

89. Zablocki v. Redhail, 434 U.S. 374, 383 (1978) (citing Mass. Bd. of Ret. v. Murgia, 427 U.S. 307, 312, 314 (1976)).

90. *Zablocki*, 434 U.S. at 375 (quoting WIS. STAT. §§ 245.10(1),(4),(5) (1973)).

91. *Zablocki*, 434 U.S. at 384.

92. *Zablocki*, 434 U.S. at 388.

93. *Zablocki*, 434 U.S. at 390.

94. Turner v. Safley, 482 U.S. 78, 96–99 (1987) (applying strict scrutiny to a prison regulation that required inmates to obtain permission from the prison superinten-dent, based on compelling reasons, in order to get married); *Zablocki*, 434 U.S. at 383 (1978); Edith Z. Friedler, "From Extreme Hardship to Extreme Deference: United States Deportation of Its Own Children," *Hastings Constitutional Law Quarterly* 22 (1994): 497–98 ("Regardless of how far the courts have expanded this penumbra of rights, its core philosophy has remained intact; the right of family association is a sig-nificant interest in fundamental rights jurisprudence. Any state action that potentially affects such rights should be analyzed under the strict scrutiny test").

95. Volpp, "Divesting Citizenship," 435–36.

96. Volpp, "Divesting Citizenship," 435–36 (quoting Immigration and Citizenship of American-Born Women Married to Aliens: Hearing on H.R. 4057, H.R. 6238, and H.R. 9825 before the H. Comm. on Immigration and Naturalization, 69th Cong. 22–28 (1926) (statement of Elizabeth Kite, scholar, Library of Congress)).

97. Volpp, "Divesting Citizenship," 436.

FIVE. CHILDREN OF DEPORTEES

1. "Remarks by the President in Address to the Nation on Immigration," The White House, November 20, 2014, https://obamawhitehouse.archives.gov/the-press-office /2014/11/20/remarks-president-address-nation-immigration.

2. Marc R. Rosenblum and Doris Meissner, *The Deportation Dilemma: Reconciling Tough and Humane Enforcement* (Washington, DC: Migration Policy Institute, 2014), 9, http://www.migrationpolicy.org/research/deportation-dilemma-reconciling-tough -humane-enforcement.

3. Heather Koball, Randy Capps, Sarah Hooker, Krista Perreira, Andrea Campe-tella, Juan Manuel Pedroza, William Monson, and Sandra Huerta, *Health and Social Service Needs of US-Citizen Children with Detained or Deported Parents* (Washington, DC: Urban Institute and Migration Policy Institute, 2015), 1.

4. There may be a greater proportion of deportees who are parents of American children among deportees from specific countries. For example, a study that ad-ministered a questionnaire to deportees upon their arrival in El Salvador found that

73 percent reported they had a child under the age of eighteen in the United States, with 90 percent of these children being U.S. citizens. Joanna Dreby, "The Burden of Deportation on Children in Mexican Immigrant Families," *Journal of Marriage and Family Therapy* 74 (August 2014): 829–45.

5. Luis Zayas, *Forgotten Citizens: Deportation, Children, and the Making of American Exiles and Orphans* (New York: Oxford University Press, 2015), 126.

6. Luis Zayas quoted in Cindy Y. Rodriguez and Adriana Hauser, "Deportations: Missing Parents, Scared Kids," *CNN*, October 27, 2013, http://www.cnn.com/2013/10/26/us/immigration-parents-deported-children-left-behind/.

7. Zayas, *Forgotten Citizens*, 171.

8. Luis H. Zayas, Sergio Aguilar-Gaxiola, Hyunwoo Yoon, and Guillermina Natera Rey, "The Distress of Citizen-Children with Detained and Deported Parents," *Journal of Children and Family Studies* 24 (2015): 3221.

9. Cervantes v. INS, 510 F.2d 89 (10th Cir. 1975) ("The incidental impact on an alien's minor children caused by the enforcement of the duly-enacted conditions on an alien's entrance and residence does not create constitutional problems"); Silverman v. Rogers, 437 F.2d 102 (1st Cir. 1970), cert denied, 402 U.S. 983 (1971); Perdido v. Immigration & Naturalization Serv., 420 F.2d 1179 (5th Cir. 1969).

10. Joanna Dreby, *Everyday Illegal: When Policies Undermine Immigrant Families* (Oakland: University of California Press, 2015), 36.

11. Cecilia Menjívar, "Transnational Parenting and Immigration Law: Central Americans in the United States," *Journal of Ethnic and Migration Studies* 30, no. 8 (2012): 301–22.

12. Dreby, *Everyday Illegal*, 37.

13. Brian Allen, Erica M. Cisneros, and Alexandra Tellez, "The Children Left Behind: The Impact of Parental Deportation on Mental Health," *Journal of Child and Family Studies* 24, no. 2 (2013): 387.

14. Allen, Cisneros, and Tellez, "The Children Left Behind," 390.

15. Allen, Cisneros, and Tellez, "The Children Left Behind," 389. In another study, 36 percent of the children whose parents had been deported demonstrated three or more psychological or behavioral symptoms, with greater severity linked to a parent's arrest in the home, cases where the child's primary caregiver was deported, and those who had been apart from a parent for more than a month. Jodi Berger Cardoso, Erin Randle Hamilton, Nestor Rodriguez, Karl Eschbach, and Jacqueline Hagan, "Deporting Fathers: Involuntary Transnational Families and Intent to Remigrate among Salvadoran Deportees," *International Migration Review* 50 (2016): doi:10.1111/imre.12106.

16. Ajay Chaudry, Randy Capps, Juan Manuel Pedroza, Rosa Maria Castañeda, Robert Santos, and Molly M. Scott, *Facing Our Future: Children in the Aftermath of Immigration Enforcement* (Washington, DC: Urban Institute, 2010), http://www.urban.org/sites/default/files/alfresco/publication-pdfs/412020-Facing-Our-Future.PDF.

17. Deysi Aldana, "My Children Need Their Daddy," *Fox News*, February 4, 2016, http://latino.foxnews.com/latino/opinion/2016/02/04/opinion-my-children-need-their-daddy/.

18. Ginger Thompson and Sarah Cohen, "More Deportations Follow Minor Crimes, Records Show," *New York Times*, April 4, 2015, https://www.nytimes.com/2014/04/07/us/more-deportations-follow-minor-crimes-data-shows.html.

19. Anthony Advincula, "After Parents' Deportation, U.S. Children Face Mental Struggles," New America Media, February 18, 2014, accessed January 29, 2018, http://newamericamedia.org/2014/02/after-parents-deportation-us-children-face-mental-struggles.php (no longer available).

20. Christina Jose-Kampfner, "Post-traumatic Stress Reactions in Children of Imprisoned Mothers," in *Children of Incarcerated Parents*, ed. Katherine Gabel and Denise Johnston (New York: Lexington, 1995).

21. Zayas, *Forgotten Citizens*, 126.

22. Chaudry et al., *Facing Our Future*.

23. Cardoso et al., "Deporting Fathers," 50.

24. Chaudry et al., *Facing Our Future*.

25. Chaudry et al., *Facing Our Future*.

26. Dreby, *Everyday Illegal*, 138.

27. Chaudry et al., *Facing Our Future*.

28. Julianne Hing, Seth Freed Wessler, and Jorge Rivas, "Torn Apart by Deportation," *Colorlines*, October 22, 2009, https://www.colorlines.com/articles/torn-apart-deportation.

29. Nina Rabin, "Disappearing Parents: Immigration Enforcement and the Child Welfare System," *Connecticut Law Review* (2011): 102. Similarly, Zatz and Rodriguez found that "although the actual numbers are unknown and probably relatively small, practically every attorney and advocate we interviewed recounted cases involving young children who were placed in foster care and then quickly adopted, with their parents' rights severed in absentia." Marjorie S. Zatz and Nancy Rodriguez, *Dreams and Nightmares: Immigration Policy, Youth, and Families* (Oakland: University of California Press, 2015), 121.

30. Rabin, "Disappearing Parents," 121–22.

31. Zatz and Rodriguez, *Dreams and Nightmares*, 124.

32. Zatz and Rodriguez, *Dreams and Nightmares*, 124.

33. Zatz and Rodriguez report an interview with an attorney who recalls a judge saying, "I will not return those US-citizen children to the squalor that is Mexico." Zatz and Rodriguez, *Dreams and Nightmares*, 124.

34. Naomi Glenn-Levin Rodriguez, *Fragile Families: Foster Care, Immigration, and Citizenship* (Philadelphia: University of Pennsylvania Press, 2017), 64.

35. Rodriguez, *Fragile Families*, 65.

36. Rodriguez, *Fragile Families*, 66.

37. Rodriguez, *Fragile Families*, 66.

38. Jeffrey Passel, D. Cohn, and Ana Gonzalez-Barrera, *Net Migration from Mexico Falls to Zero—and Perhaps Less* (Washington, DC: Pew Hispanic Research Center, 2012), 14.

39. Randy Capps, Heather Koball, Andrea Campetella, Krista Perreira, Sarah Hooker, and Juan Manuel Pedroza, *Implications of Immigration Enforcement Activities for the Well-Being of Children in Immigrant Families: A Review of the Literature* (Washington, DC: Urban Institute and Migration Policy Institute, 2015), vi.

40. Capps et al., *Implications of Immigration Enforcement*, 12 ("Research suggests that the transition to schooling in Mexico, for example, can be very difficult for children

who have attended US public schools, as they generally do not have the Spanish language skills or familiarity with the Mexican school system necessary to succeed there").

41. Juan Sanchez-Garcia, Edmund T. Hamann, and Victor Zuniga, "What the Youngest Transnational Students Have to Say about Their Transition from U.S. Schools to Mexican Ones," *Diaspora, Indigenous, and Minority Education* 6, no. 3 (2012): 157–71.

42. Sanchez-Garcia, Hamann, and Zuniga, "What the Youngest Transnational Students Have to Say."

43. Zayas, *Forgotten Citizens*, 175.

44. Jacqueline Bhabha, *Child Migration and Human Rights in a Global Age* (Princeton, NJ: Princeton University Press, 2014), 26.

45. Ortiz v. Sessions, Civil 17-00210 LEK-KJM (D. Haw. 2017).

46. Ortiz v. Sessions, 857 F.3d 966 (9th Cir. 2017).

47. *In re* Monreal-Aguinaga, 23 I. & N. Dec. 56 (BIA 2001); Sullivan v. INS, 777 F.2d 609 (9th Cir. 1985) ("deportation rarely occurs without personal distress and emotional hurt"); Jimenez v. INS, 116 F.3d 1485 (9th Cir. 1997) (family separation is "simply one of the common results of deportation or exclusion [that] are insufficient to prove extreme hardship").

48. Edith Z. Friedler, "From Extreme Hardship to Extreme Deference: United States Deportation of Its Own Children," *Hastings Constitutional Law Quarterly* 22 (1994): 513.

49. Friedler, "From Extreme Hardship to Extreme Deference," 513; Hernandez-Cordero v. United States, 819 F.2d 558 (5th Cir. 1987), 564 (Robin, J. dissenting).

50. Susan Hazeldean, "Anchoring More Than Babies: Children's Rights after *Obergefell v. Hodges*," *Cardozo Law Review* 38 (2016): 1445–46.

51. David B. Thronson, "Choiceless Choices: Deportation and the Parent-Child Relationship," *Nevada Law Journal* 6 (2006): 1196.

52. Garcia v. Boldin, 691 F.2d 1172, 1183 (5th Cir. 1982).

53. Cervantes v. Immigration and Naturalization Service, 510 F.2d 89, 91–92 (10th Cir. 1975).

54. Acosta v. Gaffney, 558 F.2d 1153, 1157–58 (3rd Cir. 1977).

55. *Acosta*, 558 F.2d at 1157.

56. Friedler, "From Extreme Hardship to Extreme Deference."

57. Capps et al., *Implications of Immigration Enforcement*, vii.

58. Capps et al., *Implications of Immigration Enforcement*, 5.

59. Moore v. City of East Cleveland, 431 U.S. 494, 503–4 (1977).

60. As Jaqueline Bhabha argues, "The place of residence has pervasive impacts and lifelong consequences: it affects children's life expectancy, their physical and psychological development, their material prospects, their general standard of living. Belonging to a particular country determines the type of education the child receives, the expectations regarding familial obligations, employment opportunities, gender roles, and consumption patterns." Bhabha, *Child Migration and Human Rights*, 69.

61. Organization of American States, Article 17.

62. Smith v. United States, Case 12.562, Inter-American Commission on Human Rights, Report No. 81/10 (2010).

63. Convention for the Protection of Human Rights and Fundamental Freedoms, November 4, 1950, Europe. T.S. No. 5; 213 U.N.T.S. 221.

64. Bhabha, *Child Migration and Human Rights*, 30.

65. Bhabha, *Child Migration and Human Rights*, 30.

66. Sanchez-Garcia, Hamann, and Zuniga, "What the Youngest Transnational Students Have to Say."

67. Maria E. Enchautegui and Cecilia Menjívar, "Paradoxes of Family Immigration Policy: Separation, Reorganization, and Reunification of Families under Current Immigration Laws," *Law and Policy* 37, no. 1–2 (January–April 2015): 32.

CONCLUSION

1. David C. Brotherton and Luis Barrios, *Banished to the Homeland: Dominican Deportees and Their Stories of Exile* (New York: Columbia University Press, 2011); Susan Bibler Coutin, *Exiled Home: Salvadoran Transnational Youth in the Aftermath of Violence* (Durham, NC: Duke University Press, 2016); Tanya Maria Golash-Boza, *Deported: Immigrant Policing, Disposable Labor, and Global Capitalism* (New York: New York University Press, 2015); M. Kathleen Dingeman-Cerda and Susan Bibler Coutin, "The Ruptures of Return: Deportation's Confounding Effects," in *Punishing Immigrants: Policy, Politics and Injustice*, ed. Charis E. Kubrin, Marjorie S. Zatz, and Ramiro Martinez Jr. (New York: New York University Press, 2012), 113 (discussing deportation from the U.S. to El Salvador); Susan Bibler Coutin, "Exiled by Law: Deportation and the Inviability of Life," in *The Deportation Regime: Sovereignty, Space, and the Freedom of Movement*, ed. Nathalie Peutz and Nicholas de Genova (Durham, NC: Duke University Press, 2010) (focusing on El Salvador); David Grabias and Nicole Newnham, dirs., *Sentenced Home* (video; Sentenced Home Productions, 2006) (exploring deportation from the U.S. to Cambodia).

2. Linda Bosniak, "Citizenship Denationalized," *Indiana Journal of Global Legal Studies* 7, no. 2 (2000): 479, 478.

3. Linda Bosniak, *The Citizen and the Alien: Dilemmas of Contemporary Membership* (Princeton, NJ: Princeton University Press, 2006), 20.

4. Ines Hasselberg, *Enduring Uncertainty: Deportation, Punishment and Everyday Life* (New York: Berghahn, 2016), 27.

5. Walter J. Nicholls, *The DREAMers: How the Undocumented Youth Movement Transformed the Immigration Debate* (Stanford, CA: Stanford University Press, 2013), 125.

6. Coutin, *Exiled Home*.

7. Leisy J. Abrego, "Legal Consciousness of Undocumented Latinos: Fear and Stigma as Barriers to Claims-Making for First- and 1.5-Generation Immigrants," *Law and Society Review* 45, no. 2 (2011): 337–70.

8. Coutin, *Exiled Home*, 135.

9. Nira Yuval-Davis, "Belonging and the Politics of Belonging," *Patterns of Prejudice* 40, no. 3 (2006): 197–214.

10. Leo Zaibert, "Uprootedness as (Cruel and Unusual) Punishment," *New Criminal Law Review* 11 (2008): 400.

11. Joseph H. Carens, *Culture, Citizenship and Community: A Contextual Exploration of Justice as Evenhandedness* (Oxford: Oxford University Press, 2000), 166.

12. Carens, *Culture, Citizenship and Community*, 166.

13. Roberto G. Gonzalez, *Lives in Limbo: Undocumented and Coming of Age in America* (Oakland: University of California Press, 2015), 9. Sociologist Leisy Abrego has compared the experiences of undocumented first-generation adult immigrants and 1.5-generation immigrants who moved to the U.S. as children. Among other things, she found that members of the 1.5 generation "had been mostly socialized in the United States, where, having had legal access to schools, they were able to develop a much stronger sense of belonging than their first-generation counterparts." Abrego, "Legal Consciousness of Undocumented Latinos."

14. Margaret D. Stock, *Essential to the Fight: Immigrants in the Military Eight Years after 9/11* (Washington, DC: American Immigration Council, 2009), 3, http://www .immigrationpolicy.org/sites/default/files/docs/Immigrants_in_the_Military_-_Stock _110909_0.pdf.

15. Yuval-Davis, "Belonging and the Politics of Belonging."

16. Hiroshi Motomura, *Americans in Waiting: The Lost Story of Immigration and Citizenship in the United States* (New York: Oxford University Press, 2006), 11.

17. Motomura, *Americans in Waiting*, 11.

18. Motomura, *Immigration outside the Law* (New York: Oxford University Press, 2014), 97.

19. Motomura, *Immigration outside the Law*, 98.

20. Motomura, *Americans in Waiting*, 81–82.

21. Motomura, *Americans in Waiting*, 97.

22. Motomura, *Americans in Waiting*, 98.

23. Cristina M. Rodríguez, "Immigration, Civil Rights and the Evolution of the People," *Daedalus* 142, no. 3 (2013): 6. Similarly, Linda Kelly argues "the proper distinction in deciding whether an alien is entitled to constitutional protection is not whether his or her case falls 'inside' or 'outside' of immigration law." Instead, Kelly argues, constitutional protections should apply on the basis of one's "'ties' or 'membership' in the U.S. or national community." Linda Kelly, "Preserving the Fundamental Right to Family Unity: Championing Notions of Social Contract and Community Ties in the Battle of Plenary Power," *Villanova Law Review* 41 (1996): 748.

24. Motomura, *Americans in Waiting*, 6.

25. Mathews v. Diaz, 426 U.S. 67, 87 (1976).

26. *Mathews*, 426 U.S. at 82–83.

27. Landon v. Plasencia, 459 U.S. (1982) at 32.

28. *Landon*, 459 U.S. at 34.

29. Motomura, *Immigration outside the Law*, 107.

30. Joseph H. Carens, *Immigrants and the Right to Stay* (Cambridge, MA: MIT Press, 2012), 9.

31. Carens, *Immigrants and the Right to Stay*, 19.

32. Motomura, *Immigration outside the Law*, 107.

33. Nicholas DeGenova, "Immigration 'Reform' and the Production of Migrant 'Illegality,'" in *Constructing Immigration "Illegality": Experiences, Critiques, and Responses*, ed. Cecilia Menjívar and Daniel Kanstroom (New York: Cambridge University Press, 2014), 42.

34. Juan Ramon García, *Operation Wetback: The Mass Deportation of Mexican Undocumented Workers in 1954* (Westport, CT: Greenwood, 1980), 228.

35. Shannon K. O'Neil, *Two Nations Indivisible: Mexico, the United States, and the Road Ahead* (New York: Oxford University Press, 2013), 35.

36. O'Neil, *Two Nations Indivisible*, 35.

37. Carens, *Immigrants and the Right to Stay*.

38. Bosniak, *The Citizen and the Alien*, 19.

39. Bosniak, *The Citizen and the Alien*, 19.

40. Stephen H. Legomsky, "Ten More Years of Plenary Power: Immigration, Congress, and the Courts," *Hastings Constitutional Law Quarterly* 22 (1995): 937.

41. Peter J. Spiro, "Trump's Anti-Muslim Plan Is Awful. And Constitutional," *New York Times*, December 8, 2015, http://www.nytimes.com/2015/12/10/opinion/trumps-anti-muslim-plan-is-awful-and-constitutional.html?_r=0.

42. Sessions v. Morales-Santana, 137 S. Ct. 1678 (2017).

43. Zaibert, "Uprootedness as (Cruel and Unusual) Punishment," 402.

44. Joseph Carens, "The Case for Amnesty," *Boston Review*, May/June 2009, http://bostonreview.net/archives/BR34.3/carens.php.

45. Trop v. Dulles, 356 U.S. 86, 114 (1958).

46. *Trop*, 356 U.S. at 94.

47. *Trop*, 356 U.S. at 98.

48. Mari J. Matsuda, "Looking to the Bottom: Critical Legal Studies and Reparations," *Harvard Civil Rights–Civil Liberties Law Review* 22 (1987): 326.

49. *Trop*, 356 U.S. at 98.

50. Zaibert, "Uprootedness as (Cruel and Unusual) Punishment," 402.

51. Peter Riesenberg and Henry S. Matteo, *Denationalization v. "the Right to Have Rights": The Standard of Intent in Citizenship Loss* (Lanham, MD: University Press of America, 1997), 78.

52. United States ex. rel. Klonis v. Davis, 13 F.2d 630, 630 (N.Y. 1926).

53. *Trop*, 356 U.S. at 101–2.

54. Susan Bibler Coutin, "Illegality, Borderlands, and the Space of Nonexistence," in *Globalization under Construction: Governmentality, Law, and Identity*, ed. Richard Warren Perry and Bill Maurer (Minneapolis: University of Minnesota Press, 2003).

55. Deborah Boehm, *Returned: Going and Coming in an Age of Deportation* (Oakland: University of California Press, 2016), 150.

56. Orlando Patterson, *Slavery and Social Death: A Comparative Study* (Cambridge, MA: Harvard University Press, 1985).

57. Lisa Marie Cacho, *Social Death: Racialized Rightlessness and the Criminalization of the Unprotected* (New York: New York University Press, 2012), 7, 8.

58. Padilla v. Kentucky, 559 U.S. 356 (2010).

59. Fong Yue Ting v. United States, 149 U.S. 698, 740 (1893) (Brewer, J., dissenting).

60. Maynard v. Hill, 125 U.S. 190, 205 (1888).

61. Loving v. Virginia, 388 U.S. 1, 12 (1967).

62. *Loving*, 388 U.S. at 12 (quoting Skinner v. Oklahoma, 316 U.S. 535, 541 (1942)).

63. Obergefell v. Hodges, 135 S. Ct. 2584, 2607–8 (2015).

64. *Obergefell*, 135 S. Ct. at 2593–94.

65. *Obergefell*, 135 S. Ct. at 2594.

66. *Obergefell*, 135 S. Ct. at 2594.

67. *Obergefell*, 135 S. Ct. at 2600.

68. Meyer v. Nebraska, 262 U.S. 390, 399 (1923).

69. William Blackstone, *Commentaries on the Laws of England* (Oxford, 1765–69), 441.

70. Immigration and Nationality Act, 8 U.S.C. § 1430 (2012).

71. U.S. Citizenship and Immigration Services, *Policy Manual: Marriage and Marital Union for Naturalization*, vol. 12, pt. G, ch. 2, 2018, https://www.uscis.gov/policymanual /HTML/PolicyManual-Volume12-PartG-Chapter2.html.

72. According to the U.S. Citizenship and Immigration Services policy manual, "under very limited circumstances and where there is no indication of marital disunity, an applicant may be able to establish that he or she is living in marital union . . . even though the applicant does not actually reside with citizen spouse." These exceptions are limited to one spouse being in the military or required to travel for work. Incarceration does not qualify.

73. U.S. Citizenship and Immigration Services, "Petition for a Spouse," in *Adjudicator's Field Manual*, ch. 21, § 21.3, 2016, https://www.uscis.gov/ilink/docView/AFM /HTML/AFM/0-0-0-1/0-0-0-3481/0-0-0-4484.html#0-0-0-389.

74. U.S. Citizenship and Immigration Services, "Petition for a Spouse."

75. Violence against Women Act of 1994, 42 U.S.C. § 13925 (2012).

76. 8 U.S.C. §§ 1154(a)(1)(A)(iii)(II)(dd), (B)(ii)(II)(dd) (2012).

77. Bridget Kinsella, *Visiting Life: Women Doing Time on the Outside* (New York: Crown, 2007) (describing her own relationship with a prisoner and telling the stories of several other women married to men in prison); Deena Guzder, "Bar-Crossed Lovers: Making a Marriage Work When a Spouse Is Serving Life," *Al Jazeera America*, February 14, 2014, http://america.aljazeera.com/articles/2014/2/14/spouses-of-the -longtermincarcerated.html.

78. Turner v. Safley, 482 U.S. 78, 96 (1987).

79. *Turner*, 482 U.S. at 96.

80. *Turner*, 482 U.S. at 95.

81. *Turner*, 482 U.S. at 96.

82. *Loving*, 388 U.S.

83. *Loving*, 388 U.S. at 12.

84. *Loving*, 388 U.S. at 2.

85. *Loving*, 388 U.S. at 2–3.

86. *Loving*, 388 U.S. at 3 ("The trial judge suspended the sentence [of one year in jail] for a period of 25 years on the condition that the Lovings leave the State and not return to Virginia together for 25 years").

87. *The Loving Story* (HBO, 2012), https://www.hbo.com/documentaries/the-loving -story.

88. *Loving*, 388 U.S. at 12.

89. Moore v. City of East Cleveland, 431 U.S. 494, 499 (1977).

90. *Moore*, 431 U.S.

91. *Moore*, 431 U.S.

92. Kerry v. Din, 135 S. Ct. 2128 (2015).

93. *Kerry*, 135 S. Ct. at 2140 (Kennedy, J., concurring), emphasis added. The "facially legitimate and bona fide reason" standard emerged in the case of *Kleindienst v. Mandel*, 408 U.S. 753, 770 (1972), where a group of university professors challenged the exclusion of a speaker on the theory that his exclusion violated the professors' First Amendment rights.

94. *Kerry*, 135 S. Ct. at 2131 (rejecting Din's "claim[] that the Government denied her due process of law when, without adequate explanation of the reason for the visa denial, it deprived her of her constitutional right to live in the United States with her spouse" and concluding "there is no such constitutional right").

95. *Kerry*, 135 S. Ct. at 2142 (Breyer, J., dissenting) (concluding that procedural due process protections apply to this right).

96. *Kerry*, 135 S. Ct. at 2142.

97. *Kerry*, 135 S. Ct. at 2139 (Kennedy, J., concurring) (indicating "the Court need not decide . . . whether a citizen has a protected liberty interest in the visa application of her alien spouse" because "the Government satisfied due process").

98. *Kerry*, 135 S. Ct. at 2139 ("But rather than deciding, as the plurality does, whether Din has a protected liberty interest, my view is that, even assuming she does, the notice she received regarding her husband's visa denial satisfied due process").

99. Zablocki v. Redhail, 434 U.S. 374, 384 (1978) ("More recent decisions have established that the right to marry is part of the fundamental 'right of privacy' implicit in the Fourteenth Amendment's Due Process Clause"); Griswold v. Connecticut, 381 U.S. 479, 486 (1965) ("We deal with a right of privacy older than the Bill of Rights—older than our political parties, older than our school system. Marriage is a coming together for better or for worse, hopefully enduring, and intimate to the degree of being sacred. It is an association that promotes a way of life, not causes; a harmony in living, not political faiths; a bilateral loyalty, not commercial or social projects. Yet it is an association for as noble a purpose as any involved in our prior decisions"); see also Carey v. Population Servs. Int'l, 431 U.S. 678, 684–85 (1977) ("While the outer limits of this aspect of privacy have not been marked by the Court, it is clear that among the decisions that an individual may make without unjustified government interference are personal decisions 'relating to marriage, procreation, contraception, family relationships, and child rearing and education'" (internal citations omitted)).

100. *Loving*, 388 U.S.

101. *Obergefell*, 135 S. Ct.

102. Hiroshi Motomura, "The Family and Immigration: A Roadmap for the Ruritanian Lawmaker," *American Journal of Comparative Law* 43 (1995): 517.

103. Bustamante v. Mukasey, 531 F.3d 1059, 1062 (9th Cir. 2008) (citing Cleveland Bd. of Educ. v. LaFleur, 414 U.S. 632, 639–40 (1974)).

104. *Moore*, 431 U.S.

105. A citizen's right to live in the United States and to enjoy "the privileges and immunities" of citizenship is guaranteed by the Fifth and Fourteenth Amendments. *See* Ng Fung Ho v. White, 259 U.S. 276, 284–85 (1922) ("To deport one who so claims to be a citizen, obviously deprives him of liberty, as was pointed out in *Chin Yow v. United States*, 208 U.S. 8, 13. It may result also in loss of both property and life; or of all that makes life worth living. Against the danger of such deprivation without the sanction afforded by judicial proceedings, the Fifth Amendment affords protection in its guarantee of due process of law").

106. Kerry v. Din, 135 S. Ct. 2128, 2142 (2015) (Breyer, J., dissenting).

107. Smith v. United States, Case 12.562, Inter-Am. Comm'n H.R., Report No. 81/10, para. 25 (2010) (citing *Berrehab v. Netherlands*, Judgment of June 21, 1988, No. 10730/84, para. 29).

108. Jacqueline Bhabha, *Child Migration and Human Rights in a Global Age* (Princeton, NJ: Princeton University Press, 2014), 51 (noting that "torn between the sovereign state's prerogative to exercise border control and the human being's right to respect for family life, [European] courts have had difficulty reaching unanimity").

109. Bhabha, *Child Migration and Human Rights*, 52, quoting European Convention on Human Rights Article 8.

110. Hasselberg, *Enduring Uncertainty*, 48.

111. Hasselberg, *Enduring Uncertainty*, 47.

112. Bhabha, *Child Migration and Human Rights*, 80.

113. Bhabha, *Child Migration and Human Rights*, 81.

114. Bhabha, *Child Migration and Human Rights*, 84.

115. Daniel Kanstroom, *Aftermath: Deportation Law and the New American Diaspora* (New York: Oxford University Press, 2012) (recommending using the European model).

116. Hasselberg, *Enduring Uncertainty*, 46.

117. David B. Thronson, "Unhappy Families: The Failings of Immigration Law for Families That Are Not All Alike," in *Deportations Delirium: Interdisciplinary Responses*, ed. Daniel Kanstroom and M. Brinton Lykes (New York: New York University Press, 2015), 38.

118. Carens, *Immigrants and the Right to Stay*.

119. Leo R. Chavez, *The Latino Threat: Constructing Immigrants, Citizens, and the Nation*, 2nd ed. (Palo Alto, CA: Stanford University Press, 2013).

120. George H. W. Bush, "Statement on Signing the Immigration Act of 1990," *Pub. Papers of the Presidents of the United States: George Bush, 1990, Book 1* (Washington, DC: Office of the Federal Register, National Archives and Records Administration, 1991), 1717–18.

121. In three recent cases, the Court declined to categorize cases based on the possession of small amounts of marijuana or possession of drug paraphernalia (a sock used

to store four pills) as aggravated felonies. Moncrieffe v. Holder, 133 S. Ct. 1678 (2013); Carachuri-Rosendo v. Holder, 130 S. Ct. 2577 (2010); Mellouli v. Lynch, 135 S. Ct. 1980 (2015).

122. Hasselberg, *Enduring Uncertainty*, 3.

EPILOGUE

1. Susan Bibler Coutin, *Exiled Home: Salvadoran Transnational Youth in the Aftermath of Violence* (Durham, NC: Duke University Press, 2016); David C. Brotherton and Luis Barrios, *Banished to the Homeland: Dominican Deportees and Their Stories of Exile* (New York: Columbia University Press, 2011), 294; Tanya Maria Golash-Boza, *Deported: Immigrant Policing, Disposable Labor, and Global Capitalism* (New York: New York University Press, 2015), 96.

2. Deborah Boehm, *Returned: Going and Coming in an Age of Deportation* (Oakland: University of California Press, 2016), 151.

3. Joseph Carens, "The Case for Amnesty," *Boston Review*, May/June 2009, http://bostonreview.net/archives/BR34.3/carens.php.

4. Hiroshi Motomura, *Americans in Waiting: The Lost Story of Immigration and Citizenship in the United States* (New York: Oxford University Press, 2006), 97.

5. Heike Drotbohm and Ines Hasselberg, "Deportation, Anxiety, Justice: New Ethnographic Perspectives," *Journal of Ethnic and Migration Studies* 41, no. 4 (2014): 551–62.

INDEX

children of deportees, 18, 69, 127–52; erosion of parental bond, 69–70, 82, 96, 132–34; in foster care, 137–39; human rights, 149–51; language barriers, 130–31; mental health, 18, 131, 134–36; in Mexico, 139–44; numbers of, 2, 127–28; and school, 130–31, 136–37, 140–43; witnessing parent's arrest by immigration authorities, 135–36

China, 118

Chinese Exclusion Act, 20–22, 25

"citizen aliens," 24

citizenship, 155, 166–67, 187, 195n3, 225n105; as affiliation, 154, 159–64, 171; becoming a citizen, 3; as contract, 154; as exercise of rights, 154, 166–68; formal definitions of, 154; identity based on, 154–59, 171; and membership, 50; underprotection of women's, 113–17

Clinton, Bill, 41

Colombia, 148

conditional permanent resident status, 32

Congress, Mexico, 87

Congress, U.S., 17, 21, 27, 31, 46, 115, 121, 153, 161–62, 169

Constitution, U.S., 14, 20–23, 31, 103, 115, 121, 123, 147, 149, 167, 168, 170, 177–81, 204n130, 204n134, 215n77; First Amendment, 122, 224n93; Fifth Amendment, 121, 225n105; Eighth Amendment, 173; Fourteenth Amendment, 22, 169, 179, 224n99, 225n105; Nineteenth Amendment, 115

constitutional rights, and lack of protections in deportation cases, 12, 20–23, 47, 168–70

constructive deportation, 103–6, 124, 142, 146–47, 149

consular waiver, 19, 110, 186

Convention on the Rights of the Child, United Nations (CRC), 150

Corrections Corporation of America, 81

Coulter, Ann, 25

Court of Appeals, United States: D.C. Circuit, 121; First Circuit, 121–22; Third Circuit, 148; Fifth Circuit, 121–22, 147; Ninth Circuit, 75, 122, 144–46; Tenth Circuit, 147–48

Coutin, Susan Bibler, 7, 157, 172

coverture, 113–14

CRC. See Convention on the Rights of the Child, United Nations

"criminal alien," 6–7, 25–31, 50, 184–88, 205n3

Criminal Alien Program, U.S. (CAP), 28, 29

culture shock, 12, 57, 118, 142, 206n15

Customs and Border Protection (CBP), 15, 18

DACA. See Deferred Action for Childhood Arrivals

DAPA. See Deferred Action for Parents of Americans and Lawful Permanent Residents

de facto deportation, 103–6, 124, 142, 146–47

Deferred Action for Childhood Arrivals (DACA), 6, 206n23

Deferred Action for Parents of Americans and Lawful Permanent Residents (DAPA), 127

demonization of immigrants, 50, 185

denationalization, 14, 169–74

Department of Veterans Affairs (VA), 76

deportation: as amputation, 111, 213n22; and attachments to United States, 50; constructive, 103, 124, 142, 147; crime-based, 6, 8, 35, 41, 164–65; as cruel and unusual punishment, 171–74; as death, 67; and financial stress, 18, 64–65, 84, 101–2, 106, 133–34, 136, 143; historical campaigns of, 24; of lawful permanent residents, 11, 46, 164; of long-term residents, 21, 32, 45–46, 67, 101, 161–64, 186, 190–91; of Mexicans, 203n124; permanent bars, 33, 187; as a prison sentence, 92, 112, 134, 185; process of, 49–54, 101; removal and returns, 44–45; and same-sex couples, 104; statistics, 34, 43–44, 201n78, 211n1, 212n14; as a tool of social exclusion, 30

Deported Veterans Support House, 159, 162–63

deportees: adjusting to life in Mexico, 88–90, 96; in border regions, 59; and homelessness, 60, 68, 71–74; and identity, 3–4, 10, 12, 14, 15, 30, 65, 86, 95, 106, 113, 117, 153–58, 172; and lack of family in Mexico, 58–59; and marriage, 14; and mental health, 67, 69–73, 118; and parental rights, 137–39; and rebuilding lives in Mexico, 13; resilience of, 187; resistance to exclusion, 155–57; and returning to the United States, 13, 155; in rural areas, 58, 118; and school, 63; social integration of, 77, 89, 99; and socialization in the United States, 158–59; and stigma, 50,

illegal entry, 93–94

Illegal Immigration Reform and Immigrant
Responsibility Act (IIRIRA), 32. *See also*
immigration reforms (1996)

illegal reentry, 18, 84, 90–95, 101, 111, 128,
130, 133–34, 143, 155

immigrant rights within the United States,
167–68

Immigration Act of 1990, 31–32, 35, 175–76, 185

Immigration and Customs Enforcement, U.S.
(ICE), 27–28, 77, 93, 101, 118, 149

immigration as contract, 163–66

immigration crimes, increased prosecution
of, 27–28

immigration enforcement: history of, 165–66;
interior, 15, 17, 45, 135–36, 203n125

immigration reforms (1996), 31–43, 104, 149,
181, 185–86

Inter-American Commission on Human
Rights, 40, 151, 181

International Covenant on Civil and Political
Rights (ICCPR), 150

interior immigration enforcement, 15, 17, 45,
135–36, 203n125

Jalisco, 10, 11

Jamaica, 7, 71, 153

"Jose," 11, 32–33, 35, 53–54, 59, 61–62, 66,
167, 173

Juárez, 52, 105

judicial discretion, 12, 32, 36–39, 104, 146;
former rules, 38–39; human rights issues,
149–51; immigration judges' perspectives,
39–40

Kanstroom, Daniel, 7, 16, 22, 35

Kerry v. Din, 103–4, 179, 180

kidnapping, 120, 124, 204n12

Kleindienst v. Mandel, 122, 224n93

La Bestia (train), 56

Landa, Nancy, 7, 63–64

Landon v. Plasencia, 162

language barriers, 61, 64

Larch, Lillian, 115

Latino Threat Narrative, 24, 116–17, 185, 188

lawful permanent residents, deportation of, 3,
11, 17, 31, 32, 37–38, 53, 108, 176, 181

legal representation and immigration cases, 19,
36, 42–43

legislative reforms, recommendations for, 15,
181–88

Legomsky, Stephen, 169

liminal nature of immigration status, 9, 51

"Lolo," 128–31, 143, 148

Loving, Mildred and Richard, 177–78,
223n86

Loving v. Virginia, 174–78

"Luis," 11, 35, 55–56, 66, 83, 141, 167, 185

lynchings of Mexican Americans, 24

Mackenzie, Ethel, 114–15

Magaña Ortiz, Andres, 144–46

manifest destiny, 23, 197n22

marginalization of deportees, 113–14, 173

marriage: bona fide, 176; and cohabitation,
175–79; constitutional right to, 174–81; and
deportation, 14, 101–25, 174–81; interracial,
177–78

Married Women's Independent Nationality
Act, 115–16

mass deportation, 2, 4, 24–27, 30, 43–44, 51,
81, 185, 189

Mathews v. Diaz, 161

Maynard v. Hill, 174

Memije v. Gonzales, 153

mental health: bipolar disorder, 73; and
children of deportees, 18, 131, 134–36; and
deported veterans, 36–37; and deportees,
36, 67–68, 70, 74–76, 98, 118, 131, 149,
207n4; and spouses of deportees, 102, 118;
and suicide, 68–69, 70, 91, 102; and treatment in Mexico, 76–77

Mérida, 11

methamphetamine, 73, 82

Mexico City, 79–80

Michoacán, 11, 88, 119

migration patterns, U.S.-Mexico, 24,
164–66

"Mike," 11, 97–98, 168

mixed-status families, 2, 11, 41, 55, 94–95,
101–20, 124, 127–52, 150–51, 162–63

Monterrey, 79–80

Moore v. City of East Cleveland, 149, 178, 180

motion to reopen, 19, 36

Motomura, Hiroshi, 160–61, 163, 165, 180

Supreme Court, United States, 20–22, 25, 46–47, 67, 103–4, 115, 122, 123, 149, 152, 161, 169–81, 204n130, 204n134. *See also specific cases*

Swing, Joseph, 27

tattoos, 55–56, 83, 85, 89, 157, 167–68, 185

teaching English, 78–79

Temporary Protected Status, 8–9

Texas Rangers, 23–24, 79

Tijuana, 2–3, 10–11, 18–19, 46, 50, 53–54, 55, 60, 69, 74–75, 77, 80, 84, 87, 90, 96, 107–8, 141, 206n16; El Bordo area, 71–72; schools in, 140; Zona Norte, 3, 73

tourist industry in Mexico, 10, 56, 77, 78, 81–83, 95, 97, 102, 107

traffic stops and deportation, 17, 101, 135–36

transnationalism, 15, 133–34

Treaty of Guadalupe Hidalgo, 23

Trop v. Dulles, 170–73

Trump, President Donald, 2, 25, 30, 44, 87, 140, 169

Turner v. Safley, 176–77

United Kingdom, 182, 186

United Nations, 93, 150

United Nations Convention on the Rights of the Child (CRC), 150

United Nations Human Rights Committee, 150

United Nations Office of the High Commissioner for Human Rights, 46

Universal Declaration of Human Rights, 149–50

U.S. Board of Immigration Appeals, 176

USCIS. *See* U.S. Citizenship and Immigration Services

U.S. citizens, consequences of deportation for, 4, 101–52, 174–81. *See also* constructive deportation

U.S. Citizenship and Immigration Services (USCIS), 176, 223n72

U.S. Commission on Civil Rights, 46–47

U.S. Department of State, 144

U.S.-Mexico border: dangers of crossing, 94, 118; fence, 53; historical enforcement patterns, 165–66; militarization of, 15; wait to cross, 1, 107–8, 141–42; wall, 25

U.S. President's Commission on Immigration and Naturalization, 190

U.S. v. Verdugo-Urquidez, 161

VA. *See* Department of Veterans Affairs

VAWA. *See* Violence Against Women Act, 176

veterans, deported, 6, 30, 36–37, 76, 134, 159

Violence Against Women Act (VAWA), 176

violence in Mexico, 119–20, 124, 143–44

wages in Mexico, differences from United States, 1, 54, 62–63, 82, 102, 106

waivers, 19, 110, 186

Yick Wo v. Hopkins, 22

Zablocki v. Redhail, 123

Zacatecas, 140

Zaibert, Leo, 158, 170–71

Zayas, Luis, 131, 136, 144